© 2014 by Design Media Publishing Limited
This edition published in February 2014

Design Media Publishing Limited
20/F Manulife Tower
169 Electric Rd, North Point
Hong Kong
Tel: 00852-28672587
Fax: 00852-25050411
E-mail: suisusie@gmail.com
www.designmediahk.com

Editing: Rebel Roberts
Editorial Assistant: YIN Qian
Proofreading: Katy Lee
Design/Layout: YANG Chunling

p16-p27, p102-p123, p188-197, p226-p235 Copyright Australasian Health Facility Guidelines (AusHFG), The Australasian Health Infrastructure Alliance (AHIA)

All rights reserved. No part of this publication may be reproduced or transmitted in any form or by any means, electronic or mechanical, including photocopy, recording or any information storage and retrieval system, without prior permission in writing from the publisher.

ISBN 978-988-15664-2-3

Printed in China

SPECIALIZED HOSPITALS
Design & Planning

Edited by Rebel Roberts

Design Media Publishing Limited

CONTENTS

006 **PREFACE**

008 **The Healing Wheel of the Environment**

014 **Pediatrics/Adolescent**
016 PAEDIATRIC/ADOLESCENT UNIT PLANNING AND DESIGN
016 Introduction
017 Planning
020 Design
028 King Edward Memorial Hospital Intensive Care Unit & Maternal Foetal Assessment Unit
036 After Hours Pediatrics II
044 One Kids Place
054 Phoenix Children's Hospital Thomas Campus
068 Ålesund Hospital, New Paediatric Unit
078 The New "Meyer" Paediatric Hospital
092 Kinderklinik Prizessin Margaret

100 **Cancer and Radiotherapy and Chemotherapy**
102 RADIATION ONCOLOGY UNIT DESIGN AND PLANNING
102 Introduction
104 Planning
111 Design
124 Emily Couric Clinical Cancer Centre

136	UCLA Outpatient Surgery and Oncology Centre
144	Banner Cancer Centre
154	Teenage Cancer Trust Ward
162	Institute Verbeeten Hospital
170	Healthcare Centre for Cancer Patients
178	Central DuPage Hospital Cancer Centre and Diagnostic Imaging Centre
186	**Obstetrics and Gynecology**
188	MATERNITY UNIT PLANNING AND DESIGN
188	Introduction
189	Planning
194	Design
198	Bumrungrad International Hospital, Women's Centre
206	Prentice Women's Hospital and Maternity Centre of Northwestern Memorial Hospital
224	**Mental Health**
226	ADULT MENTAL HEALTH INPATIENT UNIT PLANNING AND DESIGN
226	Planning
231	Design
234	Functional Relationship Diagram
236	Centre for Mental Health in Stuttgart
244	Wier 2
250	State Reference Centre for the Mental Care
262	**INDEX**

PREFACE

The healthcare profession's design philosophy is based on our commitment to improve the human experience in healthcare settings through design. This includes better experiences for patients, their family and friends, and clinicians and staff, recognising their different experiential (emotional, cognitive and spiritual) needs. Our skill as designers is in melding proven design principles with how people move through, use, and are affected by space. We take a "people-first, human-centred" approach.

Our profession and the designers within this book are experienced in highly specialized projects that include women and children's healthcare environments, Proton Therapy centres and state-of-the-art cancer centres. The approach to healthcare design begins with the development of a full understanding of the vision, business case and goals and objectives relevant to the specific project. We then form a concept that fully reflects the function and the feeling that those factors evoke. Architects, planners and designers spend significant time with hospital leadership, clinicians, staff and other key project leaders to validate and test the design responses. The resulting design is rigorously tested against the practical and operational components of the specific space type with current best practices applied. Specialized requirements for healthcare environments are often applied and refined to accommodate the project budget. And then the designers involved provide options and recommendations to ensure that the facility will serve its intended function well into the future.

The design solutions within this book are based on the contemporary concerns of healthcare providers. Among these issues are financial viability, patient safety, staff satisfaction, environmental responsibility and operational efficiency. We recognise that difficult resource allocation decisions must be made. We consider it our profession's responsibility to provide a consultative approach to enhance those decisions. We also recognise the need for flexibility and adaptability in any space or building designed, based on changing medical practice, technology and financial dynamics.
Our commitment to healthcare is inspired by our profession's mission to service the health of mankind no matter the country or culture and bring our expertise developed over many years to bear on our client's projects. We relish being challenged by the vision for a project, and to work to bring that dream to reality through architecture and interior design.

Design reflects our cultural values. Architecture is the tangible result of creating distinctive places that are inspired by design. The ultimate goal is for people to energize the spaces and buildings that grow from the deep roots of our culture and our dreams – goals that reflect legacy and aspiration. It is exciting to us personally to be challenged with a project vision and to work to bring that dream to reality. That's why we are all here – to build the dream.

Richard H. Fawell, NCARB, AIA, IIDA
VOA Associates Incorporated, China
architecture + planning + interior design

The Healing Wheel of the Environment

"The effect in sickness of beautiful objects, of variety of objects, and especially of brilliancy of colours is hardly at all appreciated. People say the effect is only on the mind. It is no such thing. The effect is on the body too. Little as we know about the way in which we are affected by form, by colour and light, we do know this, that they have an actual physical effect. Variety of form and brilliancy of colour in the objects presented to patients is an actual means of recovery." Florence Nightingale, 1885.

Evidence-Based Design
Internationally, there is an increasing focus on Healing Architecture and Evidence-Based Design (EBD). EBD is seen as a parallel to evidence-based medicine, and is defined as "the deliberate attempt to base design decisions on the best available research evidence… Evidence-based healthcare designs are used to create environments that are therapeutic, supportive of family involvement, efficient for staff performance, and restorative for workers under stress. An evidence-based designer, together with an informed client, makes decisions based on the best information available from research and project evaluations." Hamilton DK (2003) The Four Levels of Evidence-Based Practice. Healthcare Design, Nov 2003.

Evidence-Based Design and the Healing Wheel of the Environment
On the basis of EBD, the DNU consultant group has developed "The Healing Wheel of the Environment", which forms the planning foundation for the entire project. As EBD is a relatively new discipline, and limited in many respects in its scientific foundation, the logical consequence is that only "evident" areas are included in the wheel, which can be extended at any time.

The twelve components of the Healing Wheel of the Environment are:
- Empowerment and ergonomics
- Daylight

Tom Danielsen

- Single-bed rooms
- Acoustics
- Artificial light
- Access to the landscape
- Communication and logistics
- Textures
- Indoor climate
- Art
- IT
- Design and decor

Empowerment and Ergonomics
The patient must as far as possible be able to regulate the light, heating and music in the patient room. Via bedside PCs, patients will have access to their own journals and will be able to see the times of planned examinations, test results, etc. Improved ergonomic design will help to ensure less fatigue and stress.

Daylight
Daylight is not just important for our sense of well-being, but also for our health. Daylight helps to ensure that our circadian rhythms are correctly adjusted; it also lifts the general atmosphere, and has an antidepressant effect. Patients in rooms with windows, particularly windows with green landscapes outside, have shorter periods of convalescence and fewer complications, and require less pain-relieving medicine. Careful and early planning of natural light can reinforce the positive effect of daylight and help to prevent the problems that natural light can also cause, such as overheating and dazzling. Besides improving personal comfort, the conscious use of daylight also helps to save power consumption on artificial light. The optimum use of daylight thus has both an environmental and an economic dimension.

The Healing Wheel of the Environment

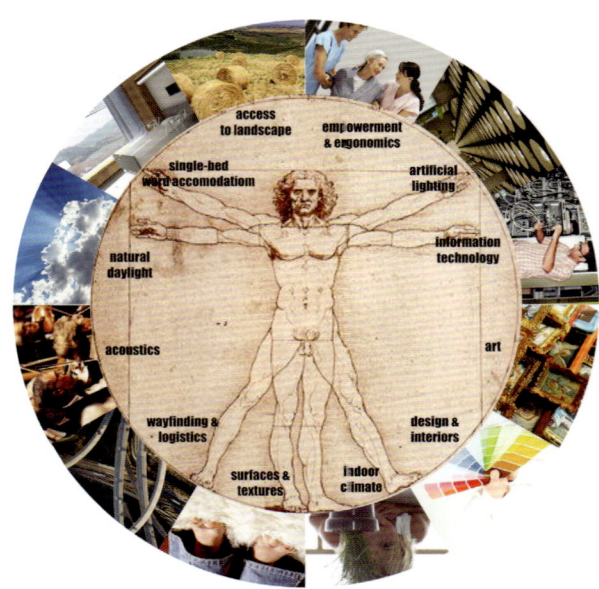

Single-bed Rooms

Research shows that single-bed rooms confer a number of benefits, including fewer hospital-acquired infections, fewer medication errors and a lower noise level. Single-bed rooms also mobilise the patients when they get up to eat, or meet other patients. They also provide privacy for conversations with hospital staff, and thereby a basis for better treatment. The arguments in favour of multiple-bed rooms are usually that they are less expensive (to build and operate), but in fact the shorter periods of admission to hospital indicate that single-bed rooms are more economic from the point of view of society.

Acoustics

A room's acoustic properties determine how sounds are disseminated there. The noise level of hospitals is notoriously high, with many simultaneous and different noise sources, such as people walking, talking or working, beep-sounds from equipment, and transportation noises – all in spaces with hard surfaces, due to cleaning requirements. A lower noise level can reduce stress for both patients and staff and help to give patients the peace and quiet they need. Good acoustic qualities contribute significantly towards a good indoor climate, and are best secured by selecting the right construction principles, an appropriate internal organisation and good surface materials.

Artificial Light

Artificial light must fulfil both functional and aesthetic needs. It must be flexible and variable and provide a sense of well-being, but must also be capable of being switched to diagnostic lighting, for example to examine changes in skin colouration. The choice of fittings and light sources must comply with both functional and atmospheric needs. Artificial light will be used in combination with daylight, and will take over the illumination function when daylight alone is insufficient.

Access to the Landscape

Patients must have access to gardens and landscaped areas. Nature has a positive effect on stress and fatigue, and its promotion of health and healing is well documented. Randomised studies have shown that a view of and access to natural surroundings can have a pain-relieving effect in itself. Gardens also cause patients to move around more, which has a positive effect on their healing, e.g. by encouraging the release of endorphins through exercise. They also provide suitable places to meet and talk with other people.

Communication and Logistics

The New University Hospital in Aarhus is in dialogue with its surroundings: the existing hospital, the future new buildings and the landscaped environment. The hospital's flow is clear, comprehensible and physically convenient for all user groups and staff. The hospital is built up around the large landscape garden, the Park, which is its most important physical landmark. The squares and arcades of the various blocks each have their own individual form and decor, and thereby their own identity. The building information will be supported by "speaking signs" – hand-held receivers which can read out signs and information boards in Danish, English, German or Spanish.

Textures/Surfaces

Surfaces influence and involve all of the senses. If we are to realise the vision of a clean, sensually rich, aesthetic, healthy and comfortable workplace, all of us – both the hospital, the occupational health services, organisations, researchers, advisers and public authorities – must work to promote a healthy working environment. All kinds of environmental factors should be given consideration in the project, and products with a positive effect on the indoor climate, including natural materials, should have preference. Efforts must be made to ensure that a large amount of the materials used can be recycled, and that the building materials are themselves based as far as possible on recycled materials. Partial or complete wood cladding should be used in some of the public areas, such as the Forum, arcades and squares.

Indoor Climate

The indoor climate of a building can influence a person's health, well-being, quality of life and productivity. In a hospital building the patients are in a vulnerable health condition, and high productivity is expected of the staff. Accordingly, the indoor climate is of considerable importance to all who spend time there. The basic principle behind the maintenance of an optimum indoor climate is that the building and its physical qualities should enhance the indoor climate as far as possible. This is primarily done through the use of heavy, well-insulated constructions and a combination of appropriate window areas, glass quality and sun screening to guard against over-heating or insufficient cooling. The building is then supplemented with technical installations such as heating and air conditioning equipment, which support the building's physical qualities. This minimises dependence on the technical installations, which, besides conferring benefits in terms of energy use, ensures an optimum indoor thermal climate. In atmospheric terms, the ideal indoor climate is achieved by utilising materials which release no gases, or only release gases in tiny quantities, and via the use of filtered and conditioned air from outside.

Art

The other components in the Wheel are "rational and evident". The rational and the irrational are inseparable; they define each other and are thereby interwoven. To meet art is to encounter something else. The appropriate relationship between the visual arts and architecture, and their modes of integration, is a perennial question. Art in the public arena offers free and enriching experiences. The construction of the New University Hospital Aarhus presents an exceptional opportunity to create original works in special places. By integrating art at as early a stage as possible, the patients, staff and visitors can be presented with larger and more complex works.

IT
The hospital of the future is a digital hospital. Wireless IT infrastructure is the natural starting-point to enable both staff and patients to easily send and receive information in digital form. Pervasive computing can make health care independent of time and place, and can improve communication and co-ordination between the various levels of the health sector.

Design/Decor
In this context, design should primarily be understood as a combination of the traditional view of design and the modern perspective on design as a rational process of problem-solving. At the New University Hospital design must contribute to improved solutions for staff, patients and relatives. The conscious use of well-designed, well-functioning products, furniture or fixtures brings benefits which extend beyond the immediate target group. Equipment design which combines advanced technology and attractive appearance with user-friendliness and good ergonomics will contribute to an improved working environment for the staff, with a reduced risk of operational errors and work-related injuries. A beautiful and friendly design without an overly mechanical appearance will also help to instil confidence and reassure nervous patients. In the same way, a well-designed patient room with a good decor and choice of materials will satisfy both the staff's need for an efficient environment and the patient's need for a friendly and confidence-inspiring space, in which elements from the domestic sphere help to call forth desirable associations and atmospheres, and in the final analysis contribute to more rapid healing and a shorter stay in hospital. The interior project, which encompasses both furniture and fixtures, must support and complement the overall vision of a modern, IT-based and efficient hospital which focuses on the individual.

Tom Danielsen,
C. F. Møller Architects Partner

Pediatrics/Adolescent

PAEDIATRIC/ADOLESCENT UNIT PLANNING AND DESIGN

1. Introduction

The Paediatric/Adolescent Unit is an Inpatient Unit with special provisions for babies, toddlers, and children and adolescents up to 16 years, specifically designed to reflect the varying physical and psychological needs of these age groups.

In Paediatric/Adolescent Inpatient Units generally, bed occupancy levels and the age/diagnosis mix of patients will vary considerably according to the Service Plan.

The design of accommodation in these units must therefore be flexible in provision of beds, cots and bassinets and in the mix of single and multiple occupancy rooms.

A mix of one-, two- and four-bed rooms provides for flexible use of accommodation.
- one-bed rooms provide accommodation for the multiple functions of isolation nursing, parent live-in and high dependency care provided there is the necessary monitoring equipment.
- two-bed rooms provide suitable accommodation for older children.
- four-bed rooms may be used for high dependency care, short term acute assessment and day care depending on the individual hospital's operational policies. They must be sized to allow for parent privacy (breastfeeding), and confidentiality.

The unit should be designed to achieve the maximum possible level of observation of patient areas. The staff station should be the focal point of the Unit and should overlook any high dependency beds.

GENERAL ARRANGEMENT
The arrangement of facilities will/may depend on the level of service but where the Hospital only has one or two inpatient units, facilities for adolescents may profitably be designed as a special "wing" of the Unit.

2. Planning

2.1 Needs of the Population

The needs of children and adolescents in hospital differ from those for adults. It is a misconception to presume that because children are smaller they will need less space. In fact, a greater amount of space is required to accommodate such activities as parent participation in care, play by and between children, ambulation and family support.

Factors specific to paediatric care which will influence space utilisation and design features include:

- The mix of beds, cots and bassinets varies constantly. All rooms therefore must be of flexible use and sized to accommodate a bed. There must be adequate and easily accessible storage of the alternative beds, cots and bassinets.
- Rooms should be large enough to allow ambulation/play space for the child, space for parents to remain with the child and to allow some privacy for the family.
- Patients' special belongings, toys and drawings should be readily accessible and visible from the child's bed.
- More isolation facilities are required than in adult wards due to a higher incidence of contagious disease among children.
- Recreational playroom and facilities for continuation of education will be required for the developmental needs of differing age groups.
- Strollers, playpens and mobile toys such as tricycles are part of the everyday environment of children and storage space will be needed for this equipment.
- The need for observation of patients by nursing staff is greater in paediatric care, especially of infants and toddlers. However, the modesty of all patients and parents should be respected and adolescents will require more privacy.
- The need for parent/patient education activities and parent counselling means that an Interview Room is required.
- There is an increased need for attention to safety precautions and accident prevention.
- Patients should have an area which is very "safe", for example, where they know they will be free from treatments and distressing procedures.
- Areas which are likely to be occupied for any length of time by staff or patients should have windows.

MANAGEMENT OF BARIATRIC (SEVERELY OBESE) PATIENTS
Obesity in children and adolescents is becoming an increasing problem. It is important to ensure that at least one bedroom and en-suite can accommodate a larger bed if necessary and easy use of lifting equipment. It may also be necessary to consider provision of a larger-than-usual examination couch in at least one Consult/Exam Room. (Also need to consider that the parent of a child may be very obese.)

ASSESSMENT BEDS
In hospitals where Emergency Units have no dedicated facilities for those children who, after initial treatment, either need a period of observation prior to discharge or where the decision to admit is as yet uncertain, an appropriately staffed Assessment Unit in the Paediatric Ward may be an option, rather than mixing children with adults. This places the child in the appropriate environment, reduces pressure on Emergency staff and is a more user-friendly option for children and their families.

2.2 Planning Models

LOCATION
Where possible, the Unit should be located on the ground floor to achieve direct access to an Outside Play Area, and to reduce the use of lifts and staircases. Where ground floor location is not possible, every attempt should be made to provide a secure open play area.

FLEXIBILITY
It is perhaps worth considering possible future use for adults with regard to room sizes, etc.

2.3 Functional Areas

FUNCTIONAL ZONES
The Paediatric/Adolescent Unit will comprise the following functional areas:
- Inpatient areas including Bed Rooms, Isolation Rooms, Play Areas, Multipurpose Activities area, Nursery and Feeding areas, En Suites and Bathrooms

- Day Stay/Assessment and Clinic Areas - if required by the Service Plan
- Parent/carer facilities
- Support areas including Staff Station, Utilities, Formula, Store, Pantry, Cleaner's and Disposal Rooms. Support rooms may be shared with adjacent units if appropriate
- Staff Areas including Offices, Meeting Rooms, Staff Change and Toilets may also be shared with adjacent units if design permits.

SANITARY ARRANGEMENTS
- En-suites are recommended for every one-bed room, with hand basin, shower and toilet to provide total flexibility in the use of each room for isolation, very ill (high dependency) patients or care-by-parent patients
- A general bathroom containing a bath, shower, two toilets (one low set), hand basin (low set) and baby bathing facilities provides for the babies, toddlers and younger children. The low set toilet and hand basin are to encourage the independence of small children. However, such a multiple occupancy space may be problematic and should be carefully considered. There needs to be space for a wheelchair and to operate a hoist.
- Separate unisex shower and toilet are recommended for older children/ adolescents
- All toilets must allow sanichair access and one toilet should provide for wheelchair access
- The use of mobile baby baths is not recommended for occupational health and safety reasons.

HAND BASINS
Hand basins are provided to facilitate the frequent handwashing required to minimise cross infection in the ward. They are located in all single-bed rooms, at the entry to the one-bed rooms (at a ratio of one hand basin to two rooms), and between each pair of two-bed rooms, in the Staff Station, in the treatment room and in the clean and dirty utility rooms.

TREATMENT ROOM
Where children share a room or even if in a single-bed room, it is preferable

to carry out more complex and potentially painful treatments/procedures away from the bedside so that the child does not a) associate their bed room with distressing activities and b) crying does not disturb other children. A parent often accompanies the child. A Treatment Room should be provided in a zone away from the bed rooms and may be designed in conjunction with the Clean Utility Room where the supplies will be located. The child may be brought into the room on the treatment room trolley but if transferred on their bed/cot, extra space will be required in the room for transfer to the treatment trolley and space to park the bed/cot outside the room. Decor should help to distract the child and allay fears – ceiling and wall graphics may be considered.

STORAGE
Storage will be required for toys and educational and recreational equipment. TVs provided at the bedside should be ceiling-mounted. Storage space should be provided to permit exchange of cribs, cots and adult beds. Provisions should also be made for storage of equipment and supplies such as patient cots and recliners for parents and extra linen for parents who stay with the patient overnight.

2.4 Functional Relationships

The Paediatric/Adolescent Unit should be located with ready access to the Emergency Unit, Operating Unit, Critical Care areas and Medical Imaging. It should be located to avoid the need for through traffic. In small units, collocation with an adult ward with swing beds may facilitate management in times of high occupancy.

3. Design

3.1 Access

EXTERNAL
Entrances to the hospital and routes to the Paediatric/Adolescent Unit should ensure minimal contact with sick or injured adult patients.

INTERNAL
Internal access to the Unit needs to be controlled by either human or physical means at all times to prevent unauthorised access or patient egress. This may be by appropriate location of Staff Station or Reception or by video surveillance and electronic door controls, particularly after hours. However, the Staff Station is not always occupied and in the absence of a ward clerk, the impact of monitoring video monitors on staffing levels needs to be considered.

3.2 Infection Control

The infectious status of many patients admitted to the Unit may be unknown. All body fluids should be treated as potentially infectious and adequate precautions should be taken particularly with small children. Linen trolley bays must have doors to prevent contamination.

3.3 Environmental Consideration

ACOUSTICS
Babies, toddlers and children are naturally boisterous at play and noisy when distressed. The sounds of children crying or in pain, the noise of unfamiliar equipment or, conversely, extreme quiet are all anxiety-provoking. Ceiling acoustic tiles, absorbent panels, curtains, upholstered furniture and carpets can be used to absorb and soften sounds in all patient and most other areas. The Treatment Room will require maximum acoustic containment to prevent the sounds of distressed children reaching those in the other patient areas. (In paediatric units, painful procedures are performed in the treatment room rather than at the bedside.) Auditory privacy will be required in the Interview Room and NUM office.

NATURAL LIGHT
Natural light is necessary to all bed rooms and to rooms such as playrooms and parent lounges.

PRIVACY VERSUS OBSERVATION
Design should allow nursing staff to have optimal observation of all patient

areas and for the children to be able to see the staff in order to feel reassured and safe. The need for observation and the safety of children must, however, be balanced against the need to protect the privacy, personal dignity of patients and their parents. This can be achieved by curtains on windows and other glazed panels and the use of bed screens.

There is a particular need for privacy for children and adolescents during:
- examinations
- treatment
- bathing
- dressing
- times of distress

INTERIOR DESIGN
In the Paediatric/Adolescent Unit it is important to use decor to positively create an environment which is as non-institutional as possible. Psychological reassurance will be provided by scaling the environment to the size of the child as far as possible. Graphics provide distraction for children and visitors and can make areas more interesting and inviting. They can be used in all patient and common areas including corridors, treatment rooms, playrooms (inside), bed rooms and lounges. Wall decorations should be at a height visible by children lying supine in bed and also some low enough for toddlers to see. Ceiling decoration should also be considered. Display panels should be provided in bed rooms for the child to decorate in his/her own way. However, swallowed pins is a real issue with children so boards that do not need pins should be provided (velcrose-type material).

WINDOWS
- The height of the windows should enable children in their cots/beds to see outside.
- Natural ventilation to all patient bed rooms (with means of restricted opening for patient safety) provides fresh air, cross-ventilation and enables the children to hear and smell the outdoors. However, insect screen must be provided to all external doors and openable windows and glass must comply with relevant regulation on safety glazing material in buildings.

- A low and wide internal window ledge will be well used by children.
- The Treatment and Tutorial Rooms will require provision for blackout.

DOORS
Door swings must be planned and arranged so that there is no danger of hitting a small child on other side.

3.4 Safety and Security

SAFETY
The design of the unit environment should be such that all possible risks to the safety of the children are minimised including risks of abduction, and take into account the natural curiosity of children.

Design and layout must prevent access by children to areas containing equipment or material likely to be harmful to them, including:
- beverage pantry and heated food trolleys
- utility rooms, cleaners rooms, storage rooms, linen bay
- resuscitation trolley
- disposal room
- treatment room
- medication room
- ward exits

In order to prevent injury whilst patients undertake their normal daily activities in the ward area, surface finishes, furniture and glazing must be of design and material appropriate to their use (e.g. rounded edges on furniture at low levels, safety glass in patient areas).

Provision of warm (thermostatically controlled) water to all areas.
Fitting of child-proof locks to all cupboards.
Designing barriers and balustrades so they are non-climbable but can be seen through by toddlers.
Provision of non-scalable safety fencing of adequate height around external

play areas especially where this is not located at ground level.
Service panels must be out of reach of small children. Similarly, nurse and emergency call buttons must be sited out of the reach of curious or mischievous hands.
Door handles out of the reach of small children.
Bedrooms to have doors with high and low vision panels and handles.
Power points in child-occupied areas must be above child height and shuttered.
Consider the use of convex mirrors to blind corners.
Care with location of main access door so that if not at the ward perimeter, it does not impede access to rooms outside.
Glass observation panels in doors need to be sized so as to enable staff to see in and low enough to be able to see a small child on the other side. As far as possible, safety measures should not cause avoidable inconvenience nor impair efficiency.

SECURITY

Security issues are of increasing importance due to the prevalence of violence and theft in the hospital environment. In designing the Unit, consideration should be given to:
- personal security of patients, parents and staff
- security of property of patients, visitors and staff
- security of hospital equipment and stores items
- drug security
- access and egress/unauthorised intrusion
- night staffing conditions
- security lighting

Egress points must be secured and should be monitored wherever possible to minimise and contain the risk of a child's unaccompanied egress or abduction from the Unit and prevent interference from unauthorised persons.

Security measures may include:
- direct staff observation
- closed circuit TV
- restricted window openings

- high level door latches
- stable doors
- locked doors. Monitoring unit access to security and safety issues need to be considered in conjunction to ensure that they do not conflict.

3.5 Non-standard Component of the Unit – Playroom

3.5.1 PLAYROOM – INTERNAL

DESCRIPTION AND FUNCTION
The Inside Playroom provides an area where children may go for play, recreation, education and remedial activities. The following designated area may be provided:
- Dining for small children
- Television
- Reading/playing board games

It is envisaged that parents and siblings will accompany their children at times. Occupancy: Up to 10 – including the Play Therapist – at 3m²/person plus storage.

Functions and activities will include:
- Structured and unstructured play activities
- Reading
- Watching television
- Drawing (chalkboard, paper, etc.)
- Board games
- Meals, snacks, drinks for patients
- Remedial therapy activities
- Education

The patients may be:
- ambulant/crawling
- in bed/cot/bassinet
- in a stroller/pram
- on a tricycle

- on crutches
- in a wheelchair
- in a playpen
- oxygen-dependent
- on IV therapy
- in traction

LOCATION AND RELATIONSHIPS
Access must allow for a bed with orthopaedic fittings.
Direct access to the Outside Play Area
Good observation from Staff Station and general nursing circulation areas required.

CONSIDERATIONS
The following are required:
- Natural light (northerly aspect where possible)
- Bright and cheerful decor
- Acoustic absorption
- Means of restricted window opening for natural ventilation when required

Corridor wall and door to be glazed to allow observation of patients.
Dividing walls may be glazed to a height suitable to allow observation of patients.

Storage (not necessarily within the Play Area) required for:
- hospital-provided toys and games
- books, education material and CDs/DVDs
- chairs (stacking, in several sizes)
- high chairs
- tricycles
- playpen (fold-away)
- strollers and prams
- computers

If paints are to be used, a small sink should be fitted.
Consider a toddler-height hand basin for use before and after meals/ snacks.

Functional Relationship Diagram – Paediatric and Adolescent Unit

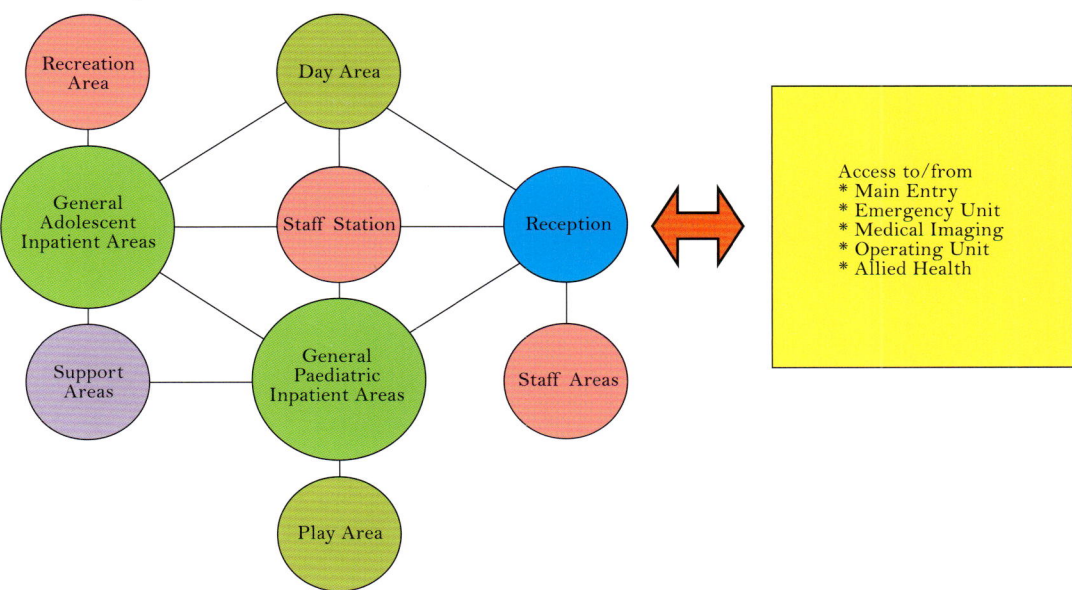

3.5.2 PLAYROOM – EXTERNAL

DESCRIPTION AND FUNCTION
An outdoor area where children may go for play, recreation, remedial activities and family visiting.

Functions and activities include:
- structured and unstructured play activities
- remedial therapy activities
- family interaction and quiet time

LOCATION AND FUNCTIONAL RELATIONSHIPS
Observation from the Staff Station
Direct access to/from Inside Play Area
Consideration should be given to external access for maintenance purposes.

CONSIDERATIONS
Threshold should facilitate ease of manoeuvring for:
- patients in wheelchairs
- patient beds/cots/bassinet
- those who have difficulty in walking

Requires protection from extreme weather conditions.
Ground area may be covered with outdoor carpet or pavers but not loose materials such as gravel or woodchips.
Non-scalable safety fence high enough to prevent removal of children is required for the surrounding area.
Access and egress should only be from the ward area.

King Edward Memorial Hospital Intensive Care Unit & Maternal Foetal Assessment Unit

Architects:
Bateman Architects
Location:
Australia
Project year:
2012
Photographs:
© Courtesy of architects

The King Edward Memorial Hospital required expansion of its Neonatal Intensive Care and Foetal Monitoring Assessment Units.

These new facilities were built to replace existing accommodation and to cater for an expected increase in future demand.

KEMH is a heritage listed site, with a group of buildings that date from the 1890's to the 1980's, and these buildings have been rendered in a diverse range of architectural styles that reflect the period of its time. Bateman Architects' design approach was to introduce a new architectural vocabulary to the surrounding architecture.

The new accommodation was achieved via a lightweight element, a "capsule", to provide the required expansion to both the NICU and MFAU. The north and south elevations of the capsule are fully glazed to allow maximum light penetration to the interior, with an external sunscreen to prevent direct sun. The west façade has windows which are offset from the external and internal skin; this gesture prevents afternoon sun penetrating directly into the building. The building is configured to make the best use of passive solar design by controlling the sun penetration and thus heat gain. Supported on circular columns this extrusion is captured and contained by a floating alucobond sheet fabric punctured by colourful openings.

1. A constricted site gave way to this building proposal; the building is an extension of the existing floor plate where space has been captured
2. Overall view of the hospital; the new and the old building are integrated
3. Side view of the reception
4, 6~9. Inspiration was taken from the colours of spring and applied internally as bright graphics in the glass splashbacks where the clinical hand basins are located. The basins serve their clinical purpose and the glass splashbacks become a colourful canvas that enriches the space
5. Corridor and staff station

A constricted site gave way to this building proposal; the building is an extension of the existing floor plate where space has been captured. The proposed new floor levels align with the existing levels so that a contiguous relationship with the internal accommodation is achieved. This allows for a logical expansion of the spaces, the most desirable relationship with the existing accommodation and provides the least amount of disruption to the hospital's operations.

Of the various health models considered for the NICU, the preferred model was a hybrid between a fully open plan model and four cot rooms. The model groups four cots into a number of alcoves, which provide a good degree of privacy

5

6

031

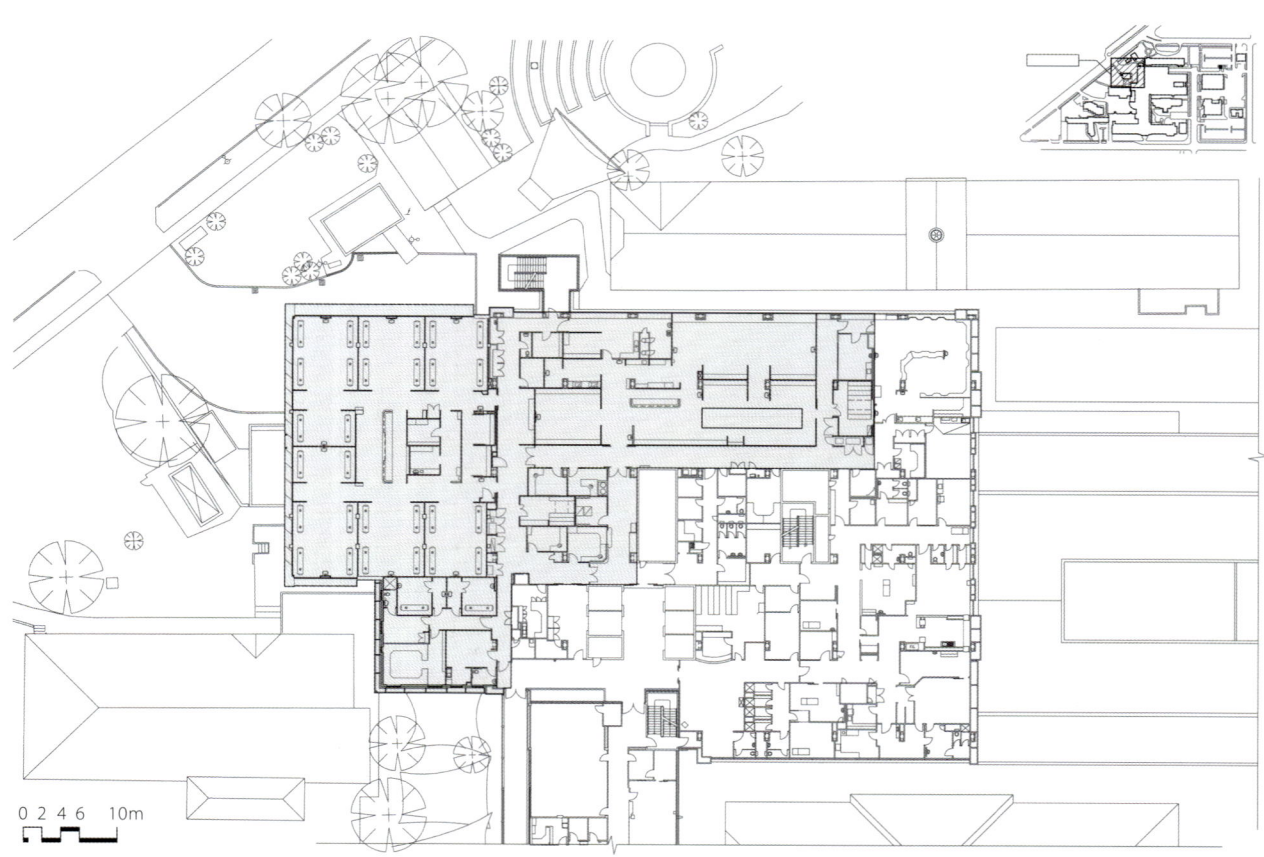

Site Plan

and acoustic control, while affording observation from a central staff base. The health planning is clear, logical and operationally efficient, which enables minimum of staff to operate the unit and reduces travel distance between spaces.

Inspiration was taken from the colours of spring and applied internally as bright graphics in the glass splash backs where the clinical hand basins are located.

The basins serve their clinical purpose and the glass splashbacks become a colourful canvas that enriches the space. This colour scheme carries through to the vinyl pattern designs so that the graphics on the glass splashback and floor vinyl speak to each other.

The environment can be characterised as light, fresh and spacious with access to views. By providing this connection the hospital is offering relief and support to its occupants.

West Elevation

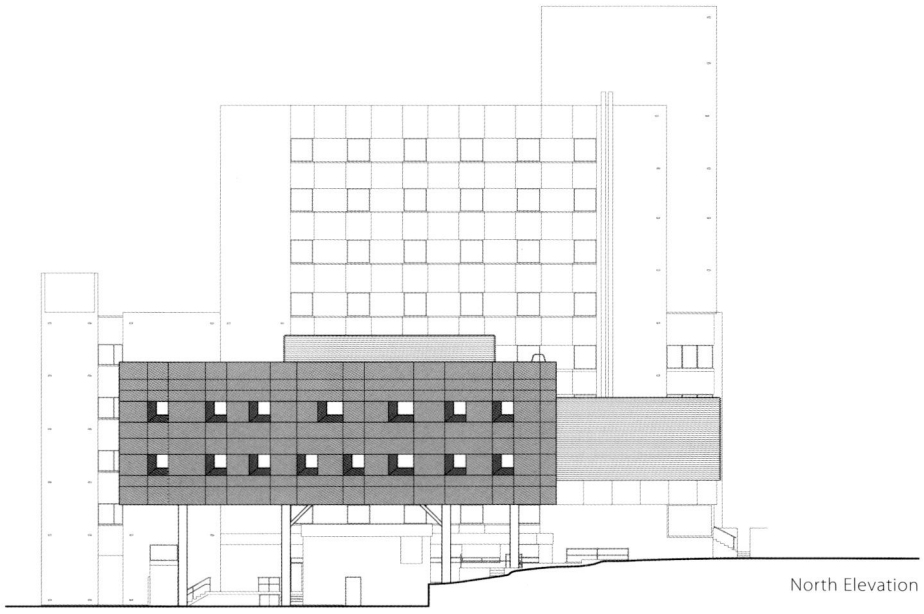

North Elevation

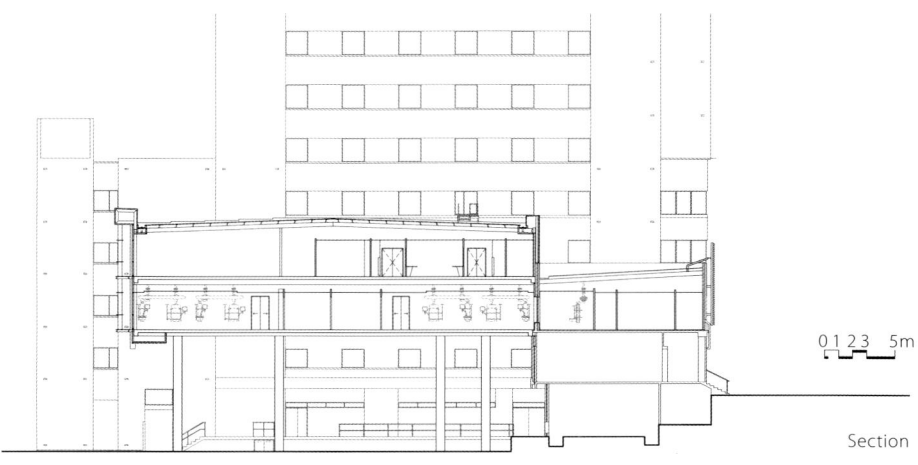

Section

Floor Plan – Level 3:
1~8. Intensive care cots
9. Single cot room 1
10. Single cot room 2
11. Nurse base
12. Clean utility
13. Dirty utility
14. Isolation room 1
15. Isolation room 2
16. Parent overnight room
17. Parent lounge
18. Clinical support office
19. Office
20. Secure reception
21. Store
22. Office
23. Office
24~26. Special care nursery
27. Nurse base
28. Clean utility
29. Baby bathing room
30. Express milk room
31. Meeting room
32. Milk fridge room
33. Work area
34. Cot clean area
35. Disposal/utility
36. Compactus store

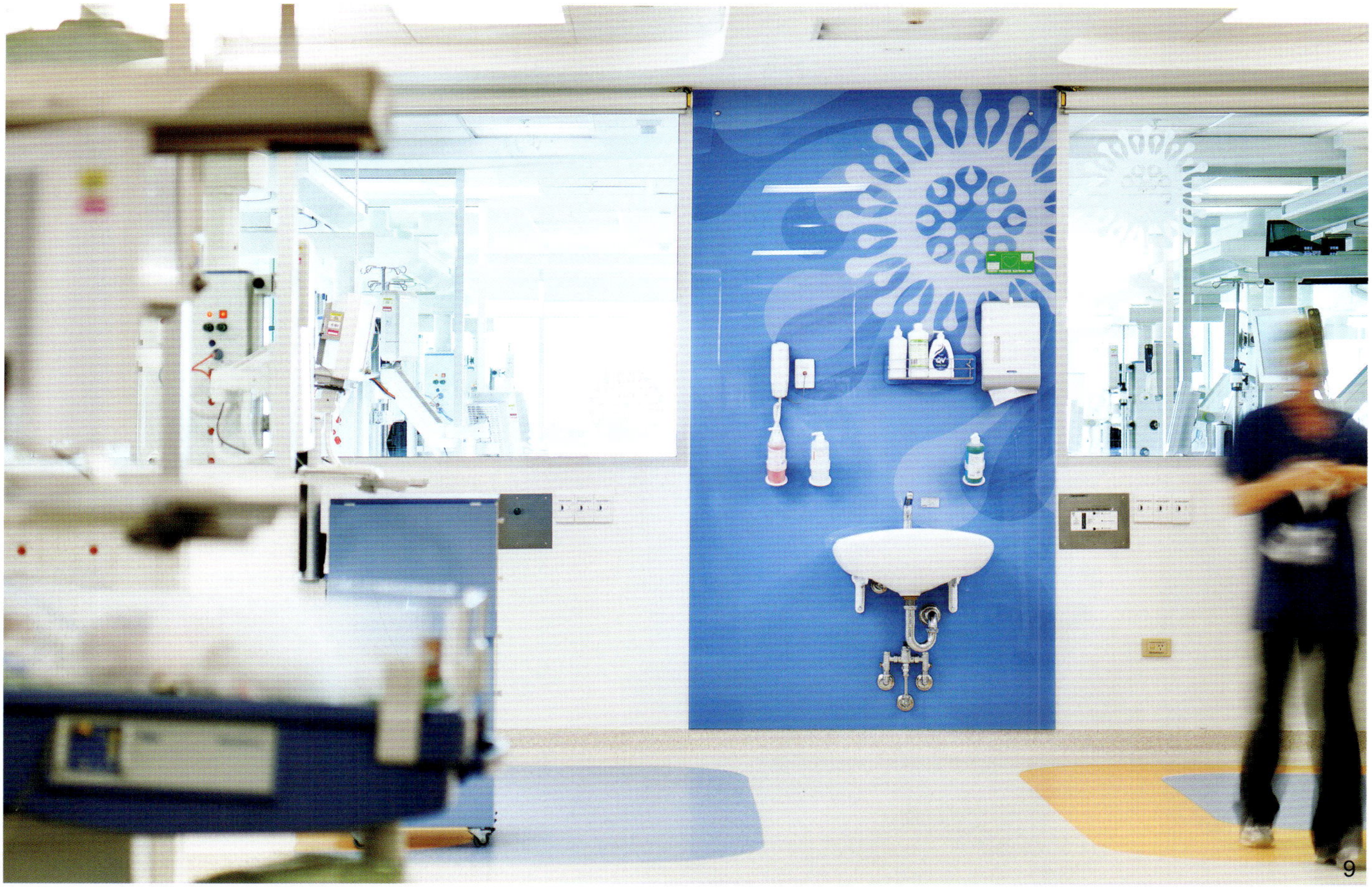

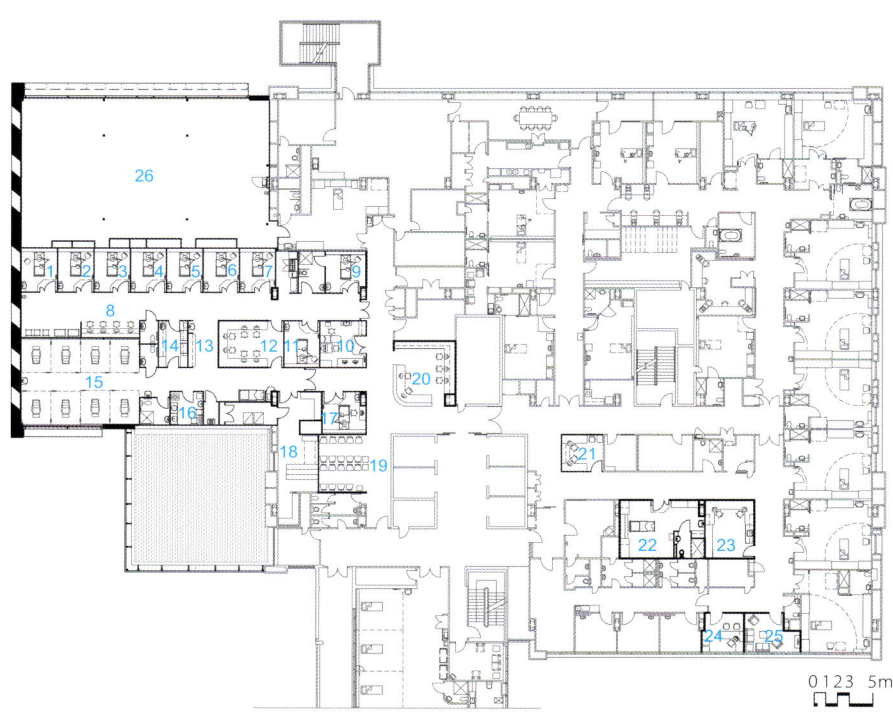

Floor Plan – Level 4:
1~7. Assessment rooms
8. Write up area
9. Assessment room with ensuite
10. Ultrasound room
11. Assessment room
12. Handover room
13. Write up area
14. Clean utility
15. Assessment cubicles
16. Dirty utility
17. Triage room
18. Store
19. Waiting area
20. Reception
21. Office
22. Birthing suite
23. Obstetrics assessment
24. Office
25. Lounge room
26. Future fitout

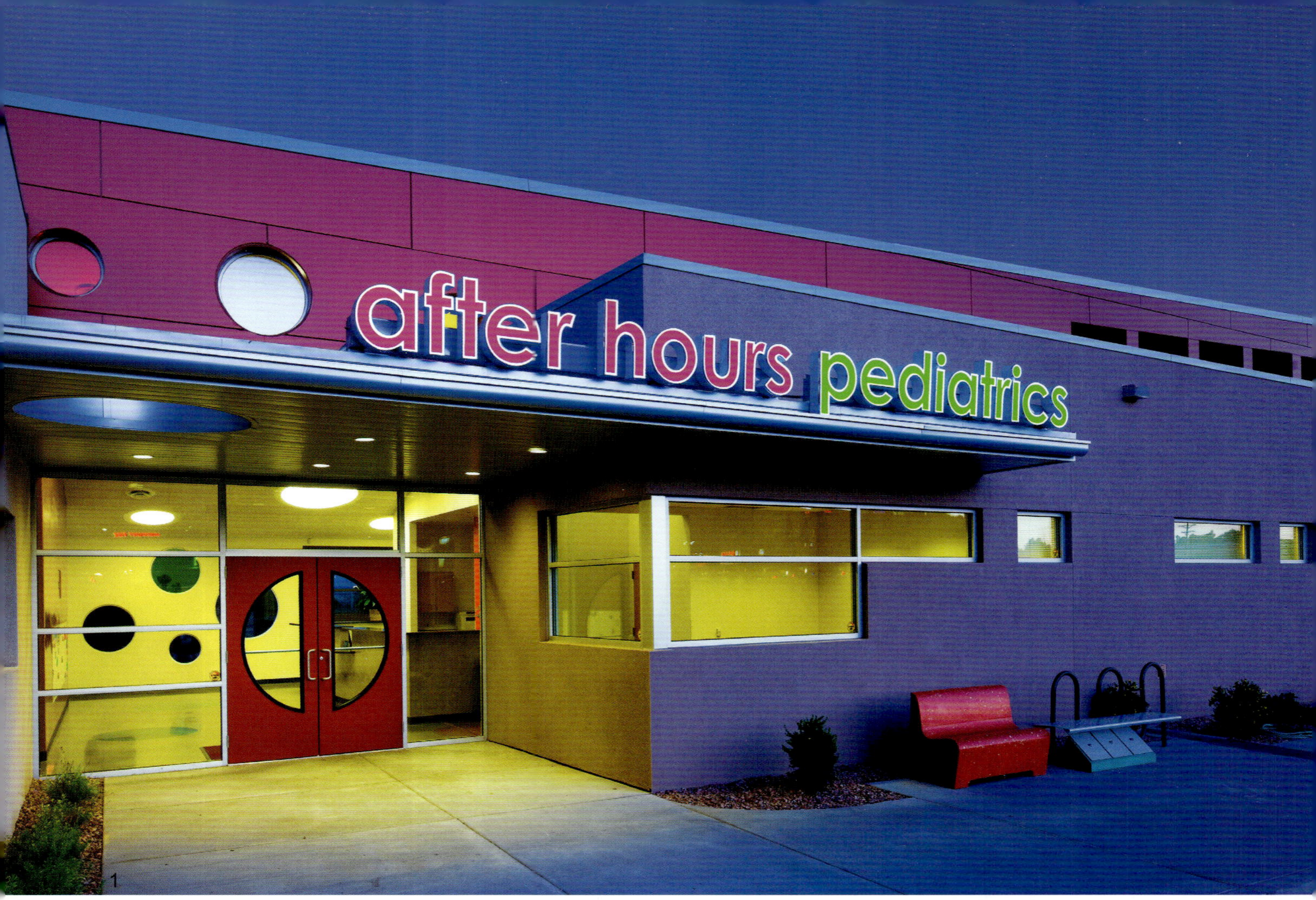
after hours pediatrics
1

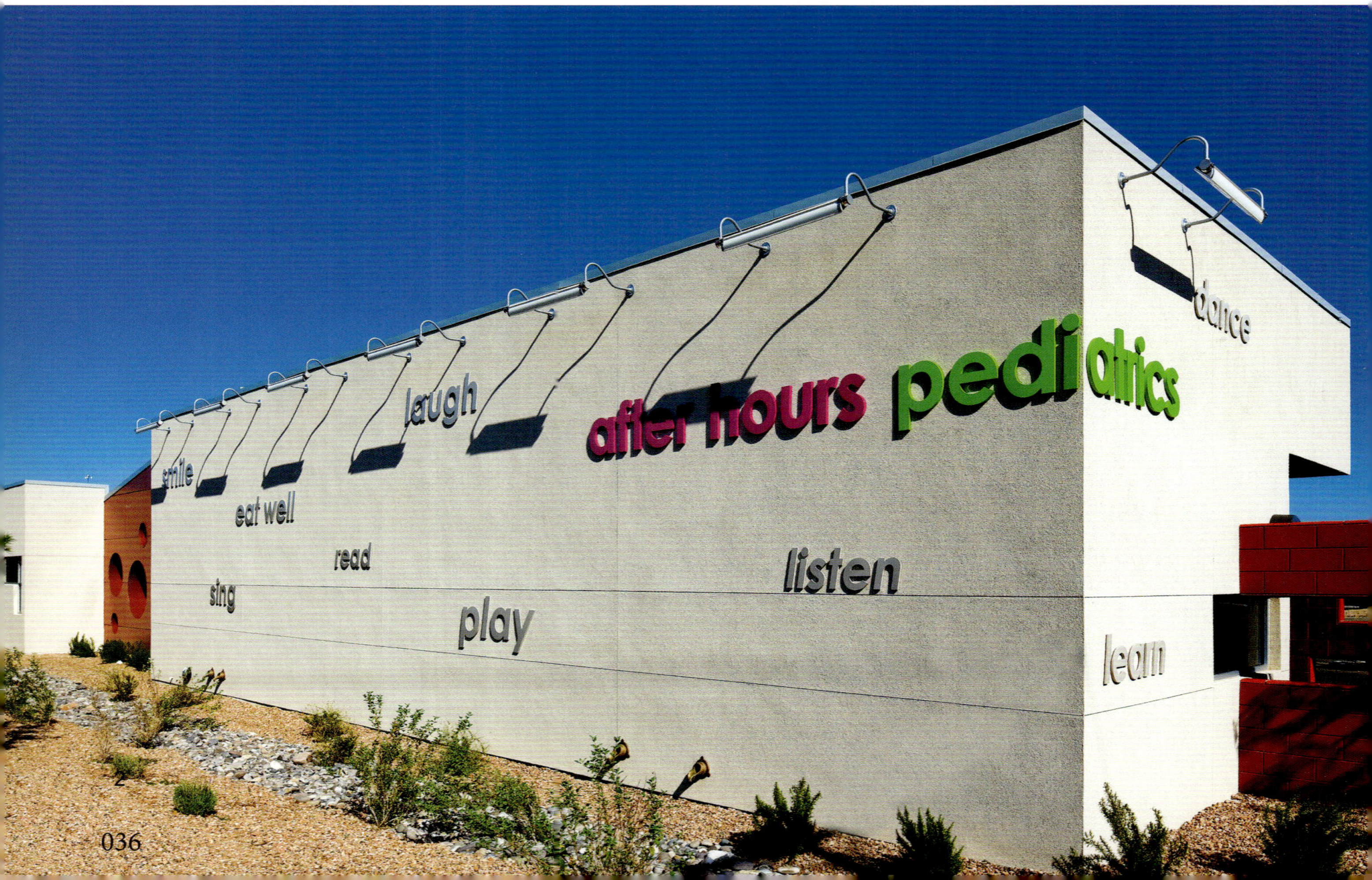
smile
eat well
sing
read
laugh
play
after hours pediatrics
listen
dance
learn

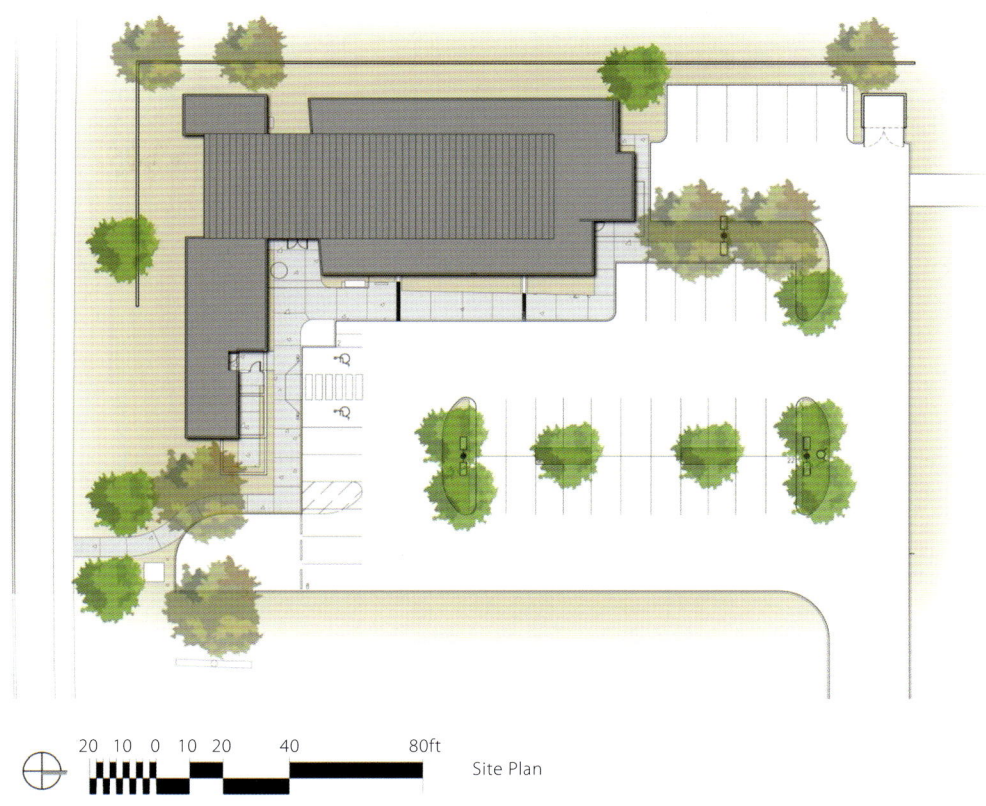

Site Plan

After Hours Pediatrics II

Architects:
Mullen Heller Architecture
Location:
Albuquerque, USA
Building area:
711.27m²
Project year:
2011
Photographs:
© Patrick Coulie

The design of After Hours Pediatrics was shaped by two driving forces: 1. a prominent site along one of Albuquerque's major arterial, Paseo del Norte, and 2. the Client's belief that "keeping kids in the game" is the best preventative medicine.

While the site enjoys high visibility along Paseo, it also presents the challenge with a high volume of traffic. To mitigate vehicular noise, the building programme was organised into two wings: an exam wing which is placed remote from the street and an administrative wing located parallel along Paseo. This arrangement provides a tremendous presence on Paseo while protecting the building entry from the busy traffic.

Inspired by the Client's emphasis on an active lifestyle, the building is punctuated with a series of circular windows of coloured glass which reference various types of sports balls, and the polished concrete floors area articulated with coloured "hash marks" representing a sports field.

To further emphasise the importance of wellness, the façade along Paseo del Norte is adorned with a playful arrangement of text art encouraging well being and a healthy lifestyle.

The building's main entry has a vaulted ceiling to provide a bright and airy environment. The circular windows which are a strong feature on the outside of the building create "spotlights" on the floor

1. Main entrance night view
2. Back façade
3. Night view from the parking lot

that move throughout the day and provide individual "stages" for children to enjoy.

Separate waiting areas for well and sick children flank the waiting area and feed corresponding exam rooms. The exam room wing is organised around a central nurse's station which provides a sense of separation between the wellness exam rooms and those for sick visits.

The exterior of the building is expressed in strong geometric forms with low bars surrounding a metal-clad wedge which rises up to allow clerestory lighting into the interior spaces. The bold colours of the metal cladding coupled with the patio wall and circular windows create a striking composition that appeals to both toddlers and the young at heart.

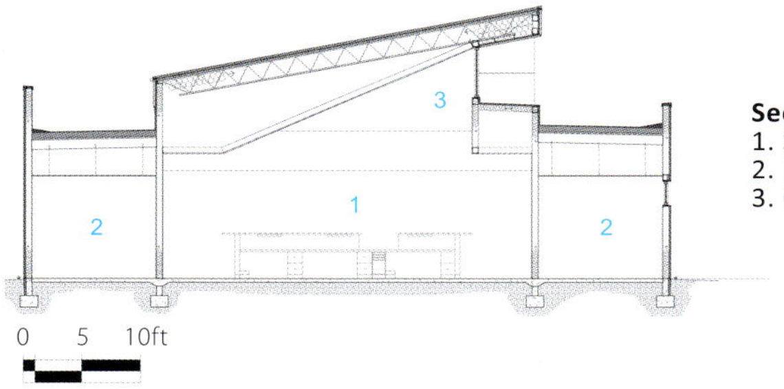

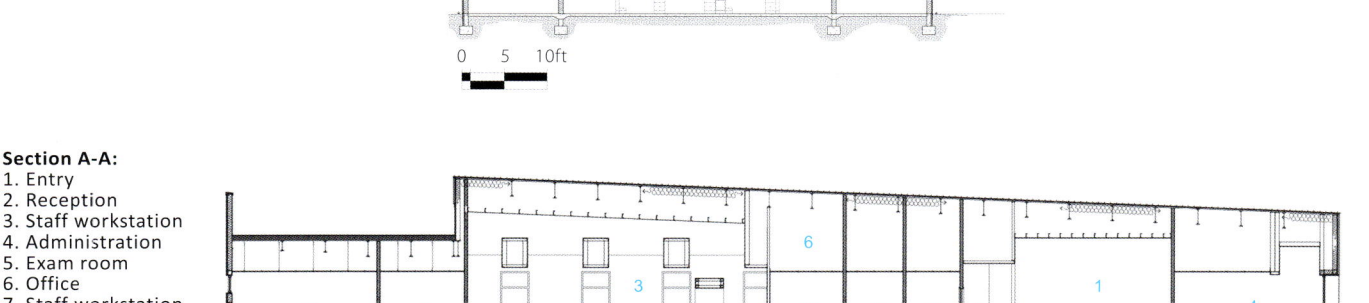

Section B-B:
1. Staff workstation
2. Exam room
3. Clerestory

Section A-A:
1. Entry
2. Reception
3. Staff workstation
4. Administration
5. Exam room
6. Office
7. Staff workstation
8. Corridor
9. Restroom
10. Lab

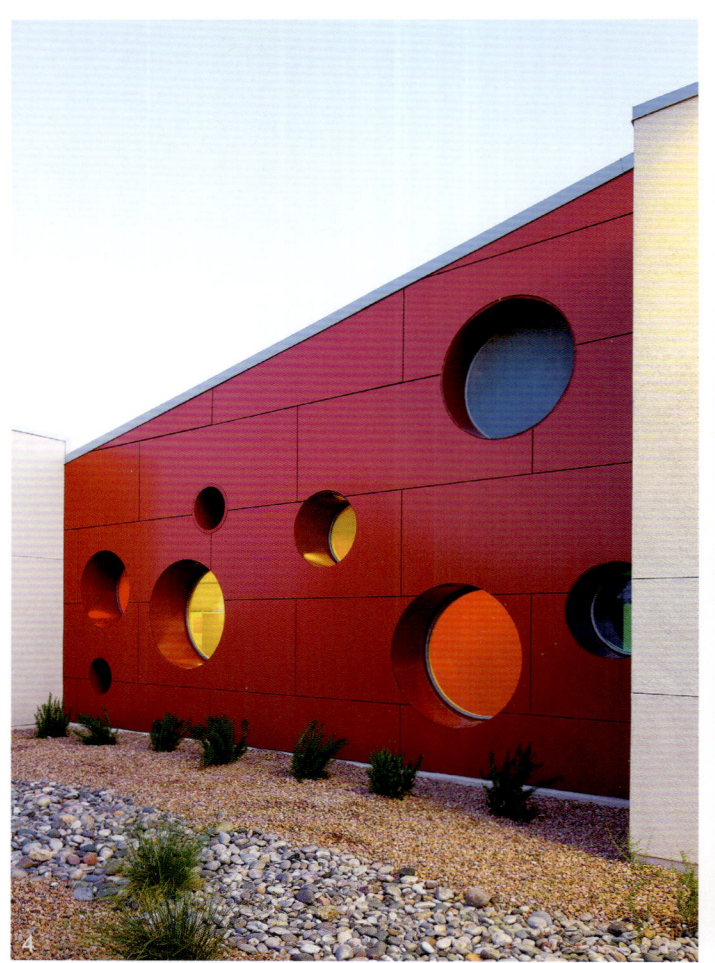

4~6. The circular windows on the outside of the building create "spotlights" on the floor that move throughout the day and provide individual "stages" for children to enjoy

7. Office area
8. Exam room

Floor Plan:
1. Entry
2. Reception
3. Waiting
4. Restroom
5. Exam room
6. Procedure room
7. Office
8. Staff workstation
9. Lab
10. Inoculation
11. Storage
12. Patio
13. Break room
14. Electrical
15. Administration

043

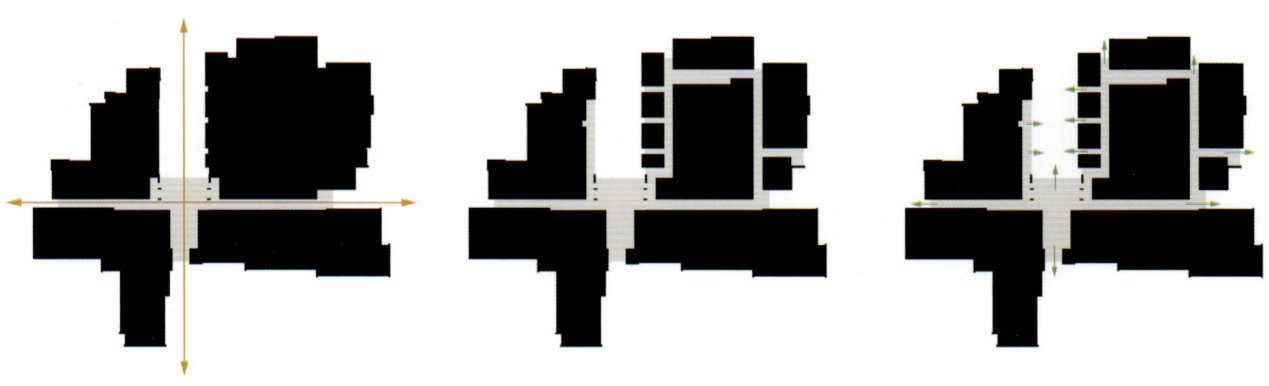

One Kids Place

Architects: Mitchell Architects
Location:
North Bay, Canada
Builiding area: 3,836m²
Project year: 2009
Photographs:
© Richard Johnson
Awards:
ARIDO Interior Design Project of the Year; Ontario Wood Works Excellence Award, 2010

One Kids Place Children's Treatment Centre in North Bay, Ontario, Canada serves children and youth with communication, developmental and physical needs, with a range of integrated services which include: occupational therapy, physiotherapy, speech language pathology, social work, therapeutic recreation and specialized medical clinics.

In contrast to many environments created for kids, the design aims not to overload the senses but rather, create a matrix of professionalism through quality materials and spatial character. Within this matrix, however, are playful elements, colour, light and textures which animate and express the energy of youth, both inside and out. These include features such as a three-metre-long saltwater aquarium to entertain the children, colourful contoured resin panels suspended above the main waiting area, and an array of artwork by local artists and craftspeople that animate the public spaces. In this environment, therapists can provide an appropriate range of stimuli and activity for children with varying needs and abilities. Spatially, the facility is organised around an intimate courtyard which provides an outdoor space, sheltered from sights and sounds of traffic, for therapy, respite and occasional celebration. The progression of space from the vestibule to the waiting area unfolds both horizontally and vertically with the vista opening to the courtyard through six-metre-high glazing accented by coloured stained glass.

North Elevation

South Elevation

1. The intimate courtyard is brought to life with coloured stained glass
2. A covered drop-off area at the entry protects visitors from the weather
3. Sun shade devices provide heat gain control while coloured spandrel panels animate the façade
4. A side entrance with a view to the main corridor beyond

All major circulation spaces of the building are visually connected to the outdoors and most notably the courtyard, providing accessibility, natural light and orientation.

The central waiting area at the heart of building features two pyramidal skylights, one of which supports a six-metre-high living green wall. In addition to its sensory appeal, the hydroponically grown plant material on the wall contributes to indoor air quality, functioning as a bio-filter through which the building's return air is mechanically drawn and purified.

In addition to the green wall, the building features a variety of other sustainable design strategies, including: strategic placement of glazing to maximise natural light control, control of excessive heat gain by sun shade devices, automated day-light harvesting, low VOC finishes, Formaldehyde-free millwork and furniture, and assorted recycled building materials.

The building is grounded to its northern context by natural materials which include: limestone (masonry, polished sills and tile), clay brick, glue-laminated timbers, cedar, maple, and slate.

5. The waiting area and main corridor feature extensive use of wood and stone
6. The waiting area provides a calming place to relax or play

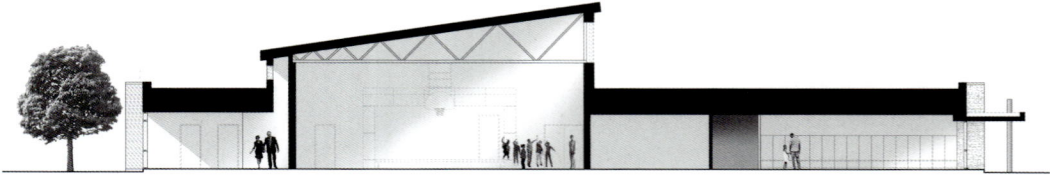

Section

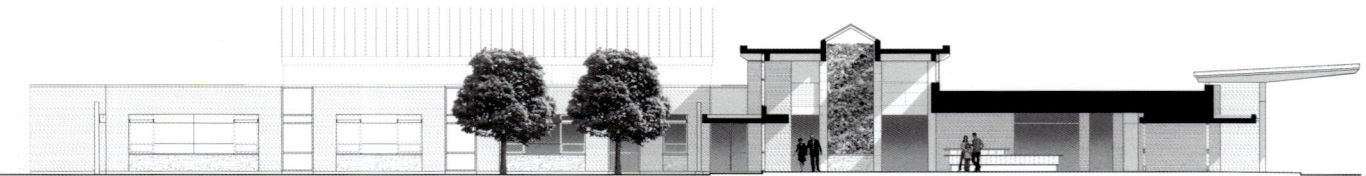

South Section

7. The main corridor features artwork by local artists and craftspeople
8. The lobby features a three-metre-wide saltwater aquarium to entertain the children

Floor Plan:
1. Lobby/waiting area
2. Pediatric clinic
3. Day clinic
4. Therapists workstations
5. Therapy room
6. Family resource room
7. Administration
8. Staff lounge
9. Gymnasium
10. Classroom
11. Courtyard
12. Services

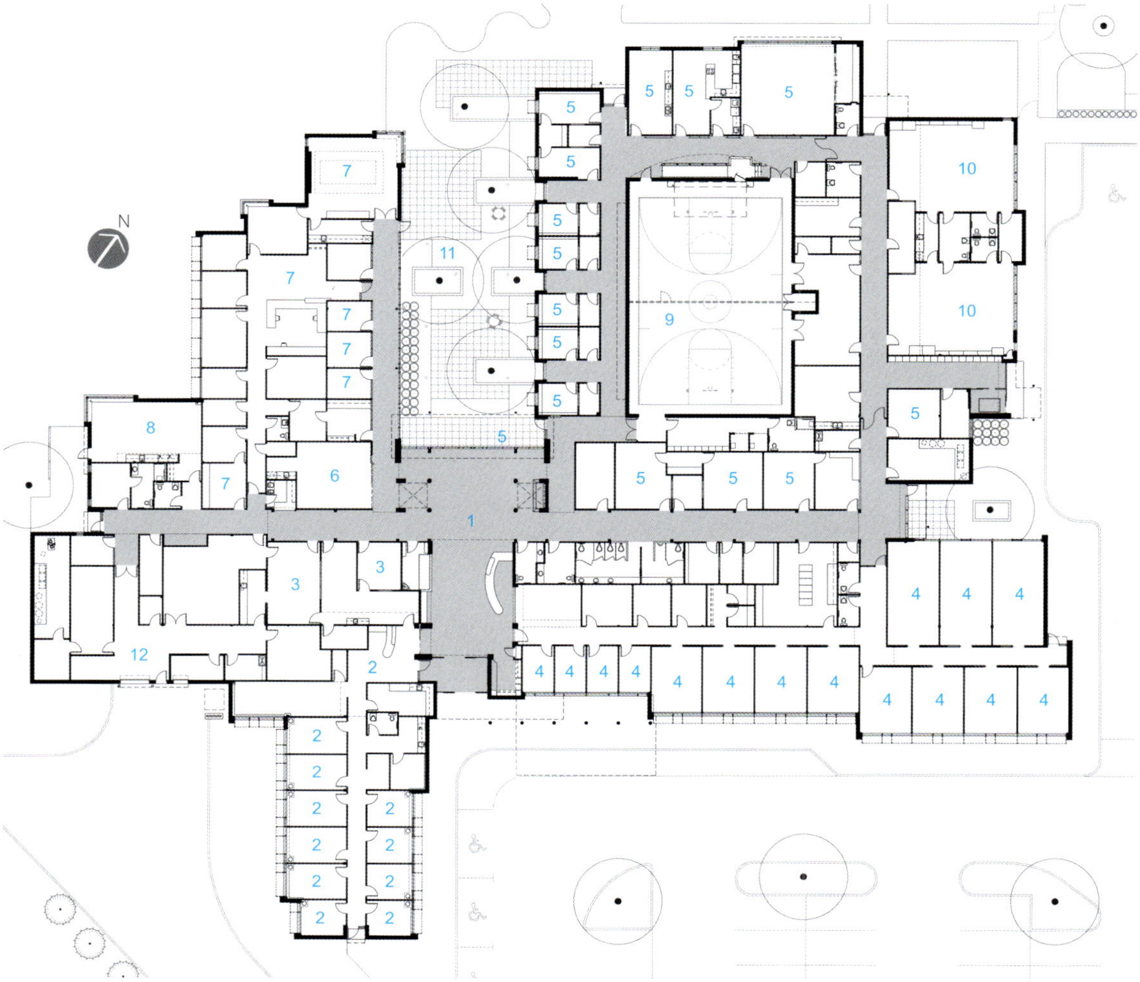

9. Classrooms are animated by bright colours and wood shelving to display the toys
10. The cubby area provides children with a personalized place to store their belongings
11. The treatment room corridor is washed with light from clerestory windows above
12. The public washrooms feature wood wall panels and slate floors

Phoenix Children's Hospital Thomas Campus

Architects:
HKS
Location:
Arizona, USA
Building area:
71,535.34m²
Project year:
2012
Photographs:
© Daryl Shields, Blake Marvin

Phoenix Children's Hospital's major expansion plan included a 71,535.34-square-metre 11-storey patient and ambulatory tower, main entry boulevard and circle drive, central plant and three parking structures. Planned with the concept of family-centred care in mind, the hospital set out to make the Phoenix Children's experience better for families and patients. The 334-bed patient tower features all private rooms for families and patients during the hospital stay. The tower also includes ambulatory care clinics, an imaging department, surgery, cath lab suite and cafeteria. Following the Green Guide for Health Care, the facility used sustainable design concepts to improve water efficiency, energy and atmosphere, materials and resources and indoor environmental quality. The site hosts a bio-filtration area in the landscape to control erosion and storm water as well as local vegetation for landscaping and xeriscape water conservation. Inside, the building features carbon dioxide monitoring, ventilation effectiveness and low-emitting materials and high performance low-E glass.

Phoenix Children's Hospital opened the first few floors of the highly anticipated

11-storey patient tower in January 2011. The newly opened space features a palm-lined boulevard entrance, three-storey light-filled atrium lobby, first-floor specialty clinic spaces and a cafeteria.

Designed by HKS, the expanded space will treat children who are seeking specialty outpatient medical care in dermatology, endocrinology, pulmonology, orthopedics and gastroenterology.

The patient care tower addition highlights a playfully sophisticated design that respects existing aesthetics while strengthening Children's brand. The campus creates a healing oasis within the desert surroundings while the tower becomes the blooming desert flower that transforms appearance from day to night.

Flowing curved forms, bold geometric blocks of colour and incredible views from within transform the pediatric patient experience to support the hospital's mission of treating the entire family. The curvilinear tower is divided into three parts to reduce the impact of its scale.

The entry court is punctuated by a large vertical sail. The three-storey atrium welcomes patients and families with shaded transparency and the colourfully animated interiors within. The southern exposure is capped by a cantilevered parapet on the southeast end reaching boldly to the community with a purple glow of hope.

Care has been taken to improve the family journey through lush and whimsical landscaping accentuated with colourful sculpture and soothing water features. The facility utilises indigenous colour, playful animal sculptures and desert flowers to visually organise each floor. Strategic day-lighting calms major spaces, punctuates corridors and creates striking vistas within patient rooms. Places of escape integrate the indoors and outdoors providing families with choices and control over the daily milieu.

1. Front façade, approach to the main entrance
2. Front view at dusk
3. Back façade viewed from the courtyard

West Elevation

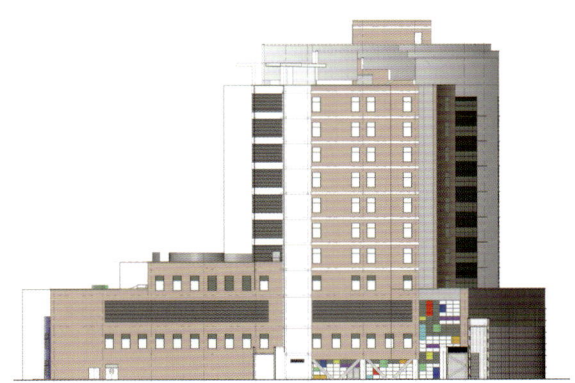

East Elevation

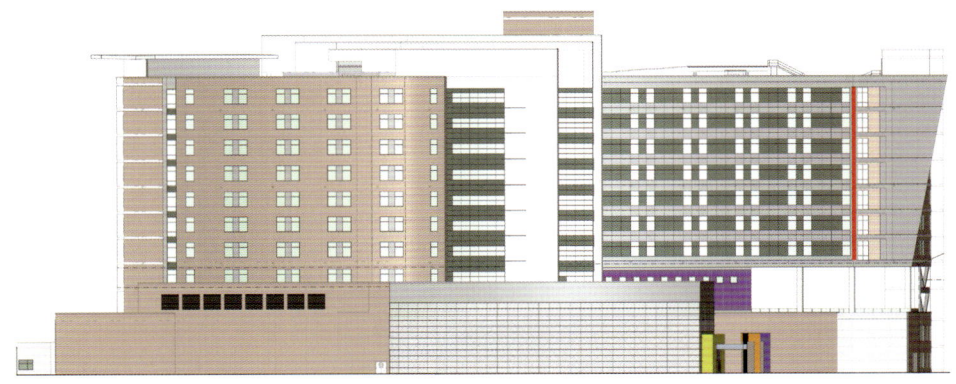

North Elevation

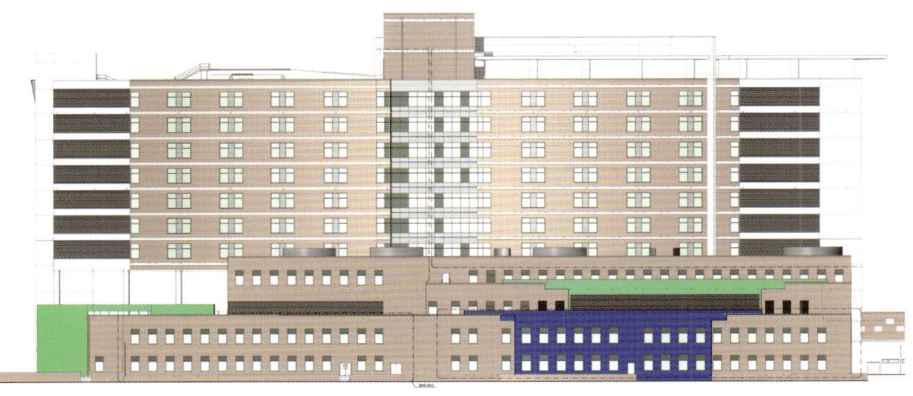

South Elevation

057

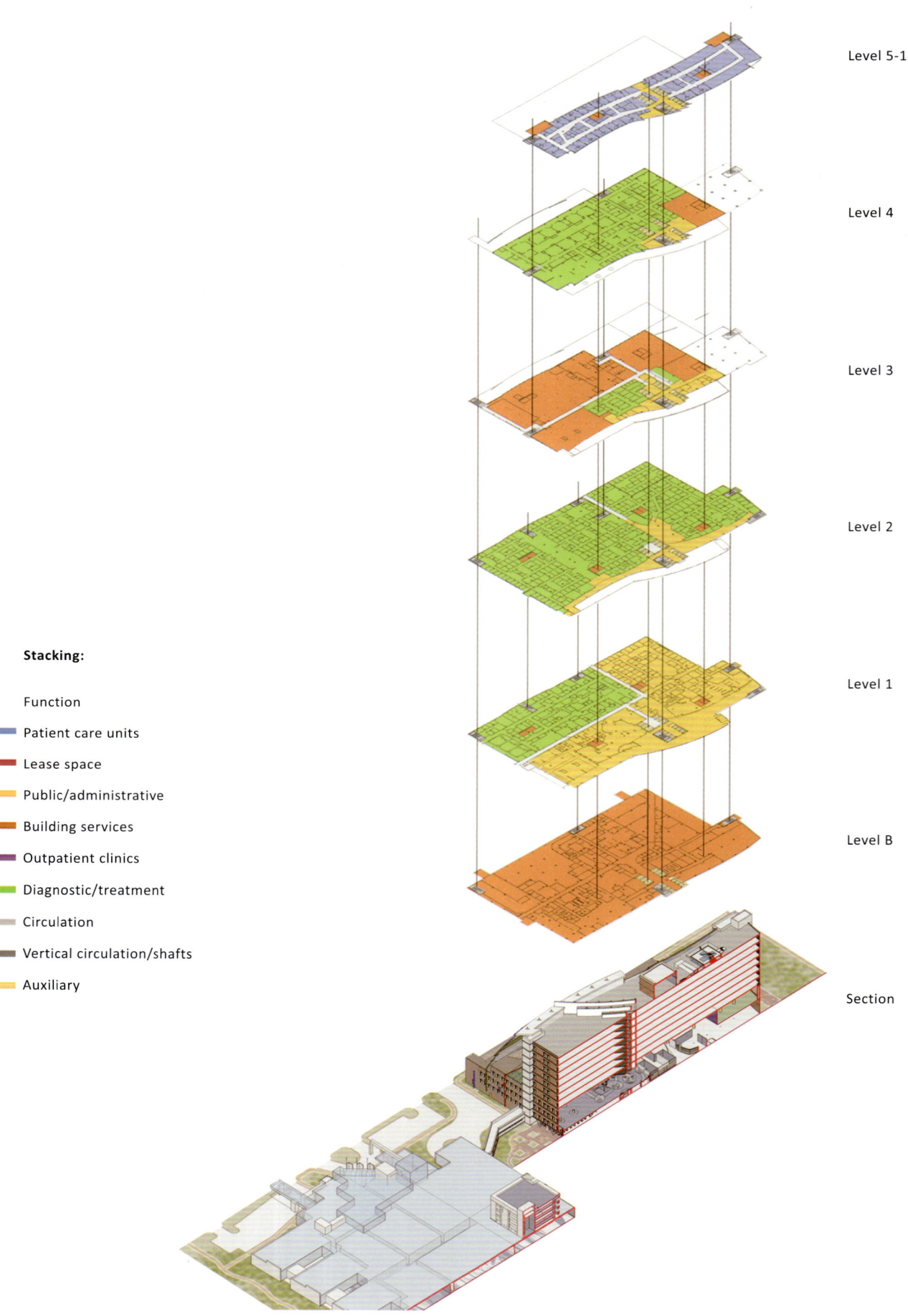

Functional Organisation:
The design team brought best practice ideas from recent pediatric projects from coast to coast and collaborated with existing and new medical, administrative and clinical staff to create efficient, innovative planning solutions with flexibility to adapt to various care model choices. Vertical stacking reduces horizontal travel for medical and support staff. The atrium links the main entrance with lifts, ancillary and public services and the day-lit path to the existing hospital. All public lift lobbies provide views to the outside and directly connect patient families to clinical and public functions. Flexible pediatric clinics are grouped in expandable modular units to ebb and flow with daily need. Invasive sedated procedures are collocated for efficient prep and recovery service. Inpatient units are de-centrally staffed as intimate clusters but each floor accommodates 48 flexible beds with family, faculty and staff support areas.

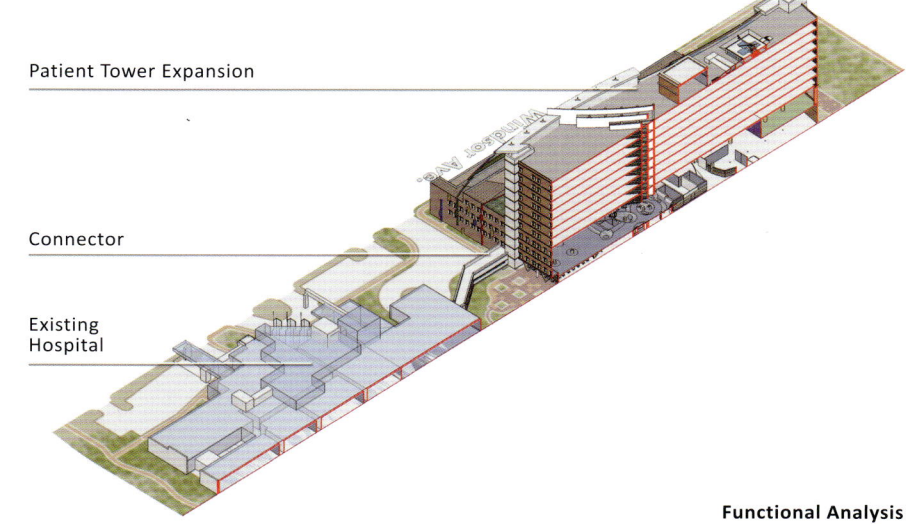

Functional Analysis

1. Mech anical
2. Shell acute 24
3. Acute 24
4. Mechanical
5. Director offices picu 48
6. Surgery/CS/Pacu
7. H.C.O.E/Cardio Diag/ Cardio Cath/Ekg/Echo/IP Pharm/ Cvicu 20/Step Down 12
8. Op Clinics/Physician Offices/ Audiology/Outpatient Rehab
9. Outpatient Pharm/ Med Record/Imaging/Dining
10. Public/admitting
11. Equipment/CEG/ EV/Kitchen/IT
12. Circulation spine
13. Unassigned
14. Behavioural 11
15. Acute 16
16. Bmt 16
17. HEM/ONC 16
18. IP Rehab/HEM,ONC,OP/ End/Hiac/Lab/IR/Conf/ED

A. Level 12 MECH
B. Level 11 SHELL
C. Level 10 BEDS
D. Level 9 BEDS
E. Level 8 BEDS
F. Level 7 BEDS
G. Level 6 MECH
H. Level 5 PICU
I. Level 4 OR
J. Level 3 CARD
K. Level 2 CLINIC
L. Level 1 ENTRY
M. Level B LOWER

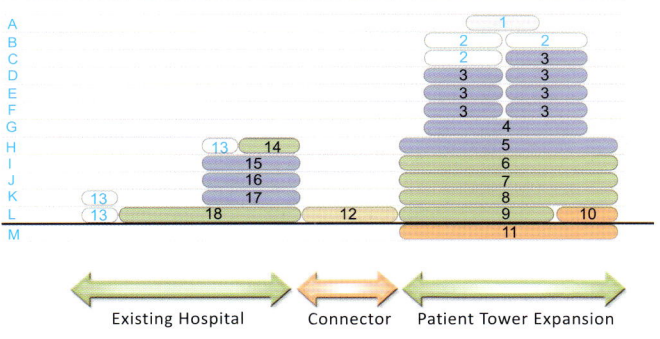

4. Entrance lobby with reception and waiting area

5. Staff station/reception
6. Corridor view

7. Corridor view

Floor Plan – Level 1:
1. Lobby
2. Admit
3. Retail pharmacy
4. Retail pharmacy
5. Servery
6. Dining
7. MRI
8. Imaging
9. C.T.
10. R/F ultrasound
11. NUC. MED. RAD
12. Offices
13. Physician offices
14. EXEC admin

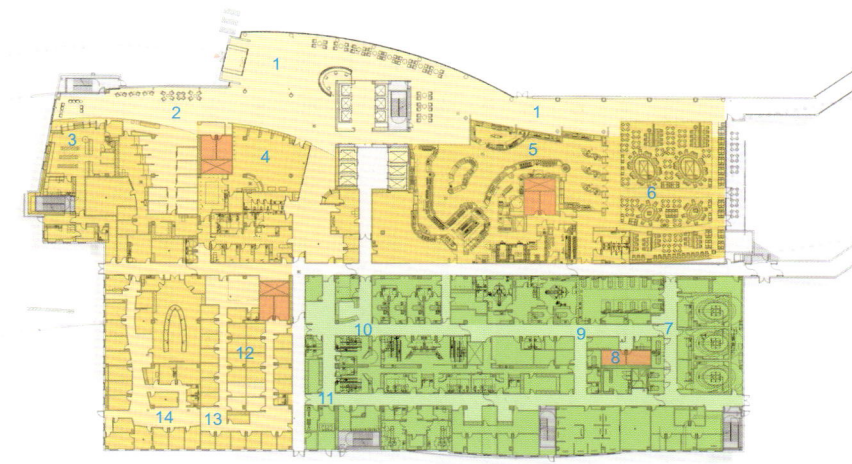

Floor Plan – Level 3:
1. Roof garden
2. Blood bank
3. Mechanical
4. NEURO DIAG
5. RT
6. S.P.D.

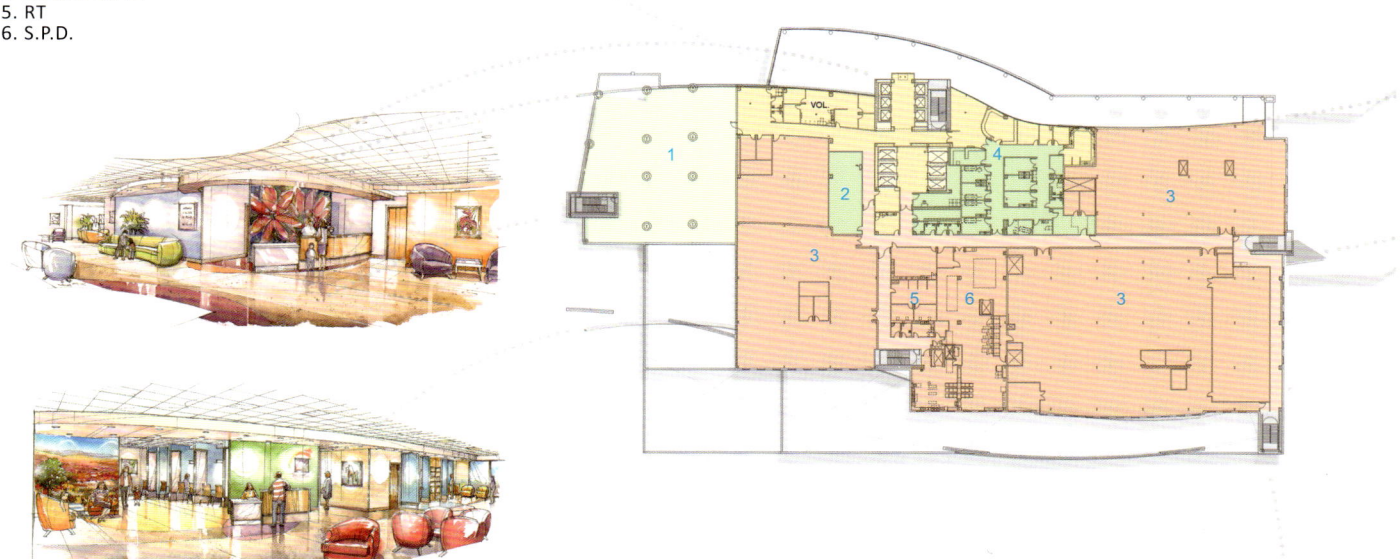

8~9. Family waiting area

Floor Plan – Level 4:
1. Family wait
2. Pre OP. recovery
3. Admin
4. Interventional services
5. PACU
6. Surgery

9

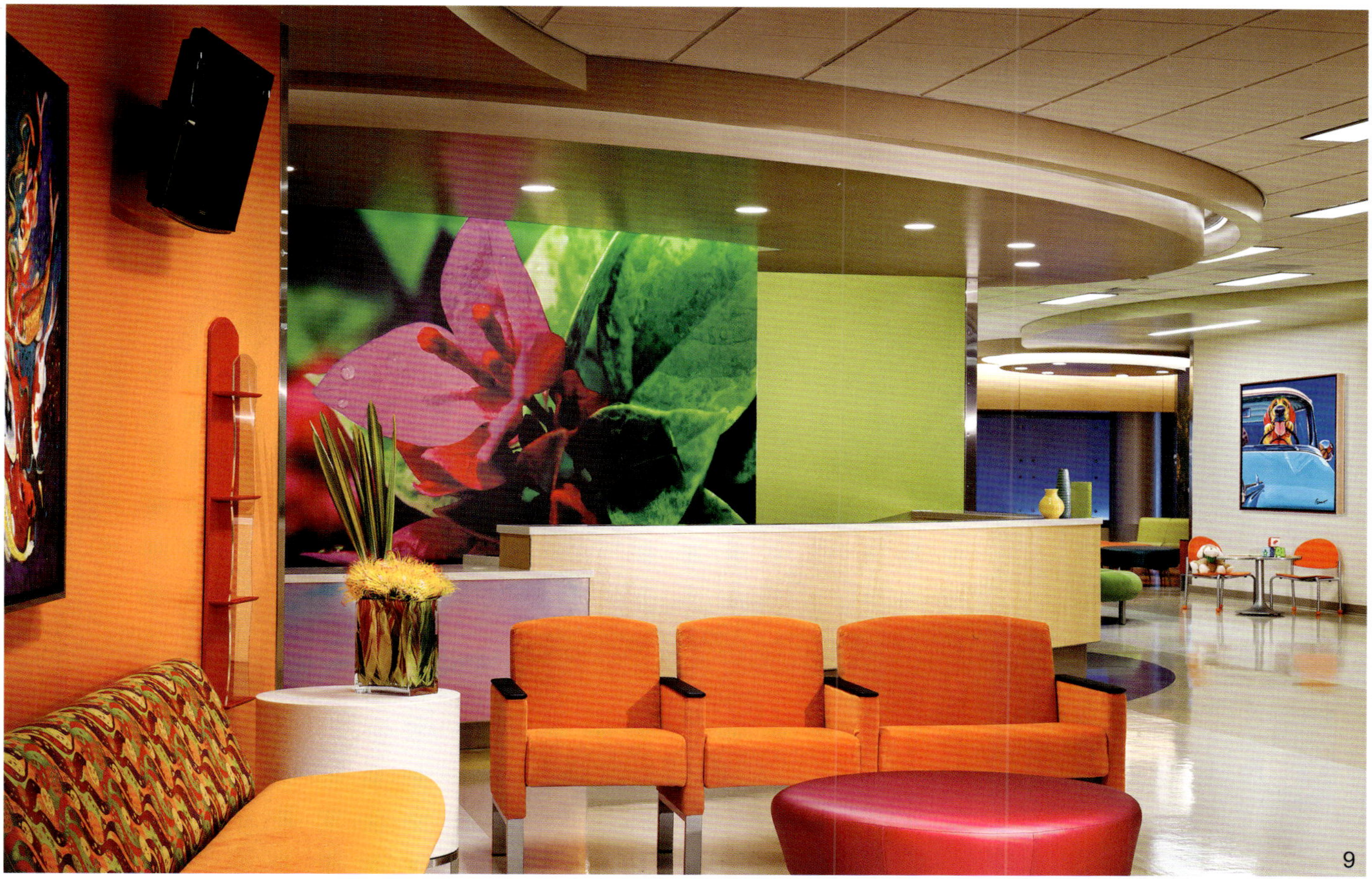

Typical Patient Care Floor

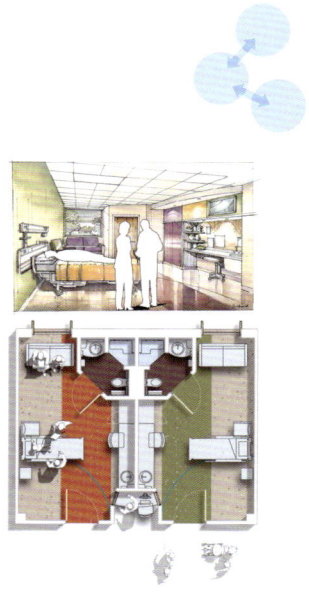

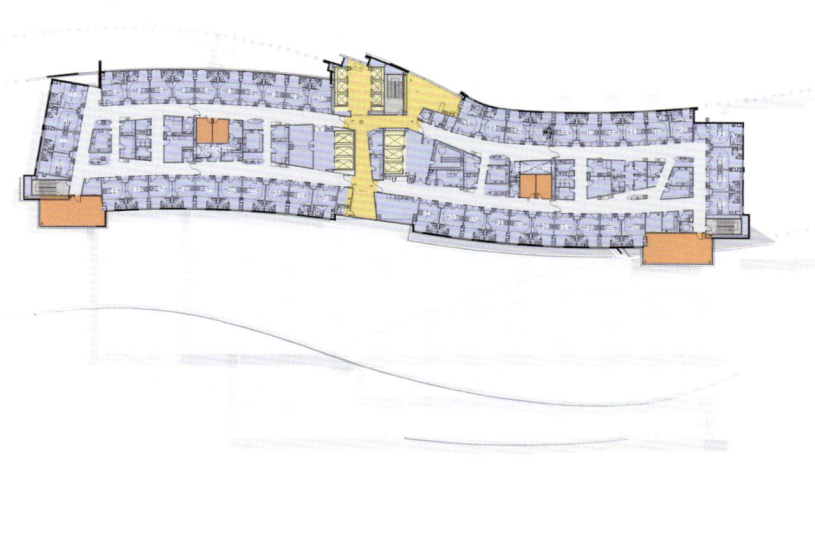

Ålesund Hospital, New Paediatric Unit

Architects:
C. F. Møller Architects
Location:
Ålesund, Norway
Construction area:
5,550m²
Project year:
2011
Photographs:
© Kim Muller

The intention of the new paediatric unit is to create a house that is not just a traditional hospital building, but a children's department based on the idea that confidence and trust is essential in any hospital stay and especially essential when children are the patients.

The project was won in 2005 under the motto "Kangaroo", which refers to a principle where the physical closeness between parents and their premature babies is part of the treatment.

The new children's department provides for sick children's different needs for stimulus from their immediate environment. They require intimacy, a sense of security, and space for play and physical activity in specially designed environments.

In addition to the neonatal ward for infants, the unit contains an outpatient paediatric ward, medical bedward, teaching facilities for school/preschool children and office space. The children's department provides a variety of treatment options for children up to 16 years.

The new wing is constructed as a free-standing building connected to existing hospital in Ålesund via a colourful footbridge. The building is laid out around a central hall separated into an indoor and

1. Courtyard and front façade
2. Side view of the building from the roadside
3. Overall building and the parking area
4. Balcony detail

an outdoor part. The attractive and light surroundings connect related functions and the building is easily comprehended by patients and visitors.

A recessed generous glass façade to the south opens the building up for views across the nearby fjord, and allows visual contact into the building. The building's primary materials are light plaster, glass and wood. The interior is brightly coloured, featuring integrated artwork on the floors and walls.

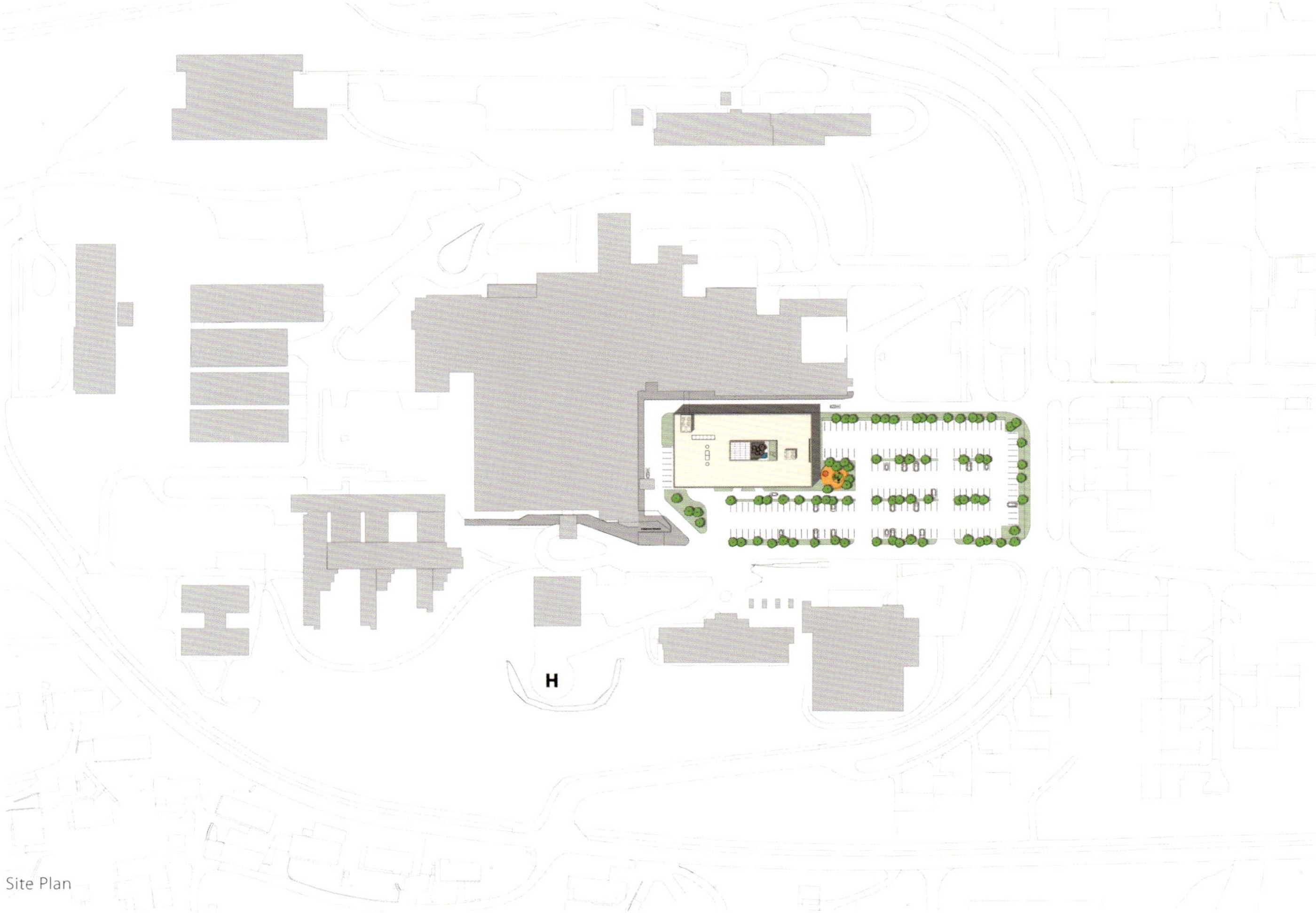

Site Plan

071

5. Main entrance
6. Atrium with colour glass wall

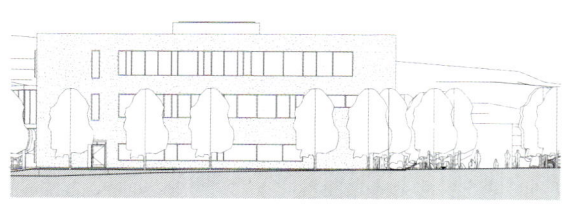
West Elevation

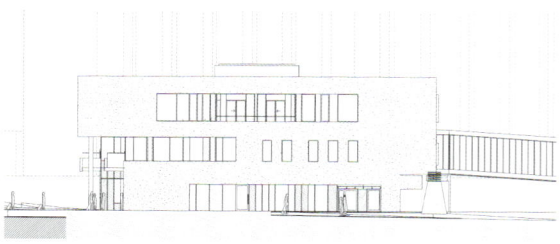
East Elevation

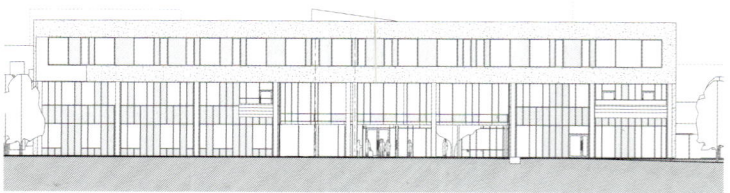
South Elevation

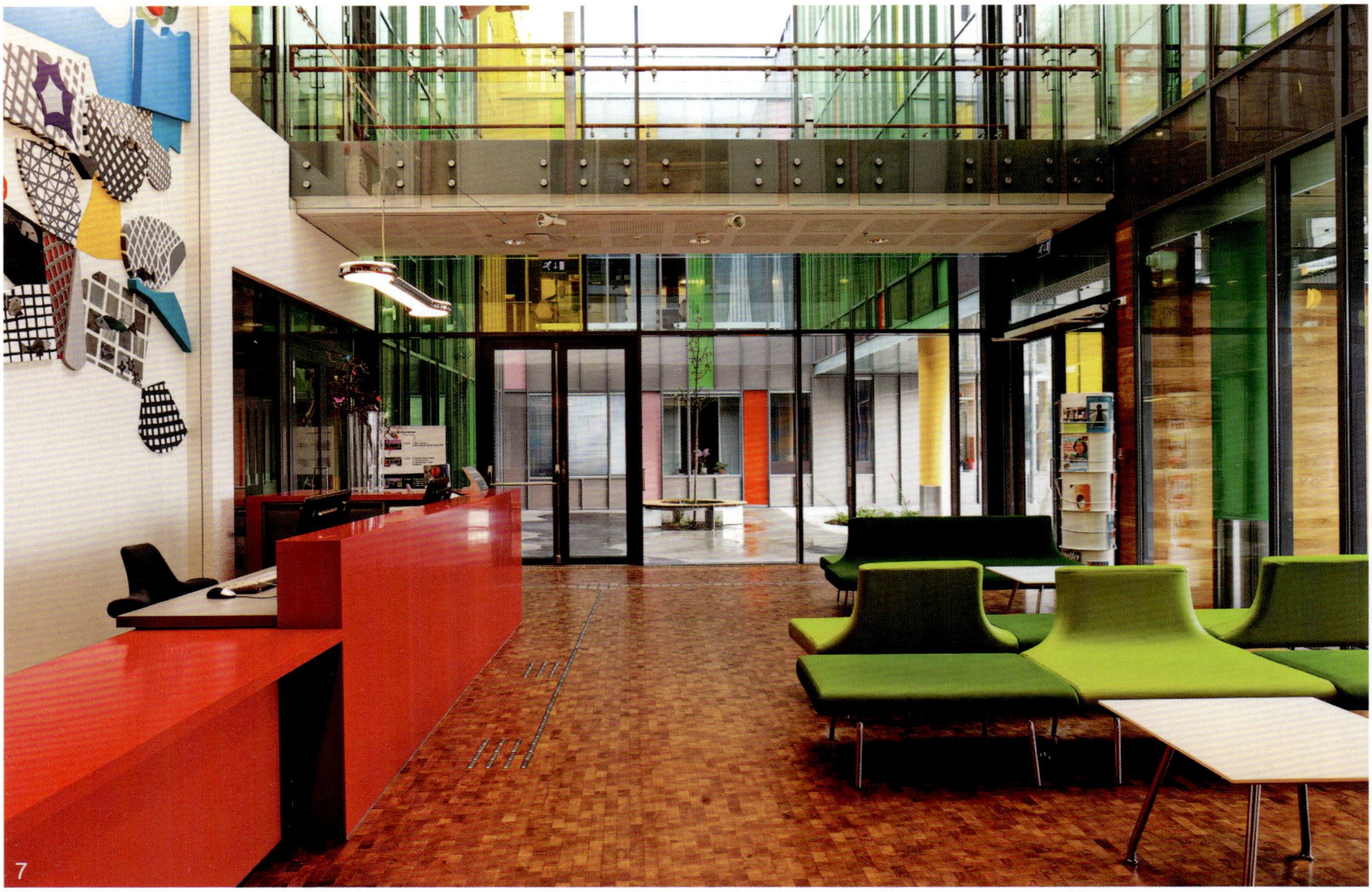

7

8

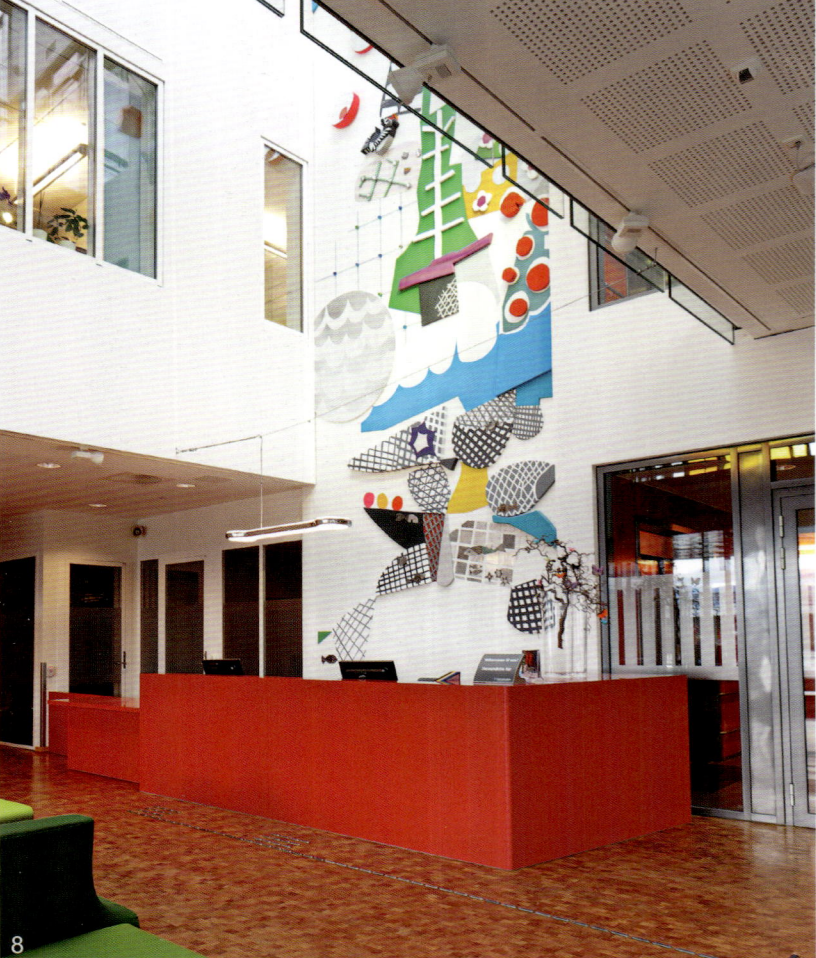

7. Entrance lobby
8. Reception
9. Corridor with playing
   and waiting area

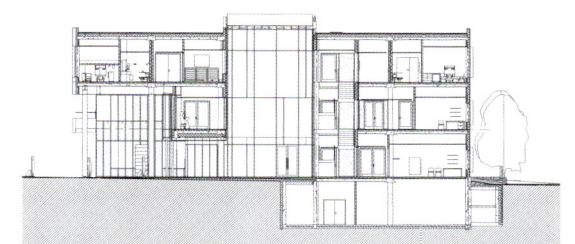

Cross Section – Entrance

Cross Section – Courtyard

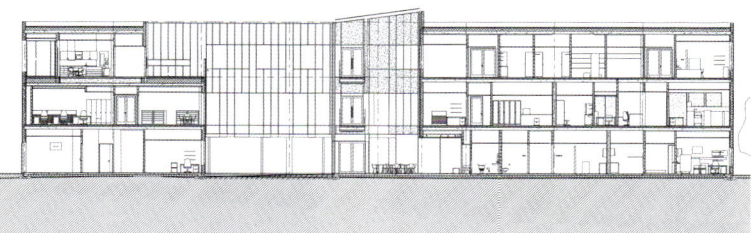

Longitudinal Section

075

10. Patient bedroom with great view to the outside

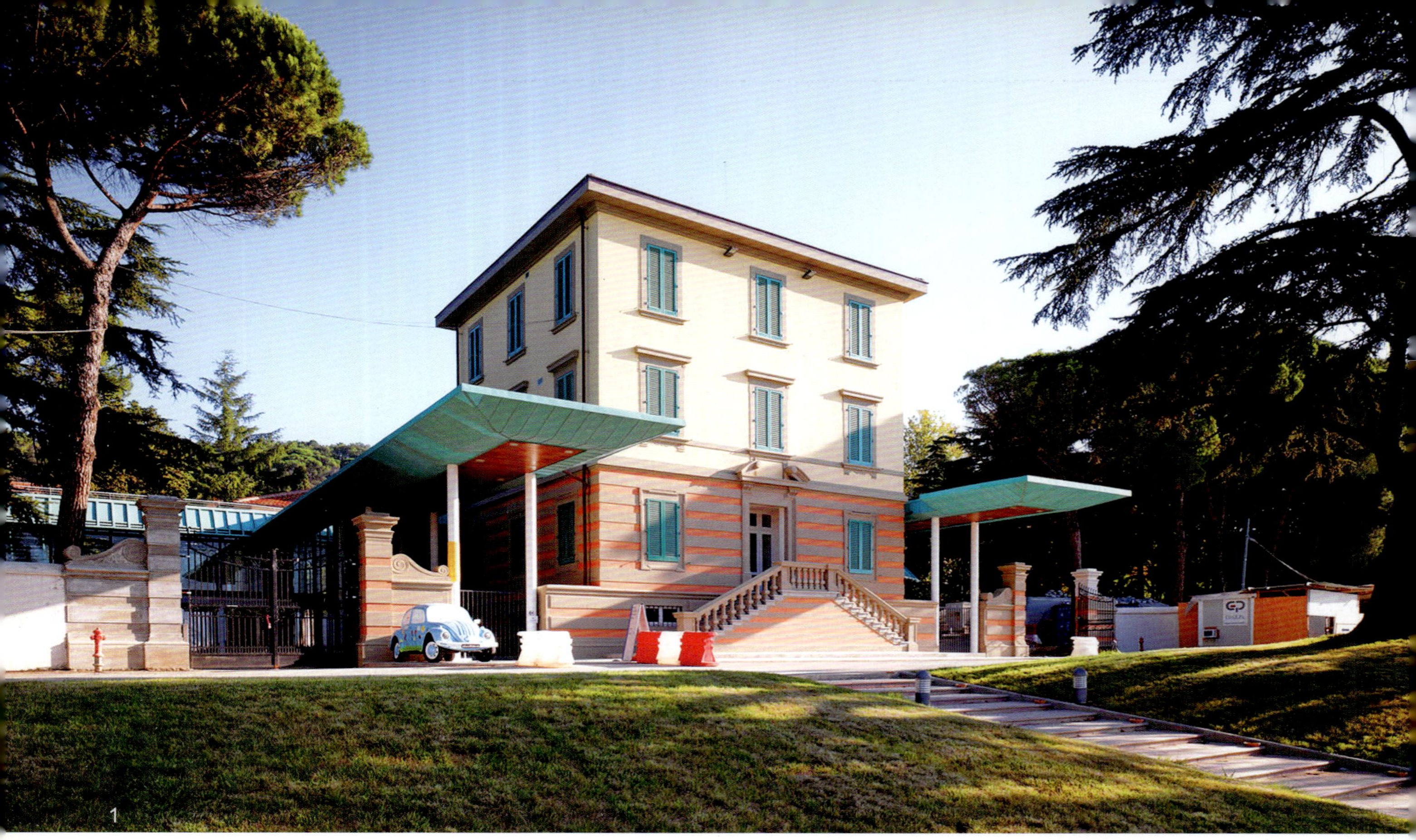
1

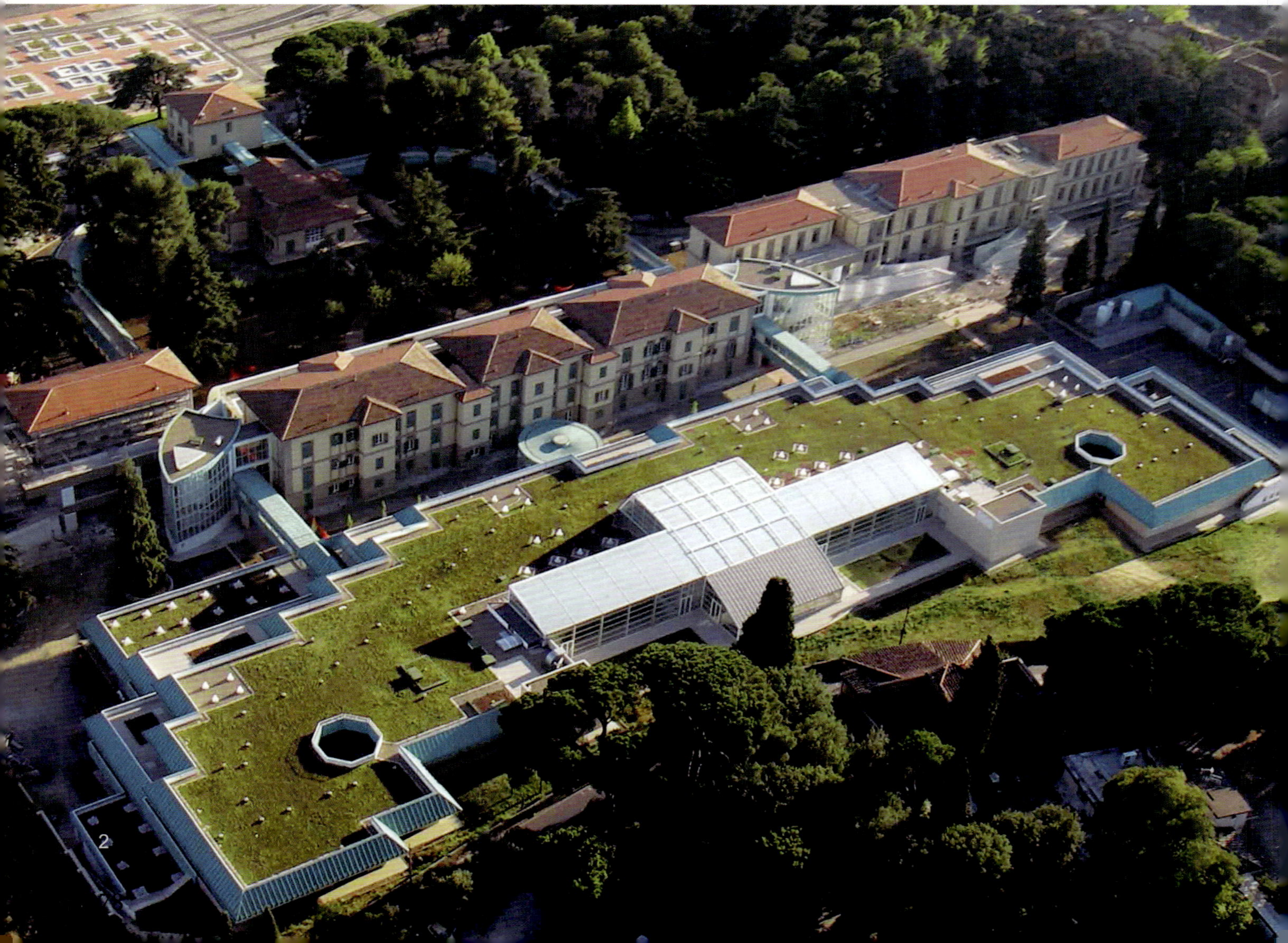
2

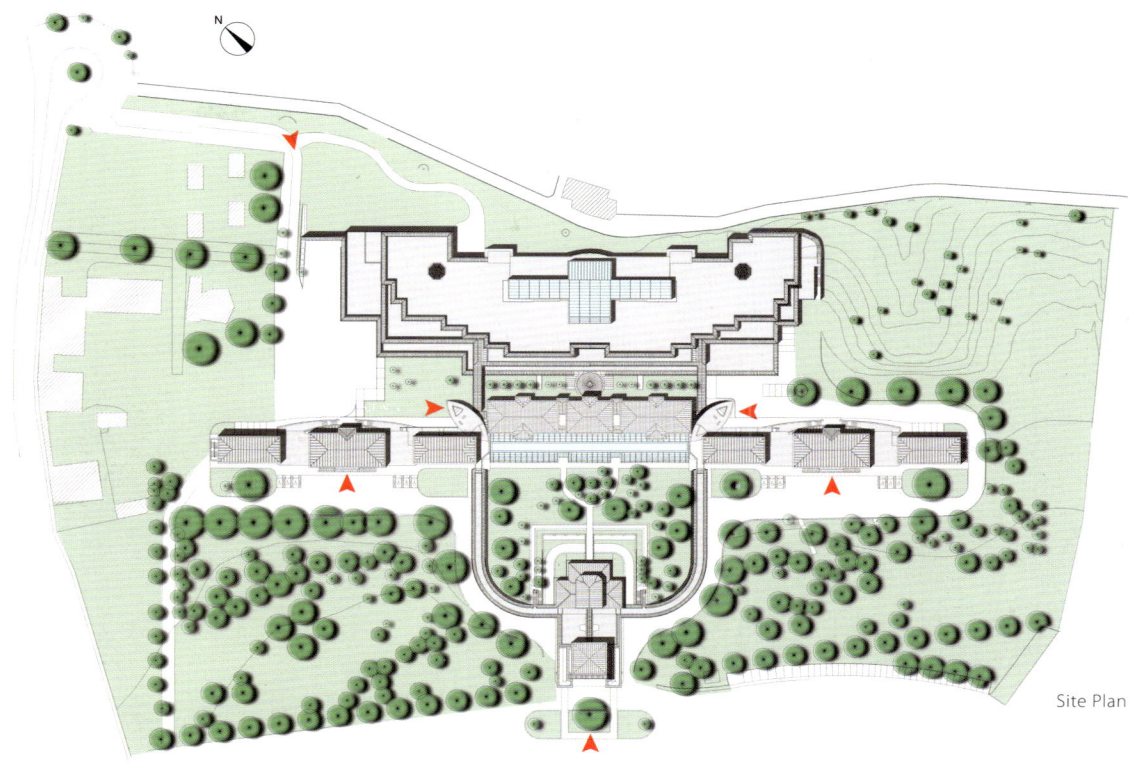

Site Plan

The New "Meyer" Paediatric Hospital

Architects: CSPE
Location: Florence, Italy
Building area: 37,000m² (11,000m² refurbishment; 26,000m² new extension)
Project year: 2007
Photographs:
© Alessandro Ciampi and Pietro Savorelli
Awards:
Financed by European Comunity; Tuscan Region Award for Sustainable Design

The new "Meyer" paediatric hospital in Florence – designed by the CSPE (Centro Studi Progettazione Edilizia) studio and Anshen + Allen, London – is the result of the experience and inter-disciplinary expertise of a diverse range of professionals who discussed their various requirements with a view to creating an ideal space for a "humanisation" of the facility. In order to provide support and monitoring for the development of the project, the Meyer Foundation was set up in 2000. The Foundation endeavours to serve as a point of reference for all the professionals and technicians who are responsible for ensuring the best possible quality of life for children, as well as the most advanced forms of treatment.

The strength of the new paediatric hub in Florence lies in the way in which it has overhauled not only the techniques used but also the look of the hospital sector by means of a mimetic solution that displays a great deal of sensitivity with regard to the hospital environment and to the surrounding built environment.

The project takes on a multitude of design issues relating to the renovation of the ancient Ognissanti villa and to the requirement to make the most of the surrounding landscape, which is constituted by a historic park and a hillside that is often praised for its natural beauty.

The overall plan of the villa, which is based on a triple-block design, could not easily be altered for use as a health facility that would meet the needs of modern-day hospitalisation. Despite this, the redesign proposal involved the renovation of the

three restructured blocks, albeit as separate units with distinct functions. The wings of the complex will play host to the University office and a care centre, while the central pavilion will house the administrative and outpatient facilities. The elevations have been painstakingly refurbished in accordance with the principle of restorative conservation, with the exception of the central façade, which is screened by a large greenhouse that floods the new atrium with sunlight. Lightweight technologies are also deployed on the roof, which features the glass "toy library" that characterises the imposing roof garden.

The new Meyer makes use of strategies that minimise the "conflict" between the new buildings, the natural environment and the pre-existing environment, without compromising the identity of the new buildings in the slightest. The first two floors are partially underground, with only the top floor being fully above ground. Moreover, the three storeys are tapered and staggered in such a way as to create overhangs with large, landscaped terraces that are "crowned" by the garden on the roof.

High technology and environmental sensitivity are the watchwords of this design, which received funding from the EU in 2000 in recognition of its use of technologies that safeguard resources and promote energy saving.

It is, then, an innovative and sustainable renovation, which goes so far as to transform the way in which the spaces are "lived" and managed. The young patients will no longer be gathered together on the basis of which doctor is treating them – rather, they will be grouped by age (0-5 years, 6-12 years) and by intensity of treatment, in order to facilitate social interaction.

Inside the new medical facility, the materials, light, colours and perception of the surrounding landscape combine to create an at once physical and psychological space that re-invents the idea of what a hospital custom-built for young patients can be like, using an approach that sees the treatment areas upgraded to include certain features that are not purely functional. The new Meyer in Florence is one of the first successful examples of a form of experimentation whereby the architecture interprets the perception of space through infant psychology in order to create what will be a true hospital for children – a hospital for the future, in other words.

1. View from the courtyard
2. Aerial view of the hospital
3~4. Courtyard

South Elevations

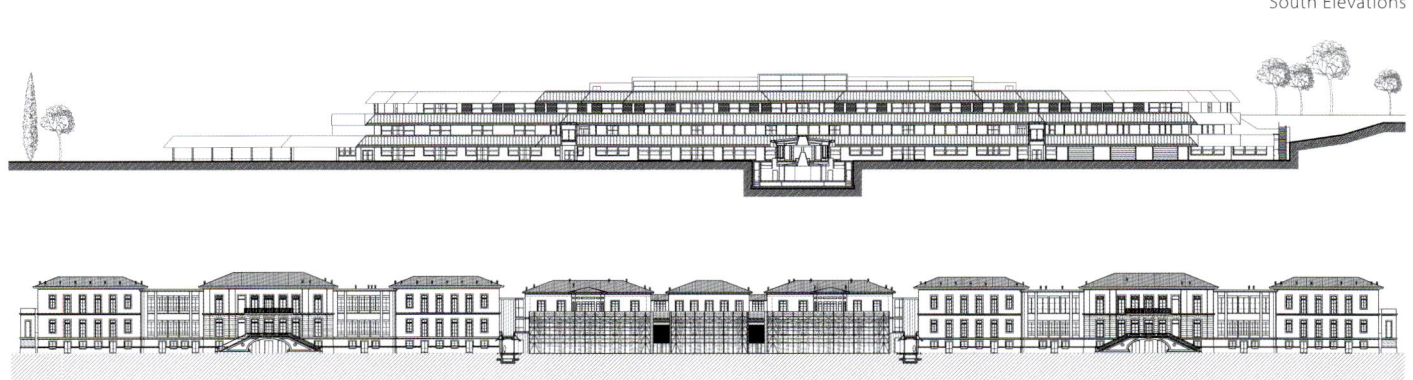

081

5. Approach of the hospital and surroundings
6. View to the interior through glass wall at night

Longitudinal Section

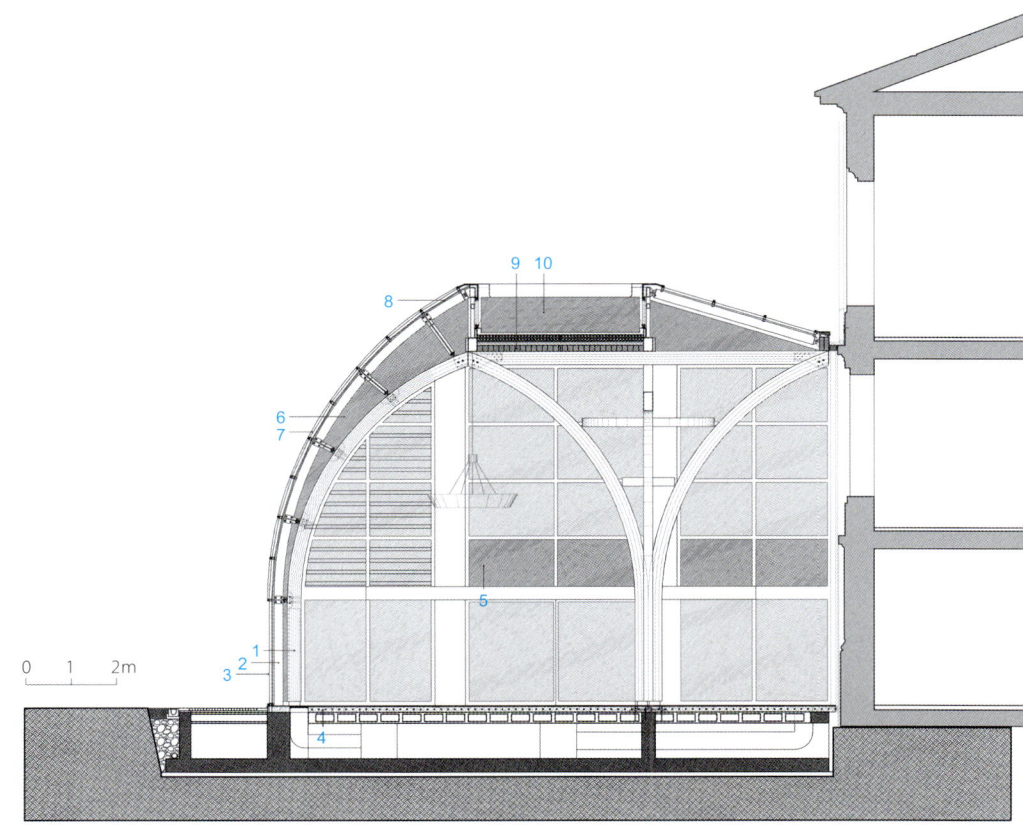

Detailed Drawing:
1. Laminated wooden pillar
2. Steel tube beam
3. Insulating glass laminated with glass
4. Concrete slab with radiant panels
5. Laminated double glazing
6. Carter prepainted aluminium sheet
7. Laminated double glazing with solar cells
8. Wiring duct photovoltaic cells
9. Wooden currents
10. PV inverter picture

7~8. The lobby enjoys sunshine

9. Green roof
10~11. Perspective view of the atrium

086

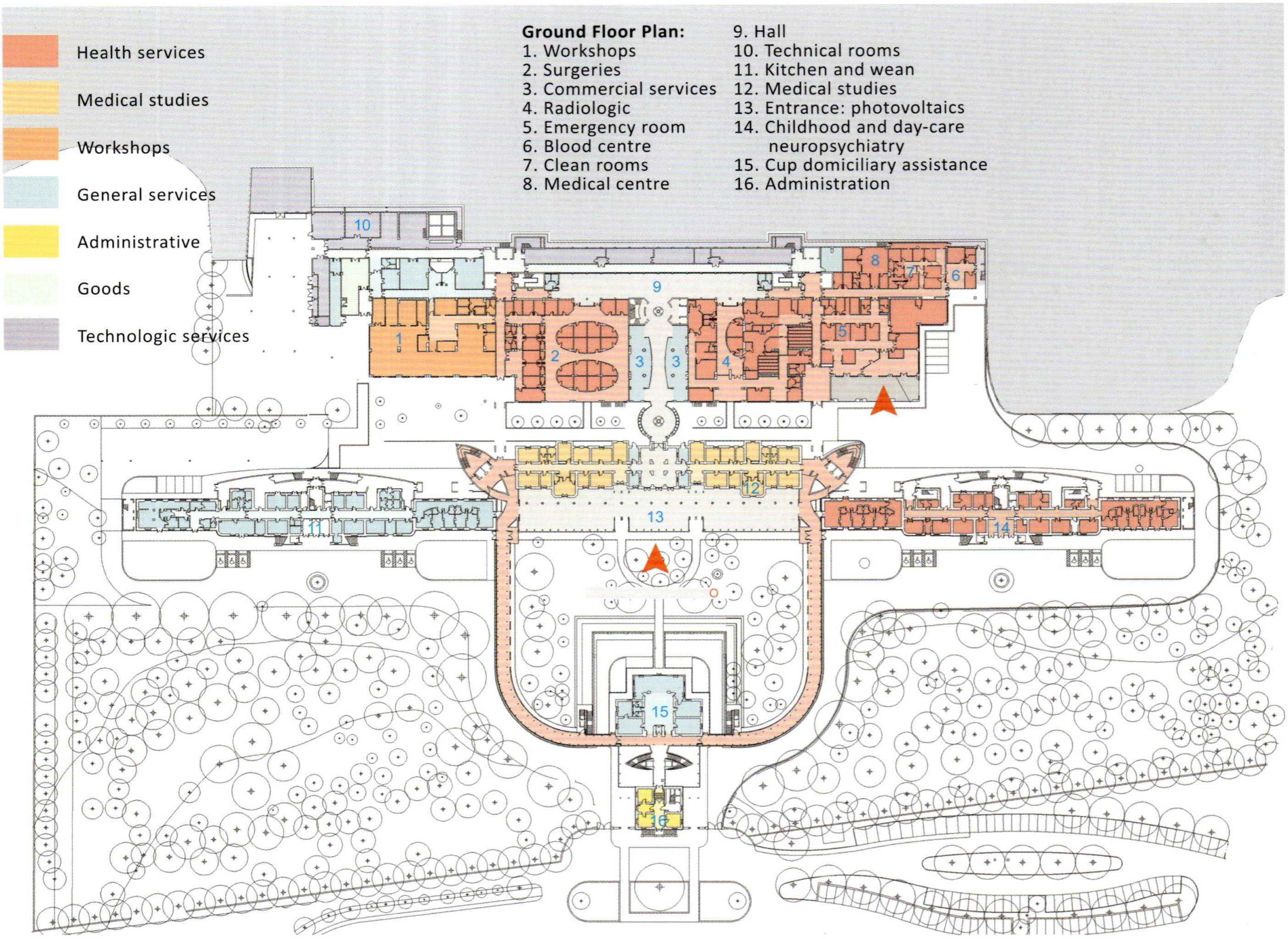

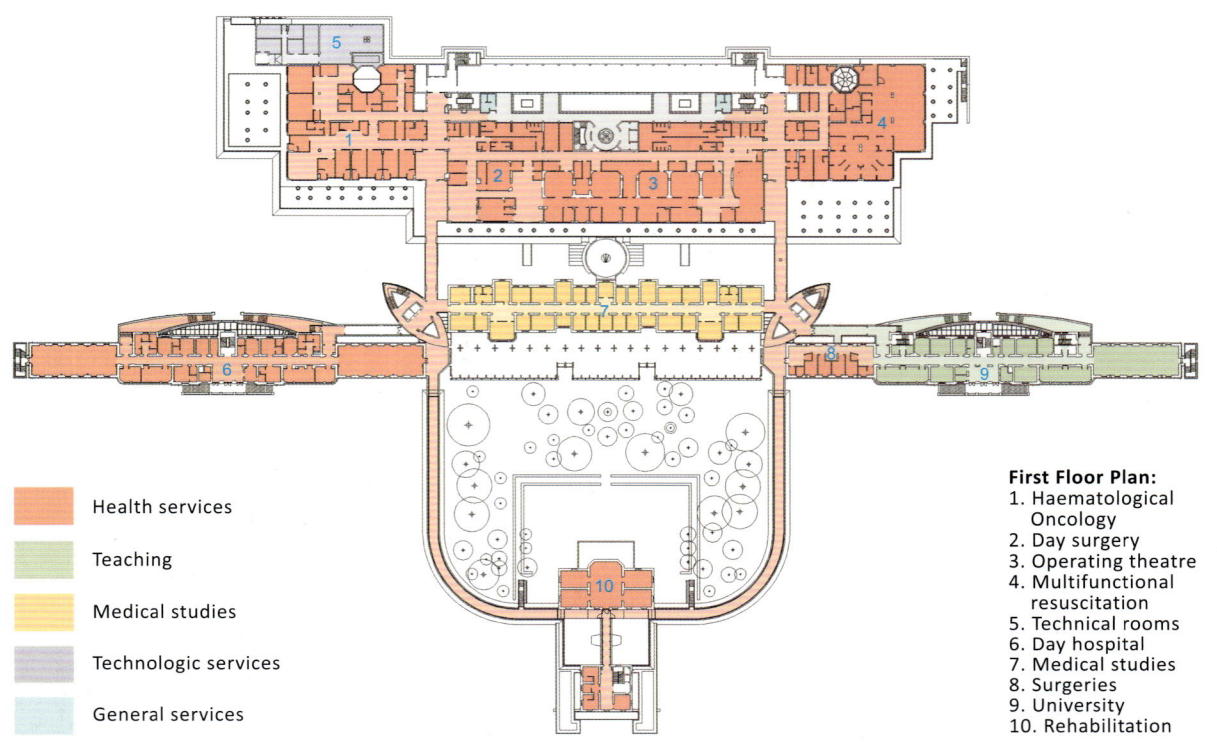

Ground Floor Plan:
1. Workshops
2. Surgeries
3. Commercial services
4. Radiologic
5. Emergency room
6. Blood centre
7. Clean rooms
8. Medical centre
9. Hall
10. Technical rooms
11. Kitchen and wean
12. Medical studies
13. Entrance: photovoltaics
14. Childhood and day-care neuropsychiatry
15. Cup domiciliary assistance
16. Administration

Legend (Ground Floor):
- Health services
- Medical studies
- Workshops
- General services
- Administrative
- Goods
- Technologic services

First Floor Plan:
1. Haematological Oncology
2. Day surgery
3. Operating theatre
4. Multifunctional resuscitation
5. Technical rooms
6. Day hospital
7. Medical studies
8. Surgeries
9. University
10. Rehabilitation

Legend (First Floor):
- Health services
- Teaching
- Medical studies
- Technologic services
- General services

12. Playing room
13. Play area

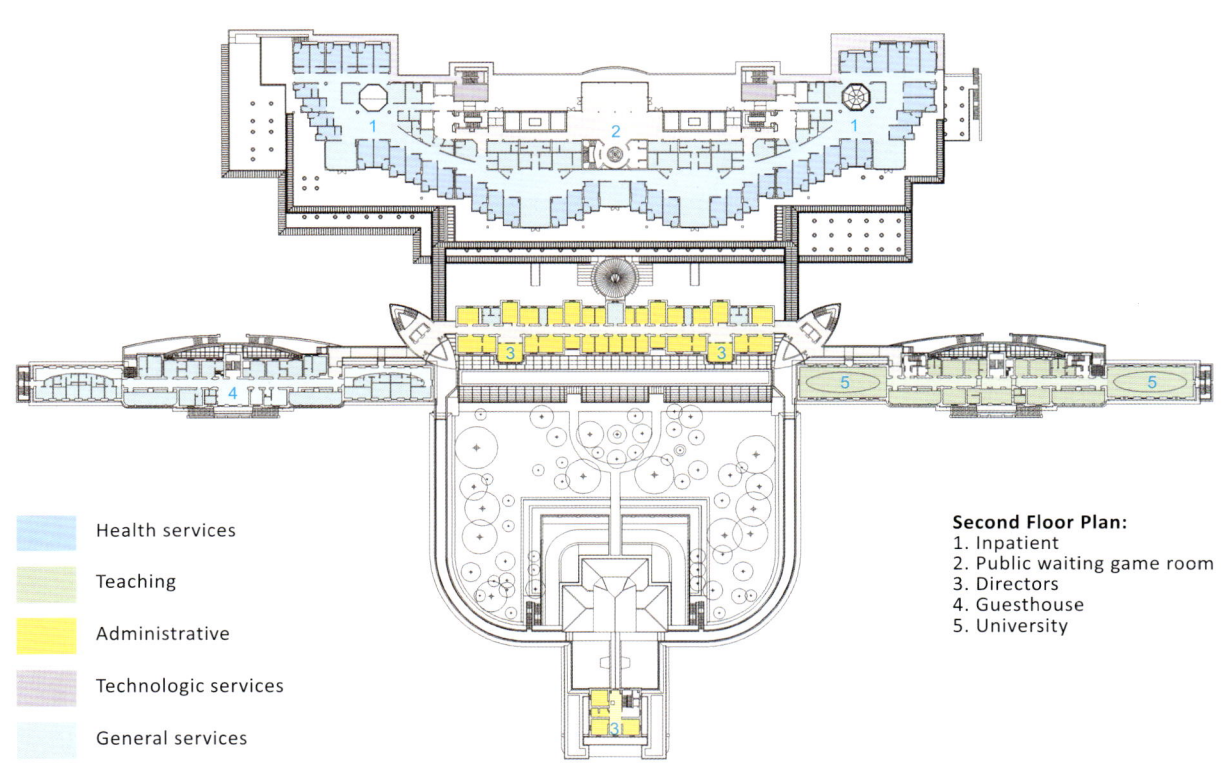

- Health services
- Teaching
- Administrative
- Technologic services
- General services

Second Floor Plan:
1. Inpatient
2. Public waiting game room
3. Directors
4. Guesthouse
5. University

14. Workstation
15. View to the corridor
16. Patient bedroom

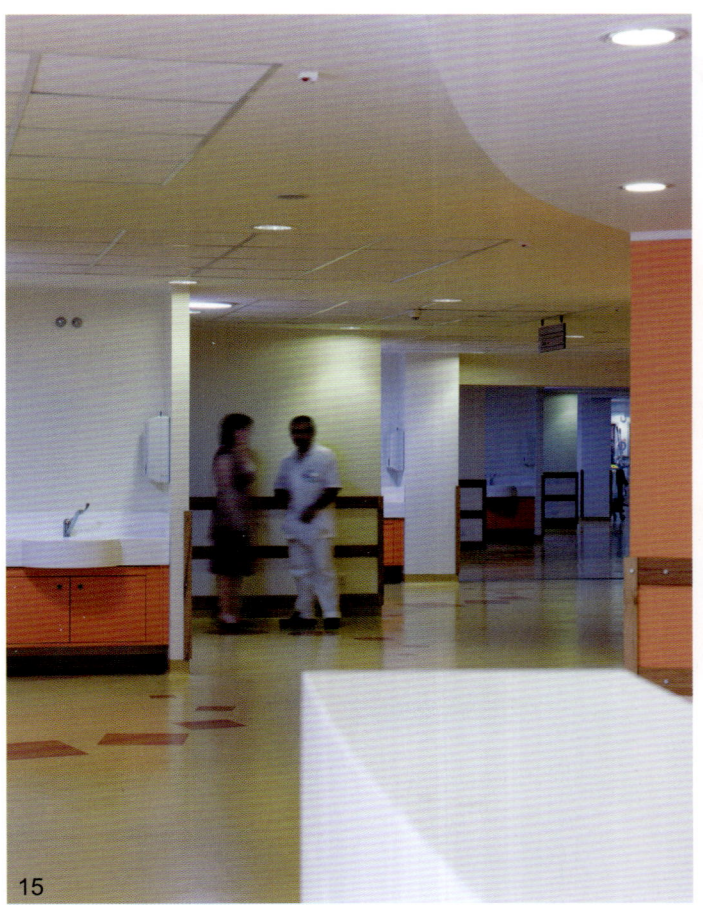

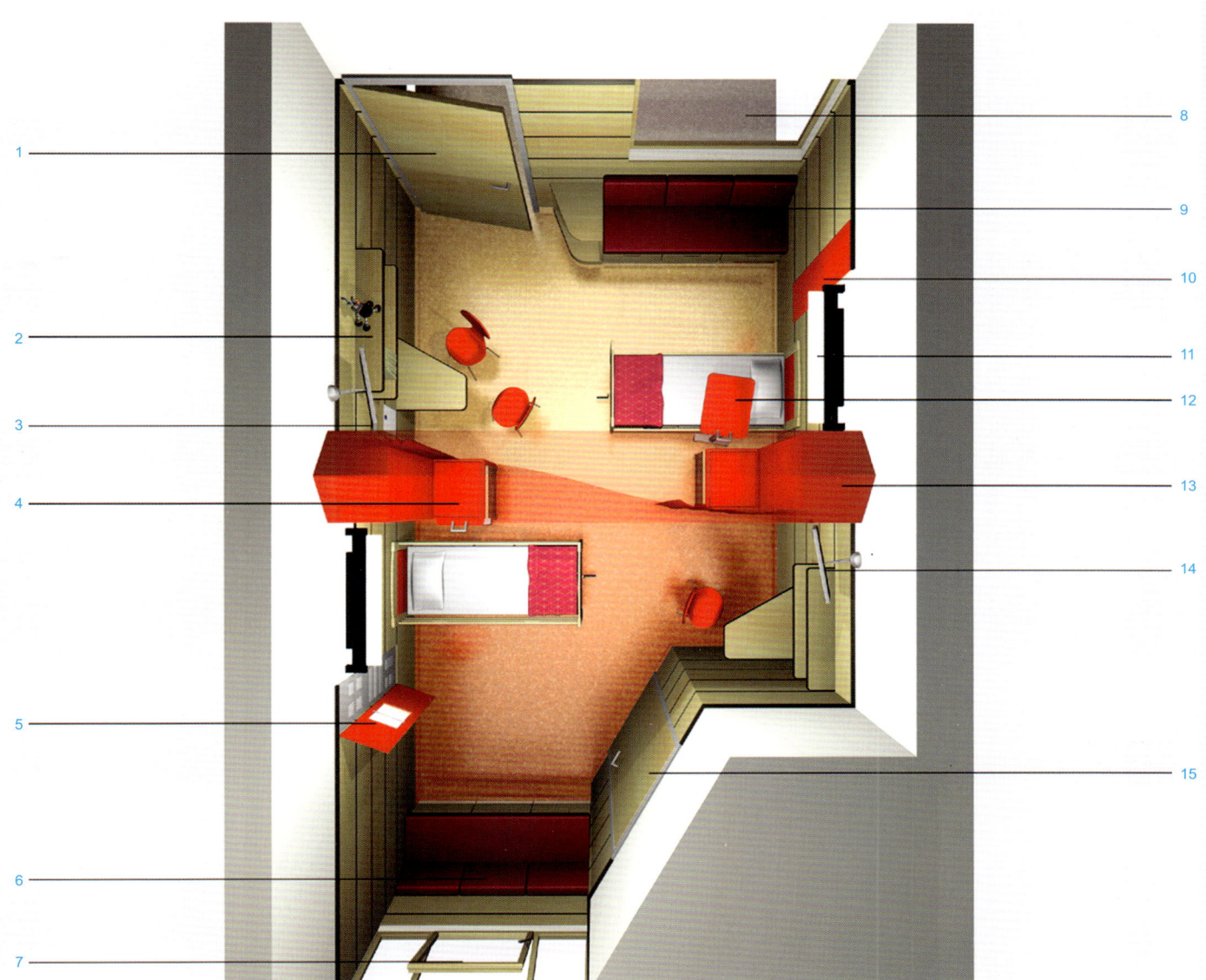

Rendering of Patient Bedroom (Above):
1. Entrance door to the room
2. Shelves and folding table
3. Television wall mount
4. Bedside table on castors
5. Door panel for access to medical gases and struggling
6. Sofa bed for parent
7. Window on green terrace
8. Access door to the toilet
9. Television wall mount
10. Closet
11. Mini cart
12. Lamp
13. Door panel for access to medical gases and struggling
14. Sofa bed for parent
15. Visual control outside

1

2

092

Kinderklinik Prizessin Margaret

Architects:
Angela Fritsch
Location:
Darmstadt, Germany
Building area:
17,860m²
Project year:
2006
Photographs:
© Dieter Leistner

The inpatient ward building of the Darmstadt Prizessin Margaret Paediatric clinics is a successful example for a contemporary childrens' hospital. All involved parties, administration, chief physician and nursing personnel, agreed to abandon the conventional hospital vocabulary. Today the building with its stylised four-leaf clover shaped floor plan integrates into the old tree population in the hospital park of Darmstadt's Mathildenhöhe.

On the ground floor, one half of the building is dug into the slope; a service tunnel links the new building with the main house. Internally, a central light funnel allows daylight to enter all storeys. The cruciform circulation of the wards, a standard solution in hospital architecture, as well as the positioning of the rooms along the façade minimises the walking distances. The nurses' lounges are located on the intersection of two clover eaves, thus providing an optimal supervision of the corridors. The hallways widen in front of the rooms to create playing and communication zones, which have a dynamic relation to the exterior via the artrium and its play of light and shadow. The light-green epoxy resin floor with white painted blossoms is equipped with underfloor heating, wihich makes playing on the floor more comfortable. Playful furnishing and decoration animate various forms of entertainment for the children.

All dimensions of the new building have

1. View to the information station
2. Waiting area outside of exam room
3. Side view of façade
4. Foyer
5. View to work station
6. View to inner courtyard from circulation

been orientated around the sickbeds as the smallest unit. The radical patient rooms are distinguished by their wedge-shaped plan and beech veneer wardrobes. An integrated settee can be used as a bed for parents, whilst a second one can be placed next to the sickbed. The warm wood and custom-made green-blue curtains, symbolising the sky and the park, generate a homely ambiance. Equally unusual are the amorphously shape bathrooms with sea-blue glass mosaics, which have been integrated into the wedge between two treatment rooms each. The balconies add to the ambiance that contributes to a quick process of recovery.

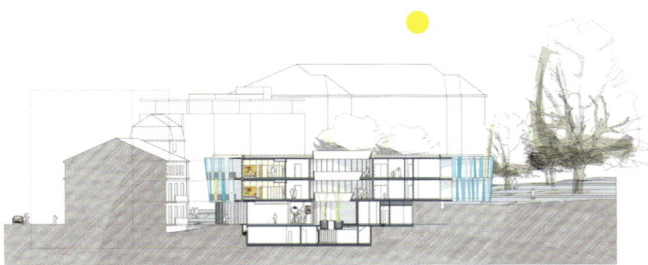

Section

Elevation

5

6

7. Doctor's room
8. Corridor

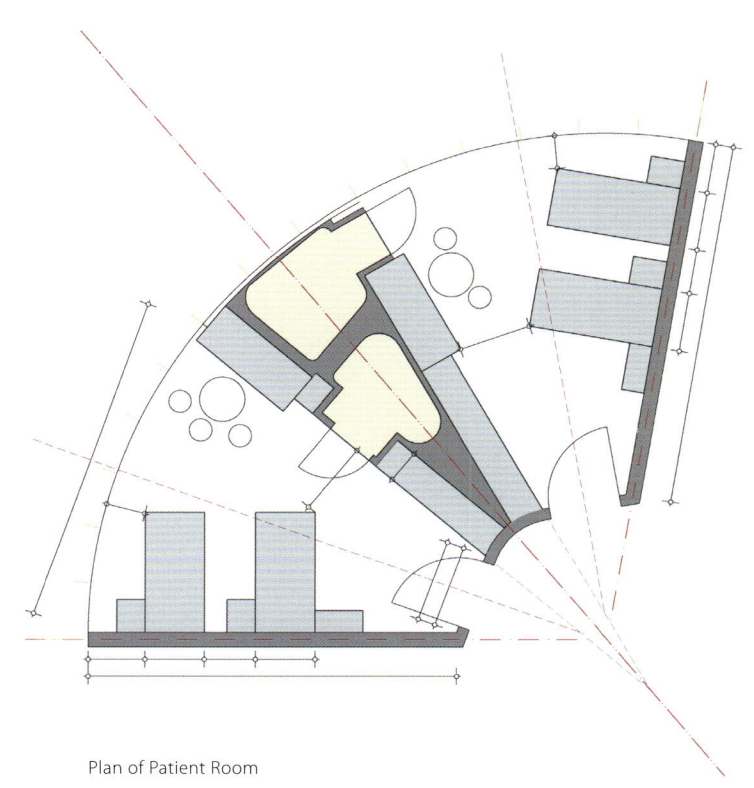

Plan of Patient Room

9

10

9. Intensive care room
10. Bathroom

Typical Floor Plan

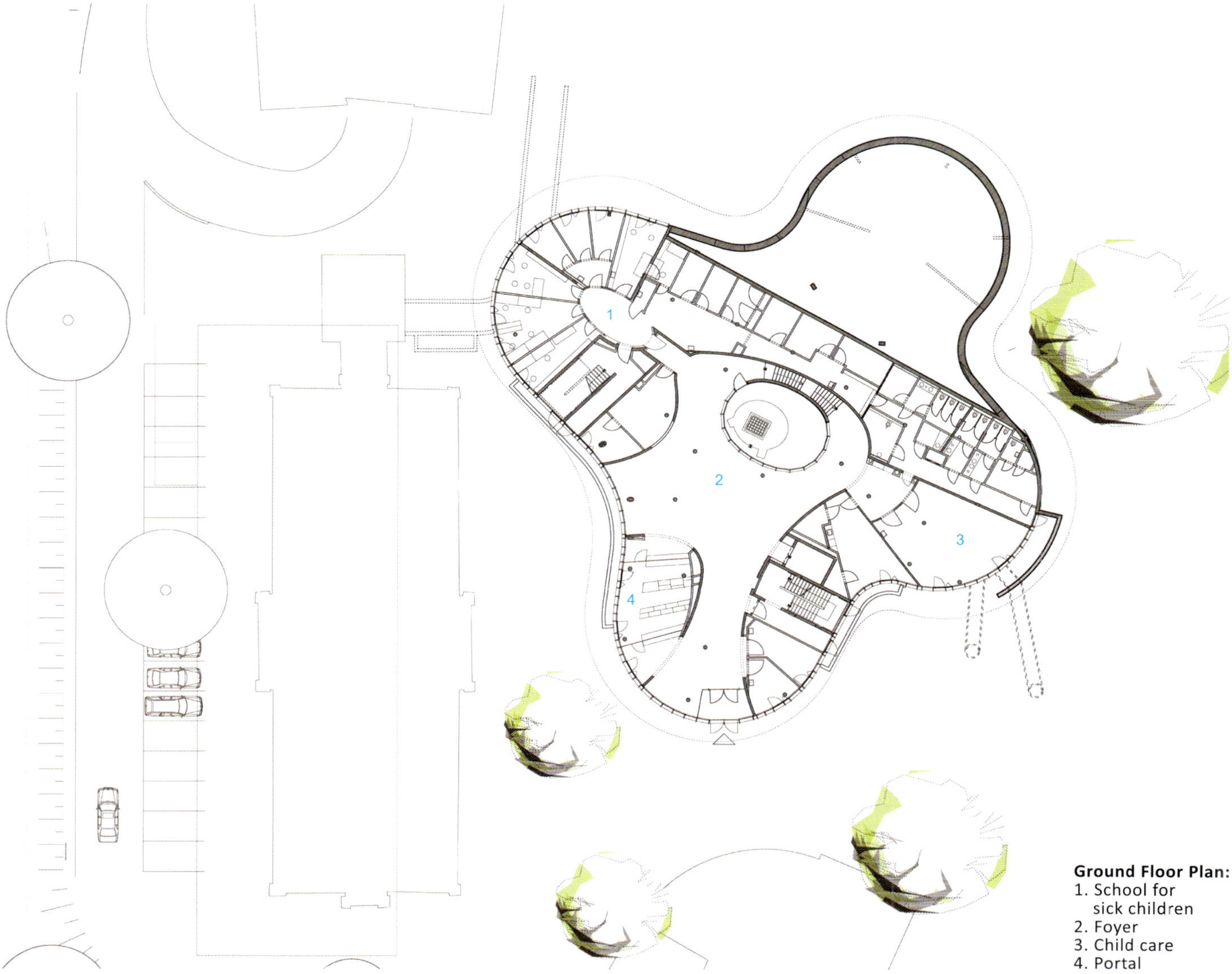

Ground Floor Plan:
1. School for sick children
2. Foyer
3. Child care
4. Portal

099

Cancer and Radiotherapy and Chemotherapy

RADIATION ONCOLOGY UNIT DESIGN AND PLANNING

1. Introduction

The purpose of the Radiation Oncology Unit is to provide facilities and equipment for treatment of patients using radioactive rays. The Radiation Oncology Unit may contain one or both electron beam therapy and radiation therapy. Although not recommended, a Simulation Room may be omitted in small linear accelerator facilities where other positioning geometry is provided. Room sizes and specifications for a Radiation Oncology Unit should accommodate the equipment manufacturer's recommendations, as space requirements may vary from one machine to another and one manufacturer to another. Radiation Oncology may also be referred to as Radiotherapy or Radiation Therapy.

1.1 Patient Characteristics

Patient characteristics:
- adults of all ages and ethnic and cultural backgrounds and children in certain centres;
- patients may be self-conscious as regards their appearance due to hair loss, lesions, disfigurement, etc.;
- patients with impaired mobility due to age or condition – or both; clinical symptoms such as pain, nausea and vomiting;
- emotional distress – anger, symptoms of loss and grief – in families as well as the patient;
- disruption to normal lifestyle. Patients undergoing radiation therapy attend daily often for up to 6-8 weeks and time spent in treatment is a major disruption to their lives. Many patients need to relocate some distance from their homes for treatment. However, the majority of patients continue their daily work and home activities as best they can throughout their treatment.

1.2 Patient Needs

Recognising the often depleted physical and emotional state of patients, their families and carers, it is important to develop a quality built environment that not only eases patient and carer anxiety but also provides staff with stimulating work environment conducive to the delivery of better patient care. As far as is practicable a non-clinical, restful environment within the radiation treatment area (bunker) and simulator areas should be encouraged by wall paintings, soft colours, etc. Planning must recognise the need for patients and their families to discuss personal matters in a private and confidential environment and to minimise concerns about appearance and loss of self-esteem.

Access is required to the following services:
- support and assistance with regard to affordable accommodation and travel that may be required for the duration of treatment particularly for patients from rural and remote areas;
- nutritional advice, advice on available alternative therapies (massage, stress management, etc.) and provision of wigs;
- palliative care assessment;
- patient and family counselling;
- education / information resources – brochures, computer access, support organisations, etc. is provided;
- parking – often highlighted by patients as the main determinant of whether or not to proceed with treatment. The perception of difficulty parking may compromise the utilisation of radiotherapy.

It must be noted that increasing survival due to early diagnosis and constantly improving technology is leading to an increase in chronicity requiring supportive care.

1.3 Design Criteria

The building both internally and externally must be accessible, approachable, friendly and non-threatening and must be appropriate to its setting and climate. As much natural light as possible should be provided, especially into public spaces, waiting areas and those treatment areas that patients and staff occupy for long periods of time. Room sizes and specifications for the linear accelerators should accommodate the equipment manufacturer's recommendations as space requirements may vary from one machine to another and one manufacturer to another.

1.4 Future Trends

The Service Plan for the project shall take into account the following trends and the degree to which these trends are to incorporated into the facility:
- combined modality treatment such as surgery and/or chemotherapy and radiation therapy occurring concurrently;
- increasing multidisciplinary patient-centred clinics and case review;
- increased formal networking and exchange of clinical data between units and extended into rural and remote communities;
- increasing use of videoconferencing;
- increased use of CT-based planning resulting in an increased amount of information for planning and an increase in time required for three-dimensional treatment planning;
- increased complexity of individual treatment plans (and number of plans per patient);
- increased requirement for accuracy in treatment. Dose escalation for tumour volumes has required greater accuracy in treatment delivery as critical organ doses may become compromised in the event of an error in field placement. Lower machine tolerances (user defined) which prevent the beam switching on in case of discrepancy between planned and actual set up assist in achieving this level of accuracy and create a significant increase in daily QA;
- technological advances in treatment improving the success rate of radiation therapy and expanding number of cancer cases for which radiation therapy can be beneficial. In NSW, this is determined by Statewide planning parameters and targets;
- capability for medium to long-term inclusion of new technologies (e.g., expansion of radiosurgery to extracranial image guided RT);
- increase in HDR (High Dose Rate) brachytherapy treatment where designated;
- use of endorectal ultrasound for staging/treatment decision-making for patients with rectal cancers;
- an increase in the number of fields as conformal therapy/Intensity

2. Planning

2.1 Planning Models

2.1.1 LOCATION

A Radiation Oncology Unit should generally be on ground level due to the weight of the equipment and shielding requirements, and for ease of installation and replacement of specialized equipment. It should be located with ready access for outpatients, including access for people with disabilities, and ambulances, and for inpatients on beds/trolleys. If the overall Centre is free-standing, careful consideration must be given to covered links between the Centre and the main hospital – for inpatients on beds/trolleys access, goods and supplies, and access to other departments such as Medical Imaging. Site conditions relating to bushfires and access by rural fire services may considerably affect configuration and location of the bunkers.

2.1.2 BUILDING DESIGN

Linear accelerator rooms require radiation protection that will include concrete walls, floors and ceiling to a specified thickness. The radiation protection needs of the unit shall be assessed by a certified physicist or radiation safety consultant.

2.2 Functional Areas

The Radiation Oncology Unit may include the following Functional Areas:
- Reception, Waiting, administrative and records areas;
- Patient treatment areas including Radiotherapy Bunkers, Treatment Planning, Simulation, Holding area, Patient Toilet;
- Film processing and storage areas;
- Support areas including Consult, Utilities, Cleaner's Room, Store, Disposal rooms;
- Staff areas including Staff Station, Offices, Staff Change and Toilets.

SUPPORT AREAS

The following optional support areas may be required:
- Quality control area with illuminated X-ray viewing boxes;
- Computer control area normally located adjacent to the Radiotherapy Room entry;
- Dosimetry equipment area;

- Hypothermia Room (may be combined with an Examination Room);
- Oncologist's Office (may be combined with Consultation Room);
- Physicist's Office (may be combined with Treatment Planning);
- Treatment Planning and Record Room;
- Provision shall be made for the following additional support areas for Linear Accelerator;
- Mould Room with exhaust hood and hand basin;
- Block Room with storage (may be combined with the Mould Room).

2.3 Functional Relationships

The Radiation Oncology Unit should be located with ready access for ambulant patients and beds/trolleys. The Unit may be co-located with Medical Imaging Units. If intra-operative therapy is proposed, the Radiation Oncology Unit should be located close to the Operating Unit or with a direct link. A ground level location is preferred due to the weight of the equipment and shielding requirements, and for ease of installation and replacement.

2.3.1 EXTERNAL
The Radiation Oncology Unit, and the Cancer Centre as a whole, has functional relationships with the following units, services and organisations:
- General Practitioners, Surgeons and Physicians;
- Community-based Services;
- Other Hospital Cancer Treatment Services;
- External Education and Research Facilities;
- Cancer Registry (if not located in the Centre).

2.3.2 INTERNAL
- Pharmacy (unless a satellite unit is located in the Centre);
- Pathology (mechanical transport system);
- Medical Imaging (CT and MRI);
- Nuclear Medicine/PET;
- Palliative Care;
- Oncology Inpatient Unit/s.

2.4 Entry/Reception/Administration

Ideally there should be one entry to the Cancer Centre leading to the main reception desk and waiting which will then divert to the sub waiting areas of clinic, planning and treatment areas. A child play area should be incorporated into the main waiting area in a safe, acoustically enclosed environment. The area should accommodate public and patient amenities. A dedicated area for patient and family resources/education facilities – including computers for patient education and completing quality of life data for clinical trials. Facilities for volunteers and transport staff should also be located in this area. Administrative functions (appointments, etc.) may be located in this area.

2.5 Clinic Suite

The Clinic Suite will be designed for multidisciplinary clinics for use by all clinical specialties. Details of anticipated occasions of service and session requirements will need to be established in order to determine the number of consulting rooms required. A room or rooms will be required for multidisciplinary clinical review of patients. Procedure room/s large enough to conduct endoscopic examinations such as head and neck examinations, pleural taps, and peritoneal drains. Space for Therapy and Dietetic consults and treatment may also be included. Waiting areas oversighted by Reception or Staff Base. Blood collection room and specimen toilet. Access to all nursing support rooms – staff base and clean and dirty utility rooms. These may be shared with the Patient Observation area if travel distances are not too great and staff do not have to cross public areas. Corridors and at least some rooms must permit trolley access. The Clinic Suite should be located on the perimeter of the Unit with direct access from the entry for easy access by outpatients and to facilitate any expansion that may be needed to accommodate the requirements of medical oncology and haematology in the future.

2.6 Treatment Planning

Facility requirements for treatment planning include:
- Simulator/CT suite;

- Resuscitation trolley bay;
- Patient & visitor amenities (change cubicles, toilets, sub-waiting, trolley bay);
- Computer planning room and brachytherapy high dose rate (HDR) planning room with server and tape storage space. Special air-conditioning is required to handle the large number of computers in this area;
- Offices/workstations for radiation therapists (working in dosimetry) and possibly trainees/students;
- QA checking and data transfer office discreet from the busy planning area for the high level of concentration required.

2.7 Patient Observation/Nursing Area

Patients are assessed weekly by a radiation oncologist throughout the course of their treatment and exam/consult rooms are included in this component for this purpose. Patient/staff interview/conference rooms are required to review the proposed treatment programme with the patient and their family. This area also includes the requirements for nursing care and care by other disciplines for:
- Education;
- Support;
- Dressing changes;
- Medication delivery;
- IV insertion and monitoring.

Curtained bed/trolley bays will be required for patient holding and recovery and each bay will require power, oxygen and suction. A staff station will oversee the bed/trolley area. A Clean Utility, Dirty Utility and storage facility will be located in this area. A resuscitation trolley bay if distance from the bay in the Simulator area is too distant.

2.8 Accessibility

2.8.1 EXTERNAL
Level, undercover access is required for outpatients and inpatients in wheelchairs, trolleys and beds. Ready access from the main hospital for food,

linen, supplies, etc. Ready access from the public car park for patients attending on a daily basis to minimise stress. After-hours access for urgent radiotherapy cases must be easy for inpatients and external (ambulance) patients.

2.8.2 INTERNAL
Access should be generous and with direct circulation systems in all patient areas to allow for the efficient movement of both ambulatory and wheelchair/stretcher/bed patients. The requirement for bed access should be carefully addressed. The treatment and planning areas should not be used as thoroughfares. Wherever possible, a separation between patient circulation and staff / materials circulation within the Unit should be attempted. Some access routes and circulation systems, particularly in the radiation treatment area, must allow delivery paths for large pieces of equipment. Height, width, and floor loads must be considered in the design of these access routes. The Radiation Oncology Unit should only be accessible to authorised persons and must be locked and an alarm activated once the area is vacated after hours. Care should be taken with wayfinding and signage to discourage accidental entry to these areas.

2.9 Infection Control

The infectious status of many patients accessing the Unit may be unknown and many may be in a severely immunocompromised or suppressed state All body fluids should be treated as potentially infectious and standard precautions should be taken. Reusable instruments and materials may be re-circulated through the usual channels to the Sterile Services Unit. It is essential that the Unit design contributes to the control of infection by way of the following:
- an appropriate overall layout to minimise cross contamination in work areas;
- efficient work flow design and detailing;
- suitable materials and finishes to facilitate cleaning;
- adequate number and location of hand hygiene facilities;
- appropriate cleaning, waste storage and waste disposal;
- appropriate isolation of space and ventilation systems which present potential hazard.

It is not generally considered necessary to provide separate waiting areas for immunocompromised patients but there shall be single rooms in the Day Unit should they be needed for this purpose.

2.10 Environmental Considerations

2.10.1 TOXIC WASTE
The following must be addressed:
- safe handling and air exchanges for chemicals in the appliance room, x-ray dark room, etc.;
- provision of effective extraction systems to areas such as medical physics laboratory with a fume hood extraction system that complies with Radiation Safety Regulations;
- drainage systems designed to meet the requirements of the relevant sewerage authority and Health Department;
- safe storage and disposal of irradiated material.

2.10.2 ACOUSTICS
Provide for the control of noise associated with activity in the appliance fabrication room so as not to disturb patients or staff. All examination, consultation rooms and offices will be acoustically private.

2.10.3 INTERIOR DESIGN
Normalisation of the environment in looks, operation and functional content whilst not compromising clinical practice or safety. Treatment areas such as the simulator room and "bunkers" should have soft colours, paintings, etc. to detract as much as possible from the isolation during treatment.

2.10.4 PATIENT PRIVACY
Provide visual and acoustic privacy for patients in all changing, consultation, examination rooms and treatment spaces. Ideally, changed patients should not have to cross public circulation space in order to access treatment areas from changed waiting areas. Patients will also require privacy to discuss billing and private health related concerns.

3. Design

3.1 Building Service Requirements

3.1.1 CONSTRUCTION STANDARDS
The flooring for a Radiation Oncology Unit shall be adequate to meet the load requirements for equipment, patient, and personnel. Provision for cable ducts or conduits should be made in the floors and ceilings as required. Ceiling-mounted equipment should have properly designed rigid support structures located above the finished ceiling. The minimum recommended ceiling height is three metres. A lay-in type of ceiling should be considered for ease of installation, service, and remodelling.

3.1.2 RADIATION PROTECTION
Cobalt and linear accelerator rooms require radiation protection that may include concrete walls, floors and ceiling to a specified thickness. The radiation protection needs of the Unit shall be assessed by a certified physicist or appropriate state agency. This assessment is to specify the type, location, and amount of protection to be installed in accordance with final approved department layout and equipment selection. The radiation protection requirements shall be incorporated into the final plans and specifications.

3.2 Safety

3.2.1 RADIATION SAFETY
The Environment Protection Authority (EPA) – part of the NSW Department of Environment and Climate Change – administers the Radiation Control Act 1990 (amended in August 2002) and the Radiation Control Regulation 2003 – responsible for regulation and control of radioactive substances, radioactive sources and radiation apparatus. Apparatus used for radiotherapy, or planning radiotherapy must be registered and operators licensed.

3.2.2 FINISHES, SURFACES AND FITTINGS
Consider the impact of finishes, surfaces and fittings on safety. In particular, consider:

- slippery or wet floors;
- protrusions or sharp edges;
- stability and height of equipment or fittings;
- choice of flooring.

3.3 Finishes

The wall surfaces in the unit areas should be washable. Non-slip flooring is essential for all work areas. The floor surface should be impervious, easy to clean, sealed with coving at the edges and have adequate drainage. Ceilings must be washable, impermeable and non-porous.

3.4 Fixtures, Fittings & Equipment

3.4.1 EQUIPMENT – GENERAL

All items of equipment will need to be itemised and larger items measured during the design phase to ensure the following:
- can be suitably housed to provide for its operation and maintenance. In particular, linear accelerator and electronic cabinet room sizes and specifications should accommodate the equipment manufacturer's recommendations, as space requirements may vary from one machine to another and one manufacturer to another. Equipment requiring services such as water and special power must be duly noted and passed to project engineers;
- doors are sized to allow passage of equipment;
- heat loads are estimated and catered for;
- weight loads are estimated and checked structurally.

Adequate space for maintenance of major equipment must also be considered. Note that electronic control cabinets are bulky and need special access to three sides.

3.4.2 SAFETY SHOWERS AND EYE WASHES

Safety shower and eye wash or eye/face wash equipment must be readily accessible where cytotoxic drugs are dispensed and administered

3.5 Building Service Requirements

3.5.1 GENERAL
High cost engineering areas which should receive careful consideration by design teams include:
- lighting and the impact of deep planning on lighting requirements;
- the number of sanitary fittings and the potential for reducing these by strategic location;
- extent of the required emergency power system;
- extent of provision of emergency doors;
- the need for and the cost benefit/implications of pneumatic transport/ communication systems;
- extent of provision of essential back-up systems (e.g. dual generators, chillers, boilers and dual electrical circuits).

3.5.2 STRUCTURAL
Radiation treatment and simulation bunkers need radiation protection built into the facility. Bunkers need special construction to ensure they meet radiation safety requirements. Ceiling mounted equipment should have properly designed rigid support structures located above the finished ceiling sufficient to support heavy ceiling-mounted equipment such as frames of data monitors. A lay-in type of ceiling should be considered for ease of installation, service, and remodelling.
Ceiling Height: A minimum 3.0-metre ceiling height in procedure rooms, with a minimum 1-metre space above for heating, ventilating and air conditioning systems.

The flooring for a Radiation Oncology Unit shall be adequate to meet the load requirements for equipment, patient and personnel.

3.5.3 COMMUNICATIONS AND INFORMATION SYSTEMS
The infrastructure for the following should be considered for the present and future expansion:
- voice/data systems;
- telephone and video conferencing capacity;

- duress call - fixed and personal (if required);
- CCTV monitoring systems of entry points;
- infrastructure for PACS, electronic records and radiotherapy information management system (RIS);
- server room;
- patient/nurse and emergency call systems (that should be consistent with existing systems);
- alarm systems – drug fridges, medical gases, entries, etc. that register in an area manned 24 hours per day;
- patient viewing cameras, treatment delivery computers and intercoms to allow the radiation therapist to monitor and communicate with the patient during treatment when the patient is alone in the treatment room.

3.5.4 ELECTRICAL SERVICES

Sufficient power for current need and future expansion of service. An emergency back-up system for the power supply should be available for high priority equipment and illumination. Provision for cable ducts or conduits should be made in the floors, walls and ceilings as required for specialized equipment. There should be a maximum distance of 7.5 metres for the cable run between the simulator and the generator; however, minimal distances are preferable to minimise the degradation of cable operation. Cable runs in the radiation treatment control area need careful planning.

3.5.5 MECHANICAL SERVICES

Appropriate air exchanges and exhausts for chemicals in the appliance workroom. Sufficient air-conditioning capacity and compressed air in radiation treatment rooms; access for future expansion of service. Appropriate air-handling systems in computer equipment rooms. General air conditioning needs to cool equipment but not blow over partially undressed patients on beds. To maintain a high level of staff concentration and to minimise the possibility of accidents, the temperature of the Unit should be maintained within a comfortable range not exceeding 25°C. Pneumatic tube system to Pathology, wards and other departments as required. Smoke detectors in radiation treatment and simulator rooms must be of the type not sensitive to radiation (i.e. photoelectric) and require special consideration.

3.5.6 LIGHTING

Lighting in the Radiation Oncology Unit will need to be of various types and will be dependent on the task. The main lighting requirements are:
- characteristics of clinical colour rendering;
- even distribution of luminance throughout the non-working areas;
- walls that do not show reflections of luminaires, particularly at eye-height of staff when working;
- fully dimmable lighting in bunkers and simulator areas;
- special three-level lighting in radiation treatment vaults;
- lasers for patient positioning in bunkers and simulator rooms with high level luminance available for maintenance and repairs.

3.5.7 HYDRAULIC SERVICES

The trade waste plumbing and drainage system must be designed to meet the requirements of the relevant Sewerage authority and the Department of Health Information of the quality of chemicals to be used/discharged must be provided by the client to the hydraulics engineer.

3.6 Non-standard Components

3.6.1 APPLIANCE FABRICATION – WORKSHOP
DESCRIPTION AND FUNCTION

Manufacture of immobilization devices. Storage space is required for the large volumes of material used to create the appliances. While the shell forming for head and neck patients is predominantly thermoplastic based, there are still patients that require plaster impressions and appliance room specific consult and mark up.

LOCATION AND RELATIONSHIPS

Direct access from the Fitting Room but away from other patient areas due to possible noise and fumes.

CONSIDERATIONS

Surge protection for electrical equipment. Dust and fume extraction. Acoustic containment.

FF&E will include:
- plaster dust extraction system and plaster trap;
- fume extraction cabinet;
- large sink and plaster trap;
- heavy duty stainless steel benching;
- shelving and cupboards;
- instruments – drill, hot wire cutter, vacuum former.

3.6.2 APPLIANCE FITTING ROOM
DESCRIPTION AND FUNCTION
Where patients are measured for immobilization devices, masks, etc.

LOCATION AND RELATIONSHIPS
Direct access from the corridor and into the Workroom. Away from other patient areas due to possible noise and fumes.

CONSIDERATIONS
Patient privacy – screen around doorway. Bed/trolley access.
FF&E will include:
- handbasin;
- plinth;
- benches & cupboards.

3.6.3 SIMULATOR/CT ROOM
DESCRIPTION AND FUNCTION
A planning simulator is a specialized x-ray machine. It may be a conventional simulator but will need an adjoining CT Room or ready access to a CT. It is expected, however, that modern units will install a CT Simulator. The simulator must have image intensification and CT inter-working capability. Computed tomography (CT) simulator combines the functionality of a conventional simulator with features and image processing and display tools of a three-dimensional radiation treatment planning (3D RTTP) system. The diagnostic C-arm mobile unit is used for similar purposes in the planning and verification of high dose rate Brachytherapy. Fan noise from various computer systems

creates significant noise making it difficult to converse with patients. Provide a large cupboard with floor-to-ceiling access to house x-ray generator and reconstruction computers discreetly within the CT room. The cupboard should have separate air flow for cooling needs.

LOCATION AND RELATIONSHIPS
Adjacent to the Control Room. Ready access to Change Cubicles, Sub-Waiting and Patient Toilets. Ready access to a resuscitation trolley (where intravenous contrast is administered).

CONSIDERATIONS
- space for a bed to enter, turn and be placed along either side of the simulator;
- lead glass viewing window to the Control Room;
- radiation screening to Standards;
- temperature and humidity control to manufacturer's specifications;
- dimmable lighting controls;
- emergency "stop" button;
- oxygen & suction on medical services panel;
- emergency/nurse call buttons;
- CCTV camera and intercom system – patient to control room;
- hand basin;
- benches;
- wall- and ceiling-mounted x-ray laser lights (that require a steel plate mounted to the building stud fixed at the floor and ceiling to ensure stability when mounted);
- x-ray transformer.

3.6.4 SIMULATOR/CT-SIMULATOR CONTROL ROOM
DESCRIPTION AND FUNCTION
Control area for the Simulator.

LOCATION AND RELATIONSHIPS
Directly adjacent to the Simulator Room.

CONSIDERATIONS
FF&E will include:
- simulator control panel;
- CT control console and computer;
- virtual simulation workstation;
- PACS viewing monitor and x-ray viewing panels for review of mammograms and x-rays of patients from rural areas;
- emergency "stop" button;
- patient viewing monitor and microphone;
- work benches.

3.6.5 PLANNING WORKROOM
DESCRIPTION AND FUNCTION
The area used by the radiation therapists who work individually using light boxes and computer terminals to produce radiation dosage profiles.

LOCATION AND RELATIONSHIPS
Ready access to the Simulator. Easy access to the Computer Server Data Storage Room for retrieval of archived data.

CONSIDERATIONS
Specialized FF&E will include:
- work benches sized to suit the planning computers;
- planning computers – 1 per staff member;
- light boxes – surface-mounted, 2 per workroom;
- plotter;
- printer;
- x-ray viewing panels – 1 per workstation.

3.6.6 MEDICAL PHYSICS LABORATORY
DESCRIPTION AND FUNCTION
Sufficient space for computers and a work area to carry out IntraBeam dosimetry measurements, dosimetry equipment QA and ultrasound and LDR brachytherapy QA.

LOCATION AND RELATIONSHIPS
Ready access to the Bunkers.

CONSIDERATIONS
Sealed vinyl floor, laminated bench tops. Hands-free telephone.

FF&E will include:
- work benches;
- light boxes;
- office furniture.

Note that IntraBeam dosimetry measurements require a shielded space. Several QA procedures may happen at one time, with one or more using radioactive sources. There must be a dedicated radioactive source handling area, including a fume hood extraction system separate from rest of the laboratory that complies with Radiation Safety Regulations.

3.6.7 ELECTRONICS LABORATORY
DESCRIPTION AND FUNCTION
Maintenance of electrical equipment divided into "clean" and "dirty" zones.

LOCATION AND RELATIONSHIPS
Part of the Medical Physics Zone.

CONSIDERATIONS
Light-coloured, antistatic flooring. Electrostatic earthing throughout the area. Hands-free telephone.

FF&E will include:
- compressed air outlet;
- benches – general and for electronic work in a clean work area;
- sink;
- peg board;
- mobile fume extraction unit;

- drill and lathe in a "dirty" work area;
- general office furniture.

3.6.8 PHYSICS STORE
DESCRIPTION AND FUNCTION
This room will house very expensive equipment and instruments for use by the physicists in the checking and calibrating of the linacs, including the water phantom machine, approximately 1m x 1m and 1,800 high.

LOCATION AND RELATIONSHIPS
Ready access to the Physics Laboratory. Easy access to a deep sink in the Cleaner's Room for filling and emptying of the water tank.

CONSIDERATIONS
Access for large items of equipment including manoeuvring the water phantom trolley. Safe for radioactive materials. Cable storage and heavy duty shelving for numerous phantoms.

3.6.9 BIOMEDICAL WORKROOM
DESCRIPTION AND FUNCTION
Maintenance and service support to an extensive range of treatment and non-treatment equipment.

LOCATION AND RELATIONSHIPS
Ready access to the Physics Laboratory and Bunkers.

CONSIDERATIONS
++Power outlets and electrostatic earthing. Sink with drip tray and spray hose. Heavy duty benching and storage.

3.6.10 LINEAR ACCELLERATOR TREATMENT ROOM (BUNKER)
DESCRIPTION AND FUNCTION
Treatment rooms or bunkers are the rooms in which EBR irradiation occurs. They require a maze-like corridor at the entrance of the room for radiation protection.

The maze, entrance and entry to the treatment room must allow access for the treatment machine, service equipment, hospital beds and gantry frames. Linacs with 18 MV photon beams generally require additional shielding at the maze entrance (i.e. neutron door); however, particular attention should be given to the bunker and maze design in an attempt to avoid the use of a maze shielding door.

LOCATION AND RELATIONSHIPS
Immediately adjacent to the Control Area so that access can be monitored. The Treatment Rooms should be located with ready access to Patient Amenities (Change Cubicles, Sub-Waiting, Toilets), Treatment Planning and support areas including film processing areas and utility rooms.

CONSIDERATIONS
Layouts shall be designed to prevent radioactive particles from escaping. Openings into the room, including doors, ductwork, vents and electrical raceways and conduits shall be baffled to prevent direct exposure to other areas of the facility. Services requirements including electrical, hydraulics, and air-conditioning will be according to the equipment manufacturer's specifications. Provide special cable access to the treatment rooms for physics measurements. Linear accelerators need special air exchanges and the floor needs protection when machines are installed.

FF&E will include:
- linear accelerator;
- oxygen & suction on medical services panel plus nitrous oxide, scavenging and medical air if GA to be administered;
- emergency "stop" switch;
- hand basin;
- benches and storage cupboards for patient machine accessories;
- laser lights for positioning;
- monitors and audio equipment for patient contact;
- ++ power outlets.

3.6.11 LINAC CONTROL
DESCRIPTION AND FUNCTION

Radiation therapists will perform all control and patient monitoring functions in the Control Room. Patient radiation treatment records and planning images may be displayed in the control room area for each treatment unit throughout the course of the therapy. Patient viewing cameras, treatment delivery computers and intercoms allow the radiation therapist to monitor and communicate with the patient during treatment when the patient is alone into the treatment room.

LOCATION AND RELATIONSHIPS
Direct access to Treatment Bunker.

CONSIDERATIONS
Cable trays must be easily removable for access by maintenance staff.

FF&E will include:
- emergency stop switch;
- intercom;
- patient viewing monitors;
- portal imaging computers;
- workstation for image and chart viewing, access to the scheduling system, and space to store treatment records (if not electronic);
- Linac control console;
- PACS monitor and/or x-ray viewing panels;
- benches/shelving units to suit equipment.

3.6.12 BRACHYTHERAPY ROOM
DESCRIPTION AND FUNCTION
A radioactive source is delivered internally through a tube or applicators implanted or inserted during surgery. The radiation source is inserted manually or, more commonly, performed by a remote after loading machine. In centres where LDR brachytherapy seed implantation is performed, the room shall be of similar size to the other bunkers and equipped as an operating room.

LOCATION AND RELATIONSHIPS
Adjacent to:

Functional relationship diagram (Radiation oncology unit functional relationship diagram)

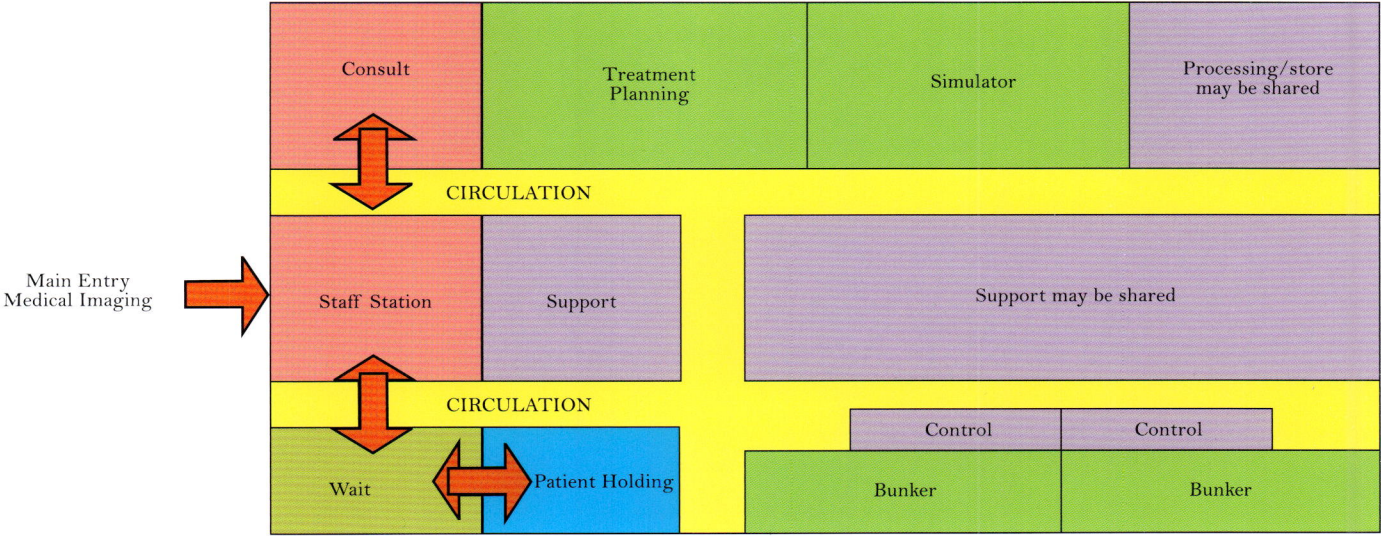

- induction bay;
- scrub room;
- recovery bay;
- seed implant store and loading room;
- other radiation treatment rooms.

CONSIDERATIONS
Radiation safety of radioactive materials. Oxygen, suction, medical air, nitrous oxide and scavenging.

3.6.13 PATIENT OBSERVATION & TREATMENT AREA
DESCRIPTION AND FUNCTION
Trolley bays where patients may be observed and assessed and a range of nursing care given such as:
- dressing changes;
- medication delivery;
- IV start and monitoring.

LOCATION AND RELATIONSHIPS
Centrally located to treatment, planning, staff station, clean and dirty utilities.

CONSIDERATIONS
FF&E includes:
- beds/trolleys;
- resuscitation trolley;
- medical gases;
- curtain screens;
- overbed tables;
- data outlets.

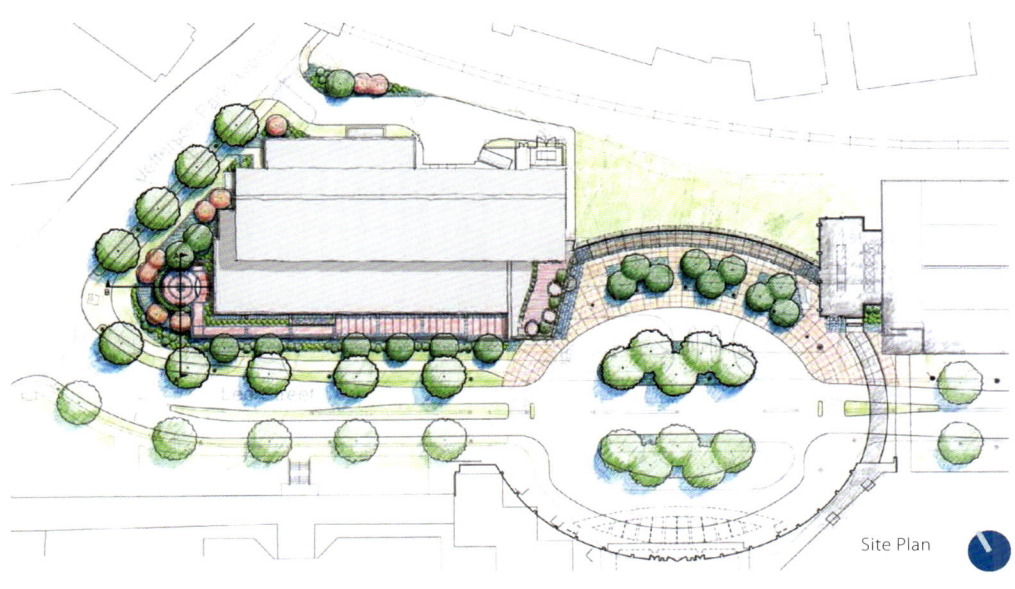
Site Plan

Emily Couric Clinical Cancer Centre

Architects:
ZGF Architects LLP
Location:
Virgina, USA
Building area:
13,935.45m²
Project year:
2011
Photographs:
© Chuck Choi Photography

Positioned as the keystone for the University Health System's new streetscape and entry precinct, the Emily Couric Clinical Cancer Centre is designed to welcome patients and families into the campus with a compelling identity and a strong new entrance.

The University of Virginia's vision of comprehensive, supportive, patient-centred cancer care is exemplified in this building with clinics, infusion, imaging, pharmacy and radiation oncology treatment areas with a full complement of patient and family support spaces. Patient support services such as social work, psychology, education and spiritual care occur throughout the building. On the ground floor, patients and family can take advantage of the meditation room, appearance centre and counselling services.

The building is organised to support clear, intuitive public circulation and way-finding. All patient corridors are located along an exterior curtain wall overlooking Lee Street and the University Health System complex. Light-filled waiting areas open directly onto circulation corridors and are organised consistently on each floor.

Each floor is themed to reflect Virginia's natural environment. This helps with way-finding, while giving each floor a unique palette that helps stitch the various functions together. The colours, materials and treatments throughout each floor reflect the theme, and corresponding pieces of art and photography are on display.

Support spaces are complemented by landscaped exterior gardens on the ground floor and a public roof garden on the third floor. This combination of clinical activities with strong patient and family support programmes reflects a vision of humane, comforting cancer treatment for patients and their families; the architectural design continues the University's vision with generous, open spaces, natural light, views, varied and interesting interior finishes, and rational, consistent planning. Patients have reported to staff that the new space is more hotel than hospital — a difficult feat considering the needs of this clinical building.

1~2. Exterior view
3. Entrance lobby with lounge area

4. Waiting area
5. Circulation with lounge area
6. Family waiting/lounge

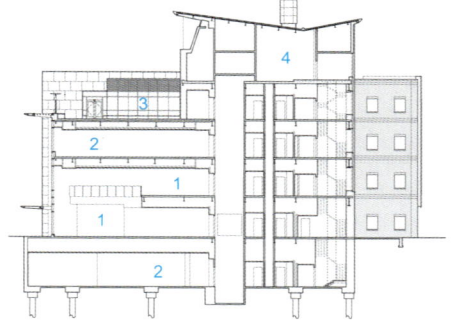

Transverse Section:
1. Lobby
2. Waiting
3. Roof garden
4. Mechanical

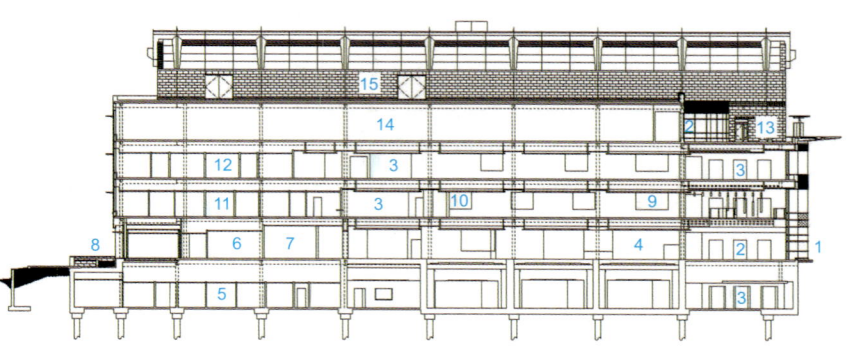

Longitudinal Section:
1. Hospital entry
2. Lobby
3. Waiting
4. Registration
5. Radiation oncology
6. Radiology
7. Meditation room
8. Terrace
9. Women's clinic
10. Pharmacy
11. Infusion
12. General clinics
13. Roof garden
14. Shell space
15. Mechanical

129

130

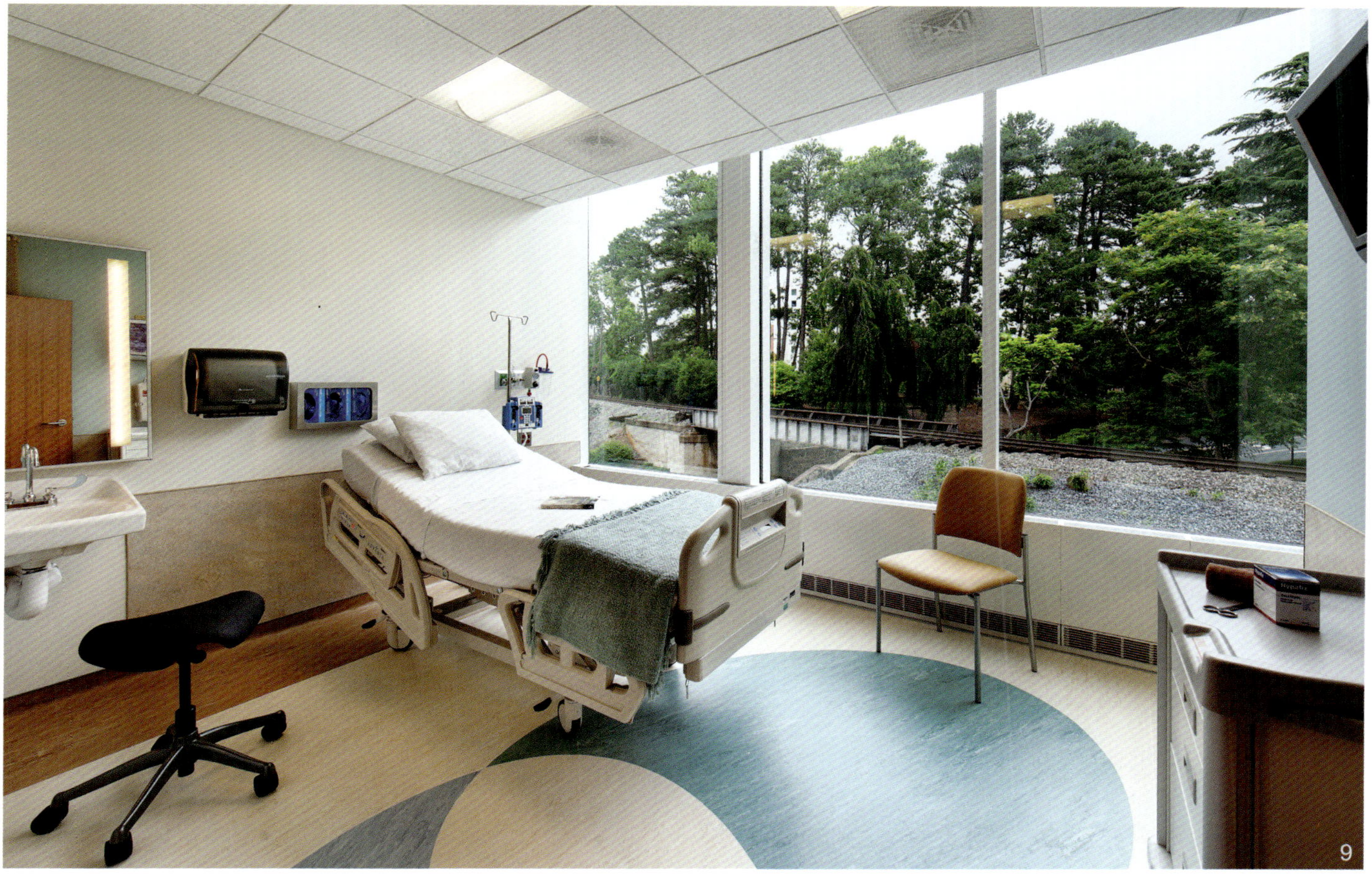

7. View to corridor with staff station and rooms for medical service
8. Staff station
9. Patient bedroom

Illustrative Section N-S Looking East at Hospital Entrance

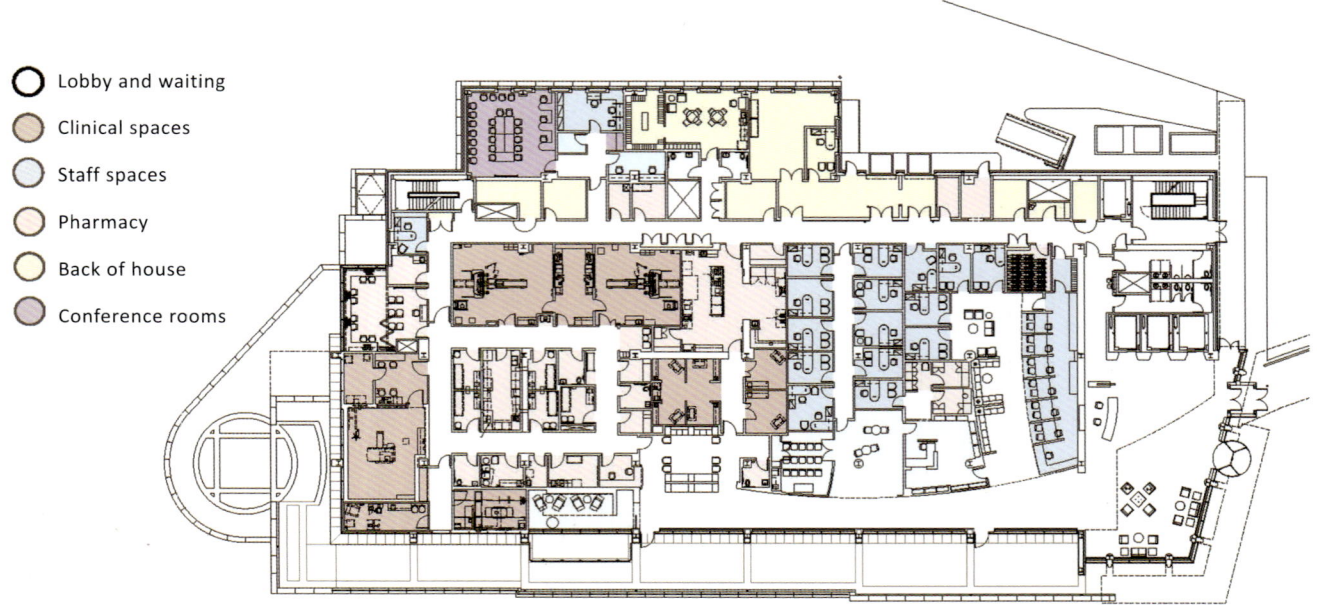

10. Lounge
11. Corridor

- ○ Lobby and waiting
- ○ Clinical spaces
- ○ Staff spaces
- ○ Pharmacy
- ○ Back of house
- ○ Conference rooms

Ground Floor Plan

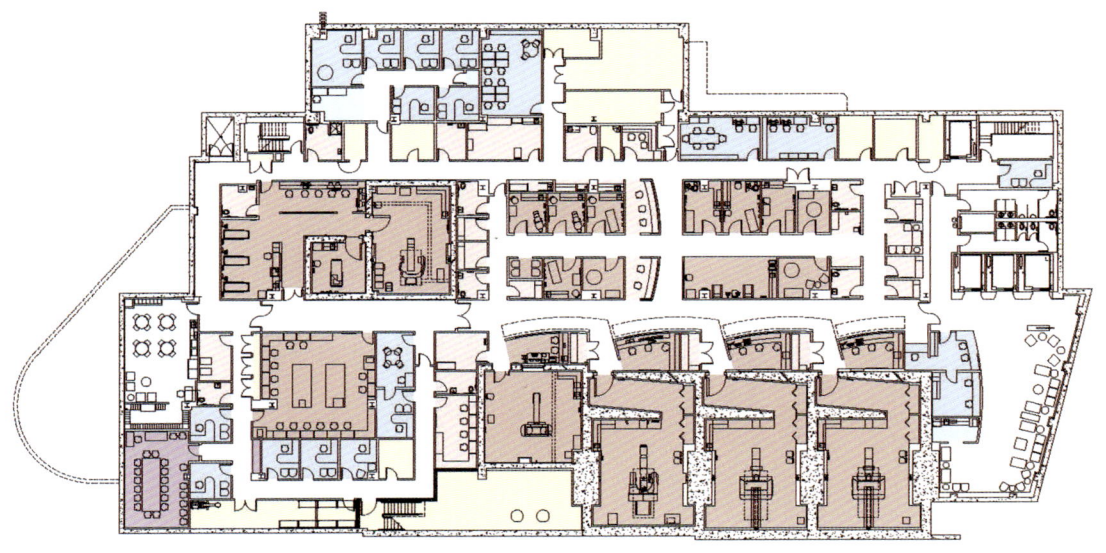

First Floor Plan

133

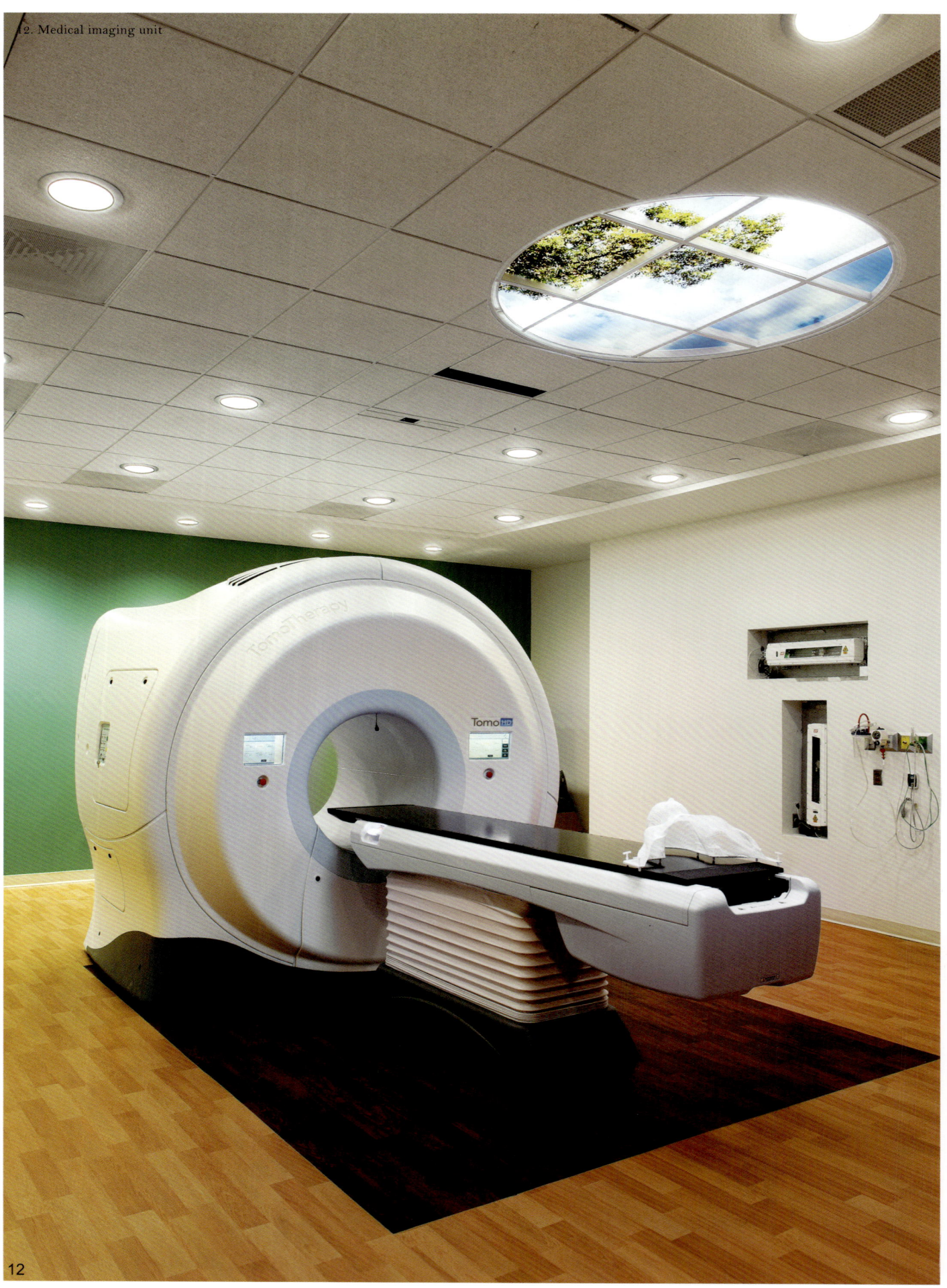

- Lobby and waiting
- Clinical spaces
- Staff spaces
- Pharmacy
- Back of house
- Conference rooms

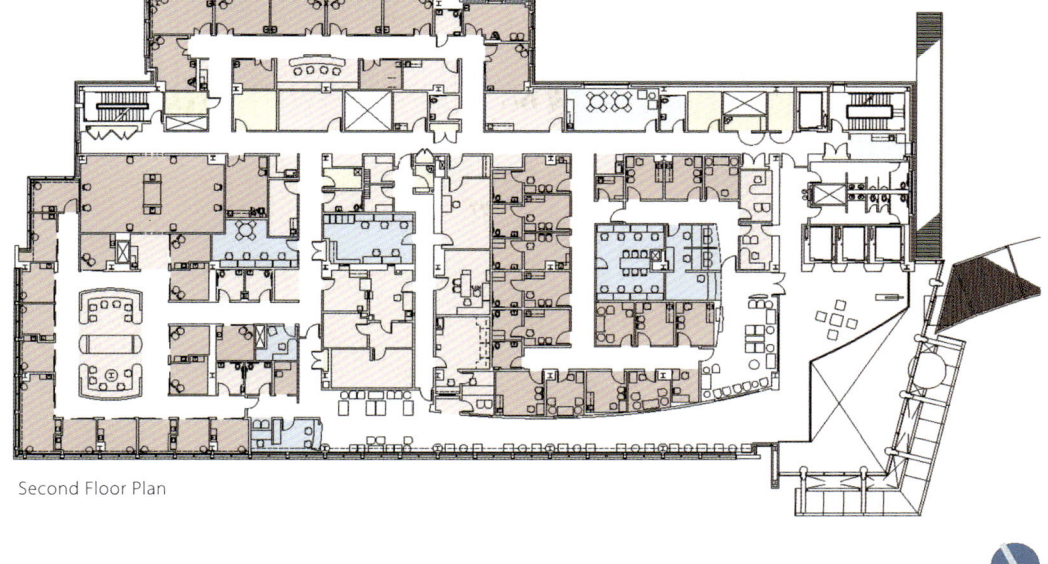

Second Floor Plan

Third Floor Plan

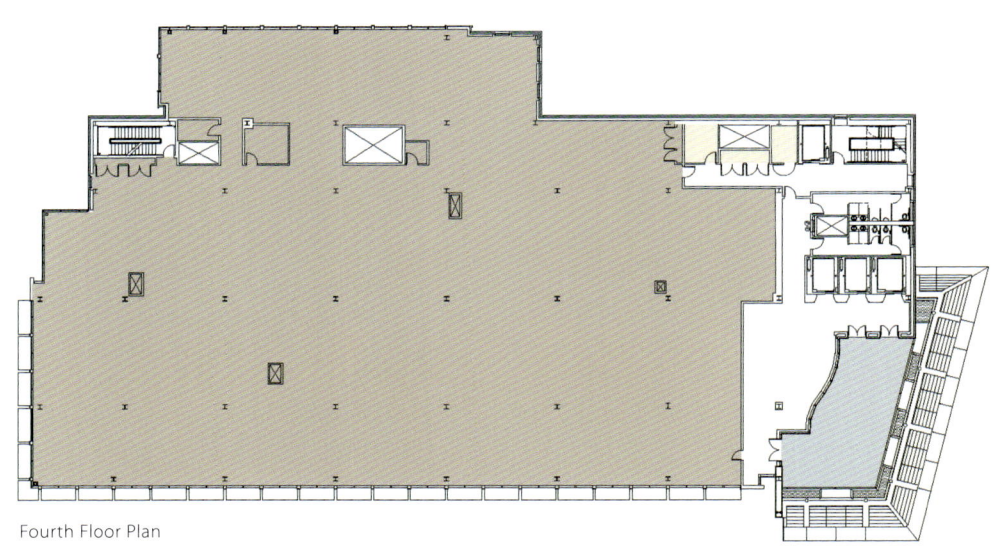

Fourth Floor Plan

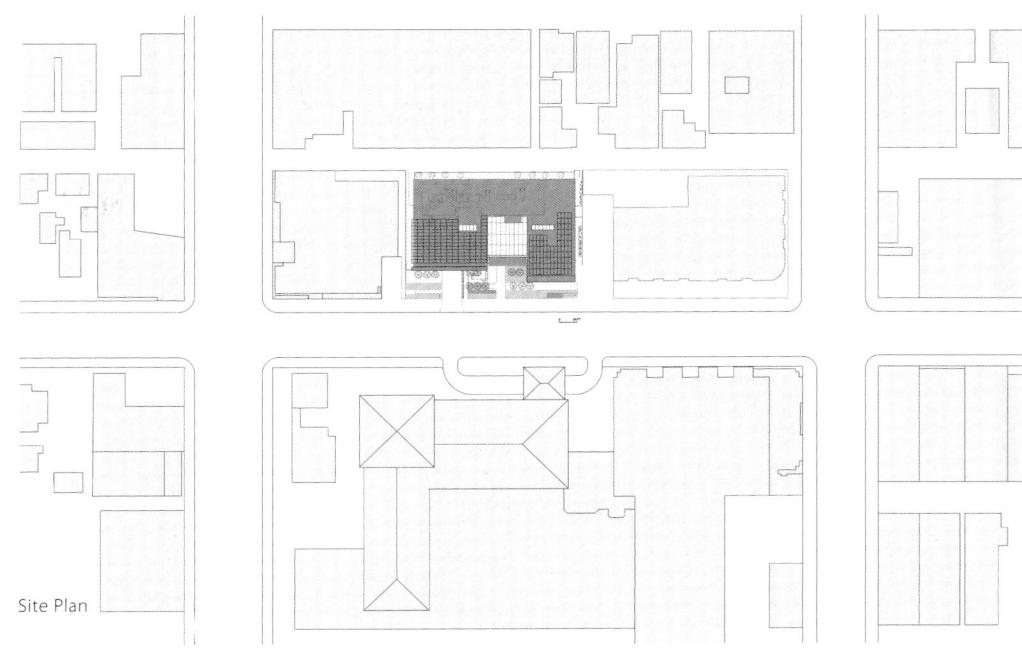
Site Plan

UCLA Outpatient Surgery and Oncology Centre

Architects:
Michael W. Folonis Architects
Location:
Santa Monica, USA
Gross area:
4,645.15m²
Project year:
2012
Photographs:
© Tom Bonner
Awards:
2011 AIA Healthcare Awards

The Outpatient Surgery and Oncology Centre in Santa Monica expresses the continuation of early California Modernist sensibilities and incorporates extensive sustainable, green-building strategies. Primary design considerations included the creation of a distinctive and articulated massing, the maximal inclusion of natural day lighting and ventilation throughout the building, and a strong indoor-outdoor connection. The project will be registered for LEED Gold Certification for New Construction and is anticipated to be the first Outpatient Surgery and Oncology Centre in the nation to achieve this rating.

The three-storey building links two distinct wings via a central, full-height, expansive and light-filled lobby. The lobby is enclosed with a full-height mullion-less glazing system and covered in a fritted glass skylight, allowing light to flood the central common area of the building. Both first and second floor exterior glazed elevations incorporates the artful expression of louvre systems, awnings, light shelves, shading fins and fritted glass across the building façade systematically facilitates and moderates the allowance of natural light into the core of the building, diffusing harsh direct sunlight and providing privacy to the many areas of the building where it is required. The roofline is layered with photovoltaic panels and articulated by the shade awnings and height variances of the lobby and buildings wings. These panels provide approximately 100,000

3D Section Diagram

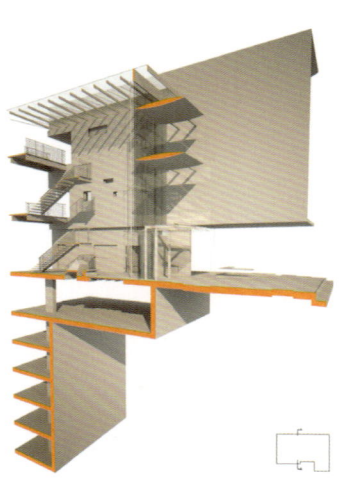

watts of solar array capacity to supply approximately 25 percent of the building's electricity.

The indoor-outdoor connection is enhanced by providing access to landscaping visually through sight lines from the building common areas and waiting rooms, and physically through accessible entryways to exterior landscaping, and through landscaping elements brought into the building. The vertical massing of the building has allowed an increased setback from the street to incorporate more landscaping on the streetscape. Patient and guest waiting rooms along the first floor of the building connect to ground-level exterior patio gardens, allow visitors and guests to sit indoors or outdoors. These landscape and seating areas help accentuate the front plaza.

1. View of building from the 16th Street
2. Aerial view of building
3. Front façade and main entrance, night view
4. View from the third floor bridge looking into atrium space
5. Transparency, view from the second floor bridge looking into atrium space

6. Third floor waiting room
7. Ground floor waiting room

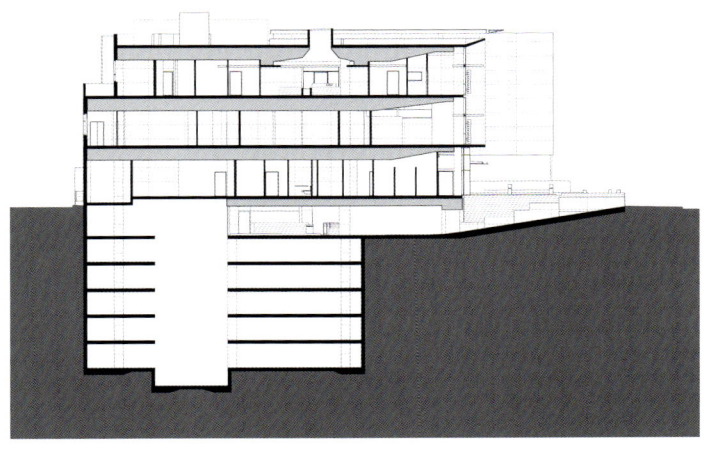

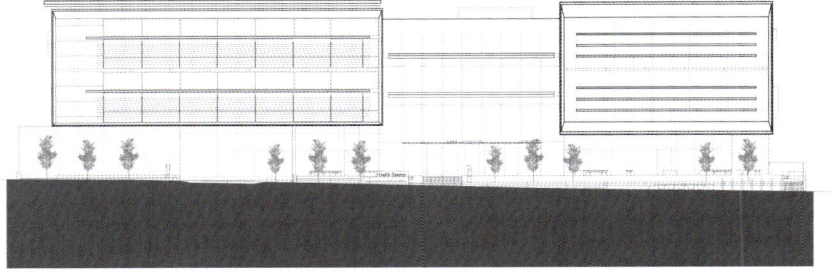

Sections

141

8. Second Floor staff lounge
9. Preparation and recovery rooms

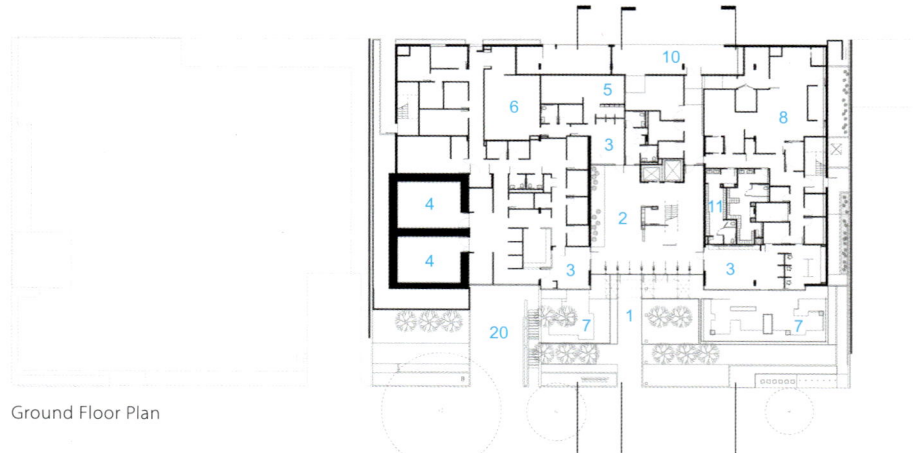

Ground Floor Plan

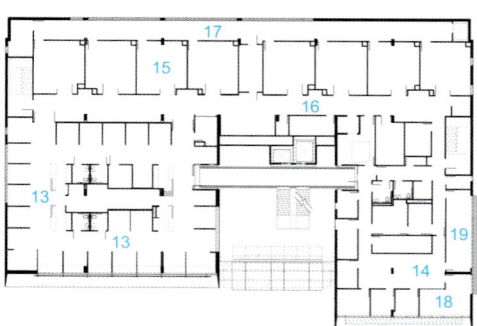

First Floor Plan

Second Floor Plan

1. Main entry
2. Lobby
3. Waiting room
4. Linac
5. Pharmacy
6. Lab
7. Patio
8. Sterile processing
9. Exam rooms
10. Loading dock
11. Staff lockers
12. Bridge
13. Prep + recovery
14. Offices
15. Operating room
16. Service corridor
17. Sterile corridor
18. Doctors lounge
19. Staff lounge
20. Driveway

143

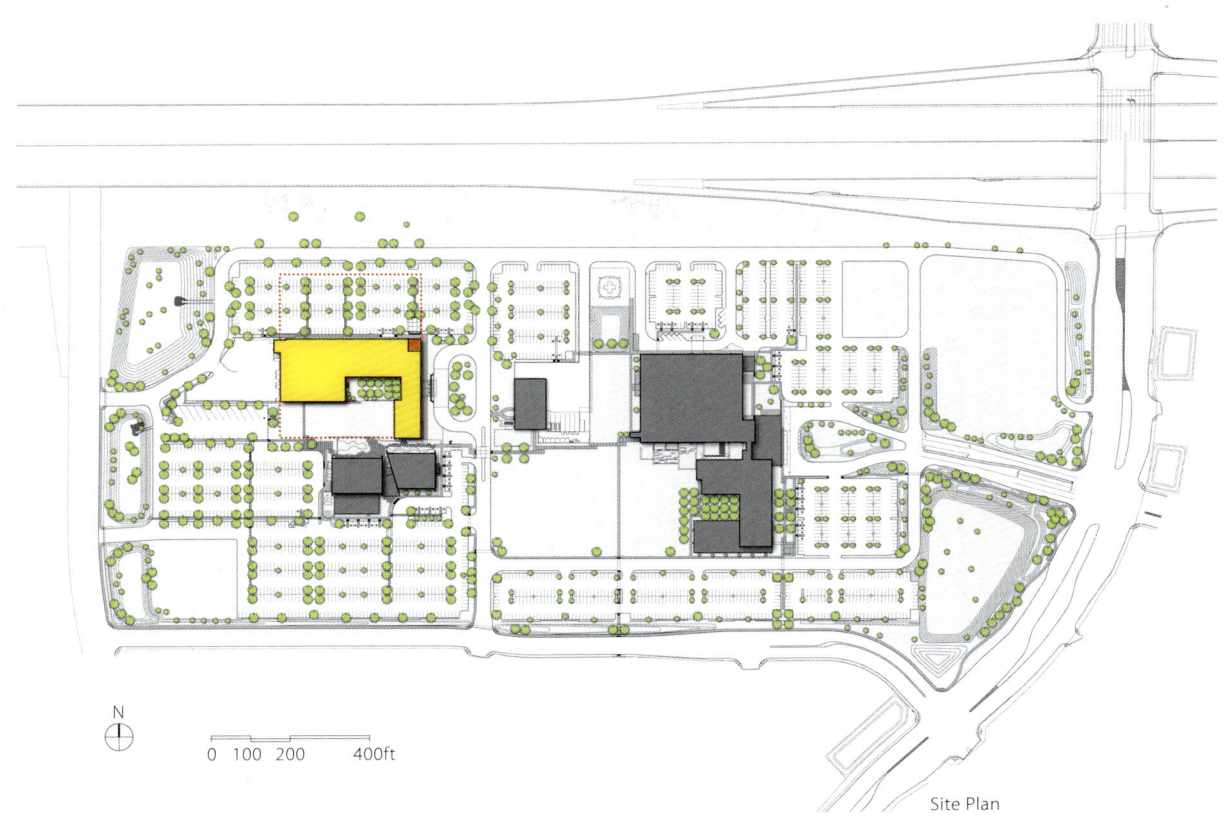

Site Plan

Banner Cancer Centre

Architects:
Cannon Design
Location:
Gilbert, USA
Building area:
12,356.10m²
Project year:
2011
Photographs:
© Mark Boisclair Photography,
Bill Timmerman Photography,
Mark Skalny Photography

With a design that merges the "high tech" world of medicine with the "high touch" needs of cancer patients to provide customised, holistic care, the Banner MD Anderson Cancer Centre focuses on outpatient care, with a unique environment incorporating natural light, artwork, water features and views of nature. The north entry includes an iconic four-storey Lantern of Hope clad in aluminium panels cut in a leaves-and-branches pattern over a white fabric scrim, which is illuminated at night in colours corresponding to the different cancer disease awareness groups.

The Centre was designed with Hope. A patient-centric experience focused on the cornerstones of convenience, accessibility and healing. Central to this design vision is logical way-finding and separation of "front-of-house" public/patient spaces from "back-of-house" staff spaces. Integral to the design was the connection to nature, including the Lantern of Hope, whose pattern reflects the Palo Verde tree, often referred to as a "nurse plant".

Orientation of public circulation corridors and waiting areas is towards the exterior along the courtyard with treatment areas located to enjoy the view of the mountains in the distance. Balconies are available in multiple locations to provide areas of respite. Spaces that cannot include exterior windows, such as radiation oncology, brings the outside in through the use of window-like nature murals.

Concept Diagram

Lighting Study

Detailed Diagram

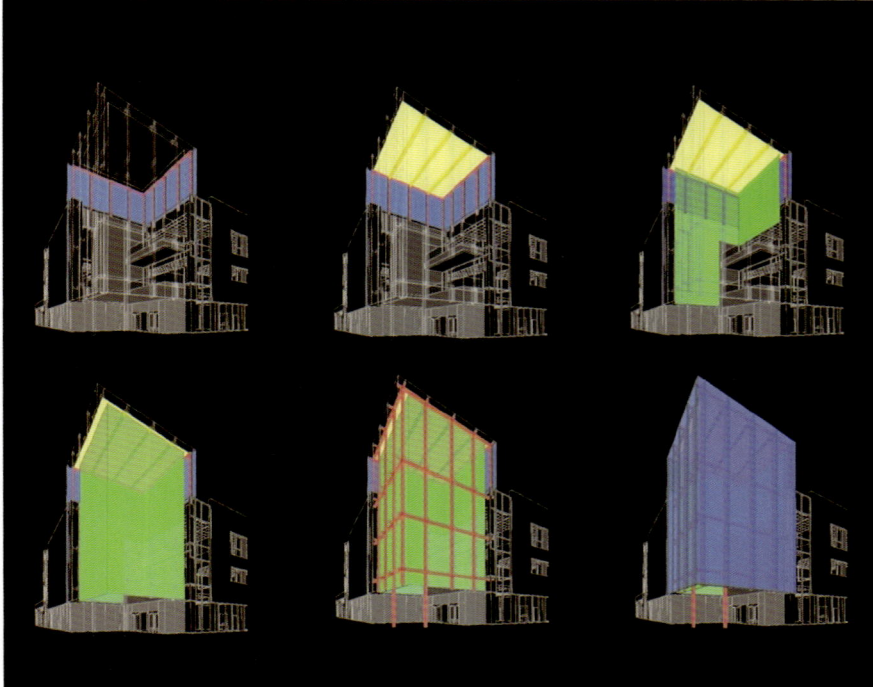

 Watercut Aluminium Panels:
Panels are copper bread blasted to create a matte natural finish.

 Structure:
A structural frame sits between the fabric and the metal providing support for the lantern. Two columns offset from the corner allow the lantern to float.

 Tensile Fabric:
With a 40% light transmittance light trickles through the patterned exterior metal during the day. At night, the fabric is illuminated with colour-changing LEDs.

 Transparent ETFE Membrane:
A transparent membrane with minimal structure allows the maximium amount of daylight and views to the sky.

1. Building view from the yard
2. Main entrance
3. Night view of exterior
4. Lobby and waiting

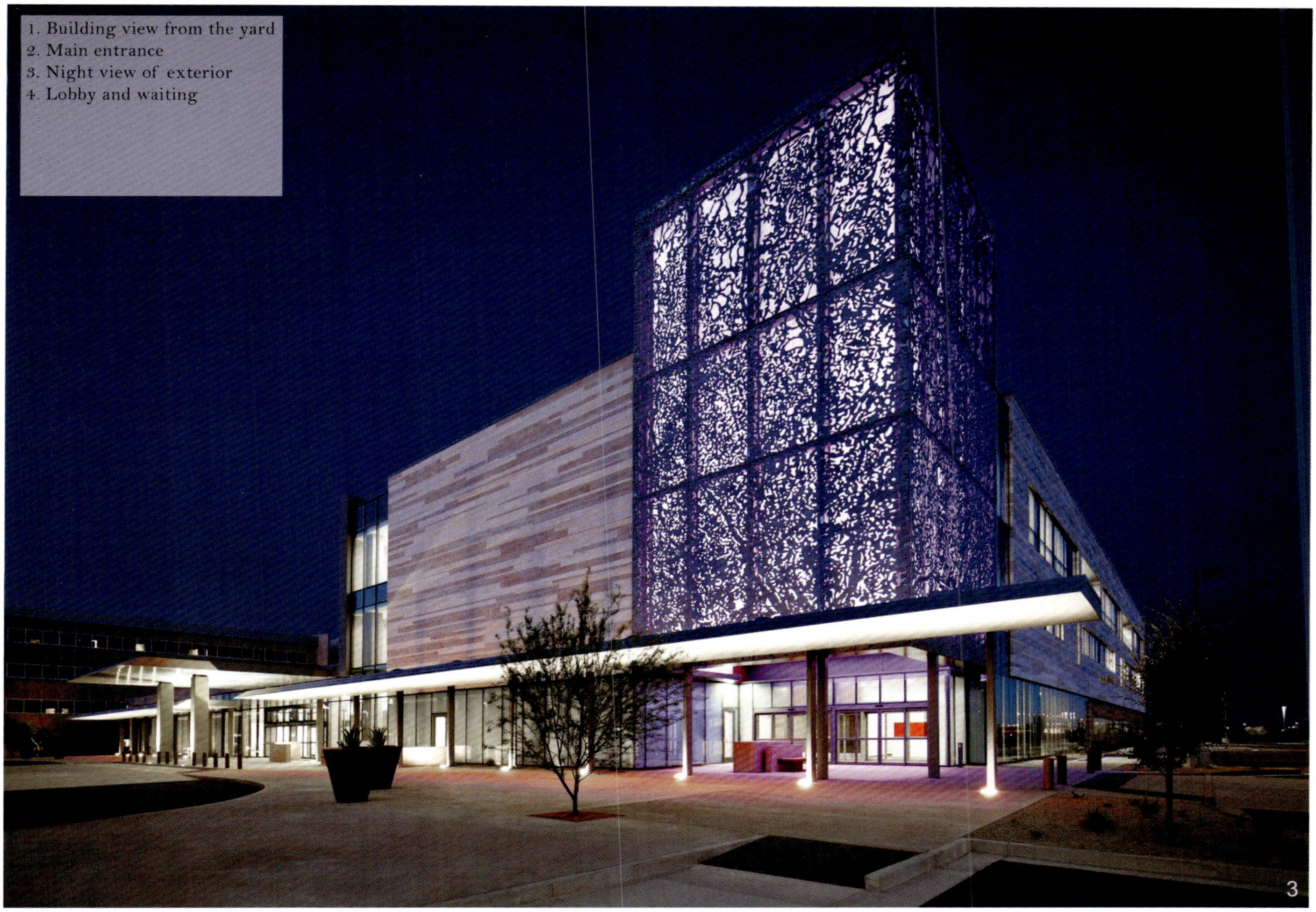

3

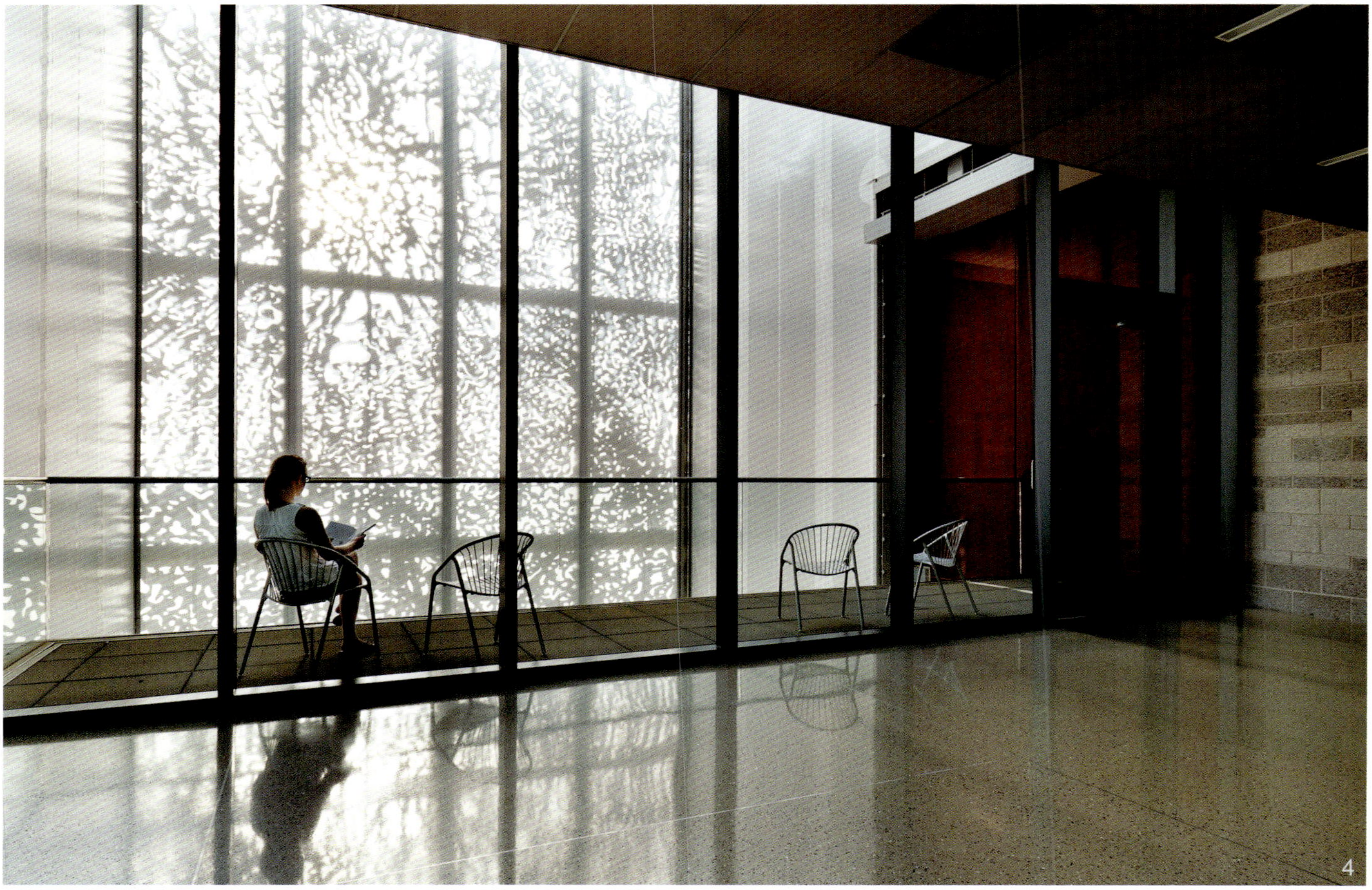

4

5. Courtyard with lounge area
6. Entrance lobby and reception

Distinct Identity

The design of the Centre extends Banner Health's signature brand established in recently opened hospitals in the area. The materials selected for the exterior, such as the ground and split-face CMU block, signature drop-off canopy, metal cladding and EIFS, build upon the Banner brand. Equally important was for the Cancer Centre to have a distinct identity, highlighted by the landmark Lantern of Hope. Pre-weathered zinc cladding that defines the entry canopy, pergolas and courtyard elevations tie with the aluminium panels on the Lantern of Hope. The interior materials also utilise a balance of Banner brand with distinctive elements such as custom glass panels and focus on nature elements to inspire hope.

Lighting the Lantern of Hope

Soaring 64 feet high and visible from the highway, the "Lantern of Hope" is a critical architectural element rising above the facility's open-air entry area. Designed to be a transition area from the desert environment to a place of healing, the lantern also lights up at night. Seamlessly integrating the lighting as well as the layered construction of inner fabric, superstructure, and the 32 massive one-inch-thick water-jet cut aluminium panels was a significant design challenge. During the design process, computer simulations and full-size physical mockups were used to achieve the "lantern-like" effect at night and the internal "tree-like" dappled shadows from the balconies during the day.

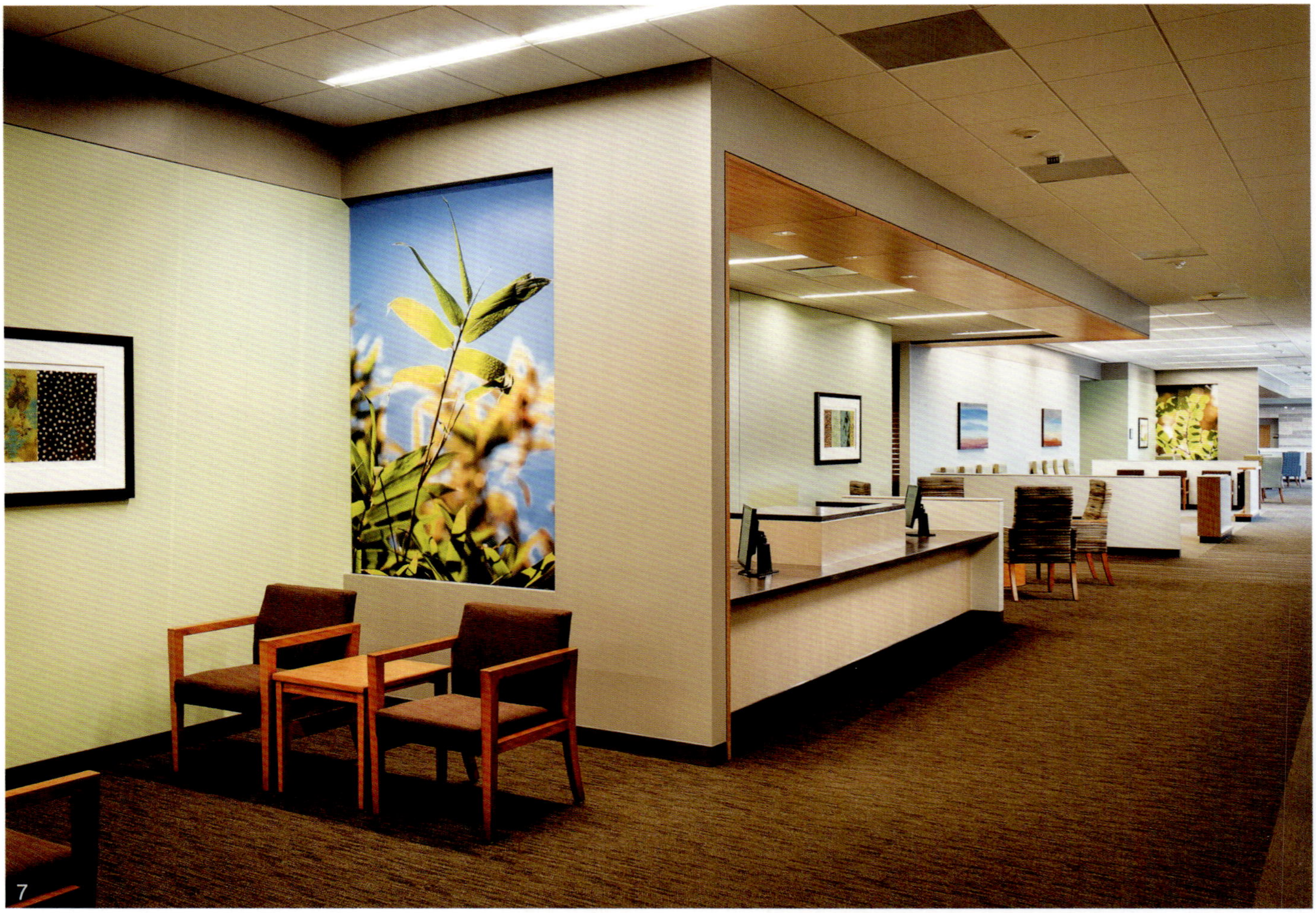

7

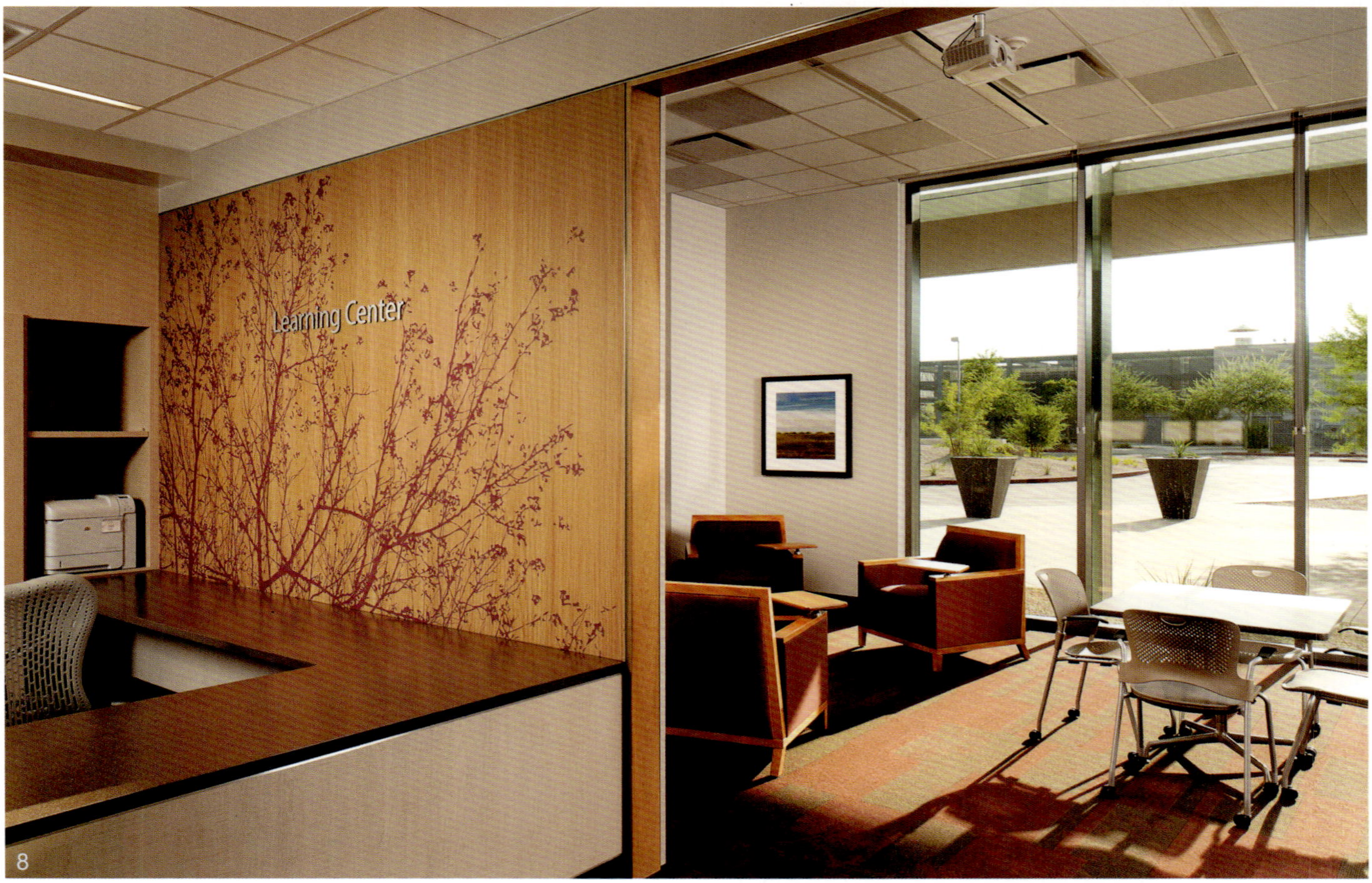

8

7~8. Staff station and waiting
9. Workstation

10. Medical imaging unit
11. Corridor

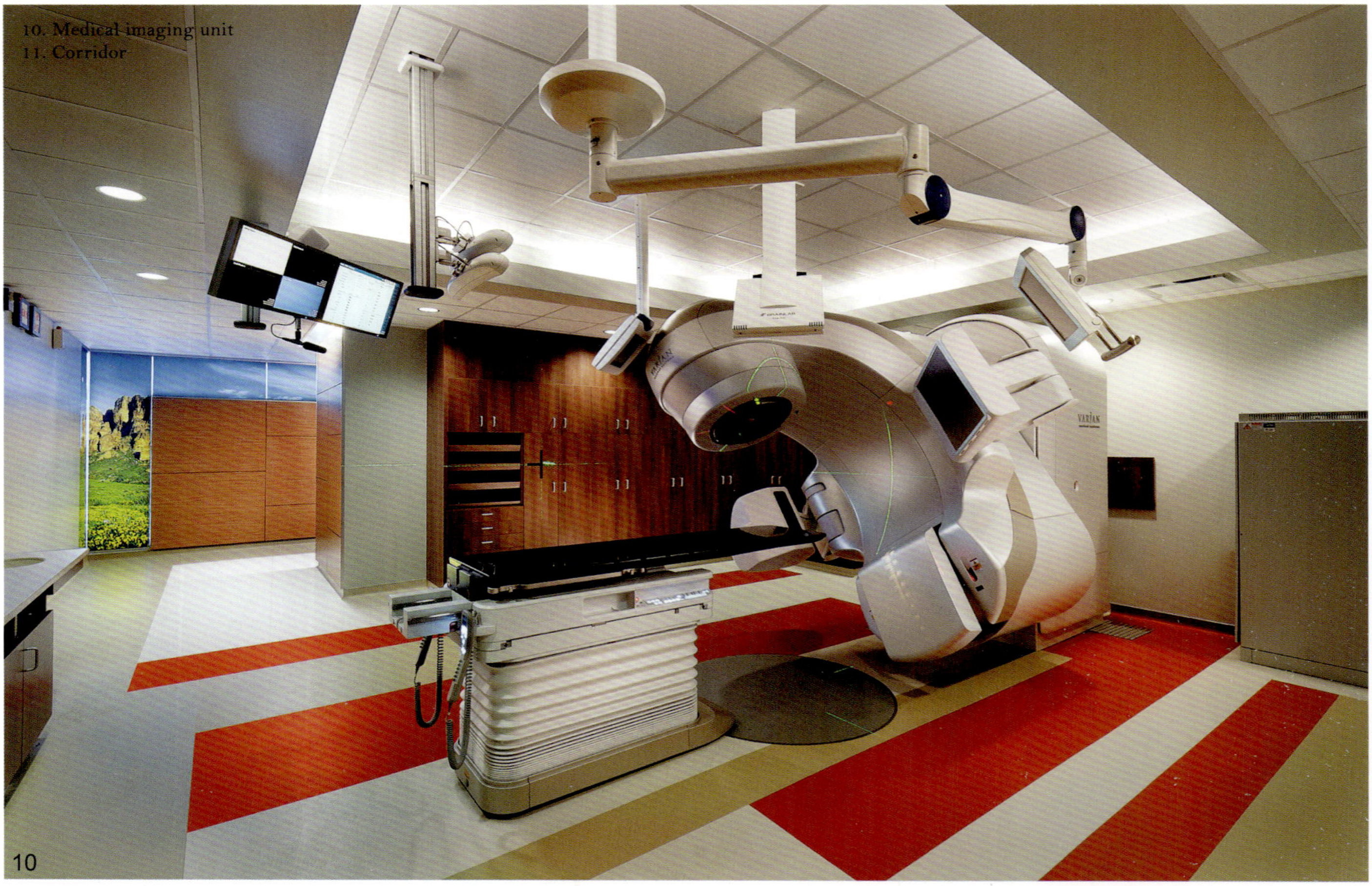

10

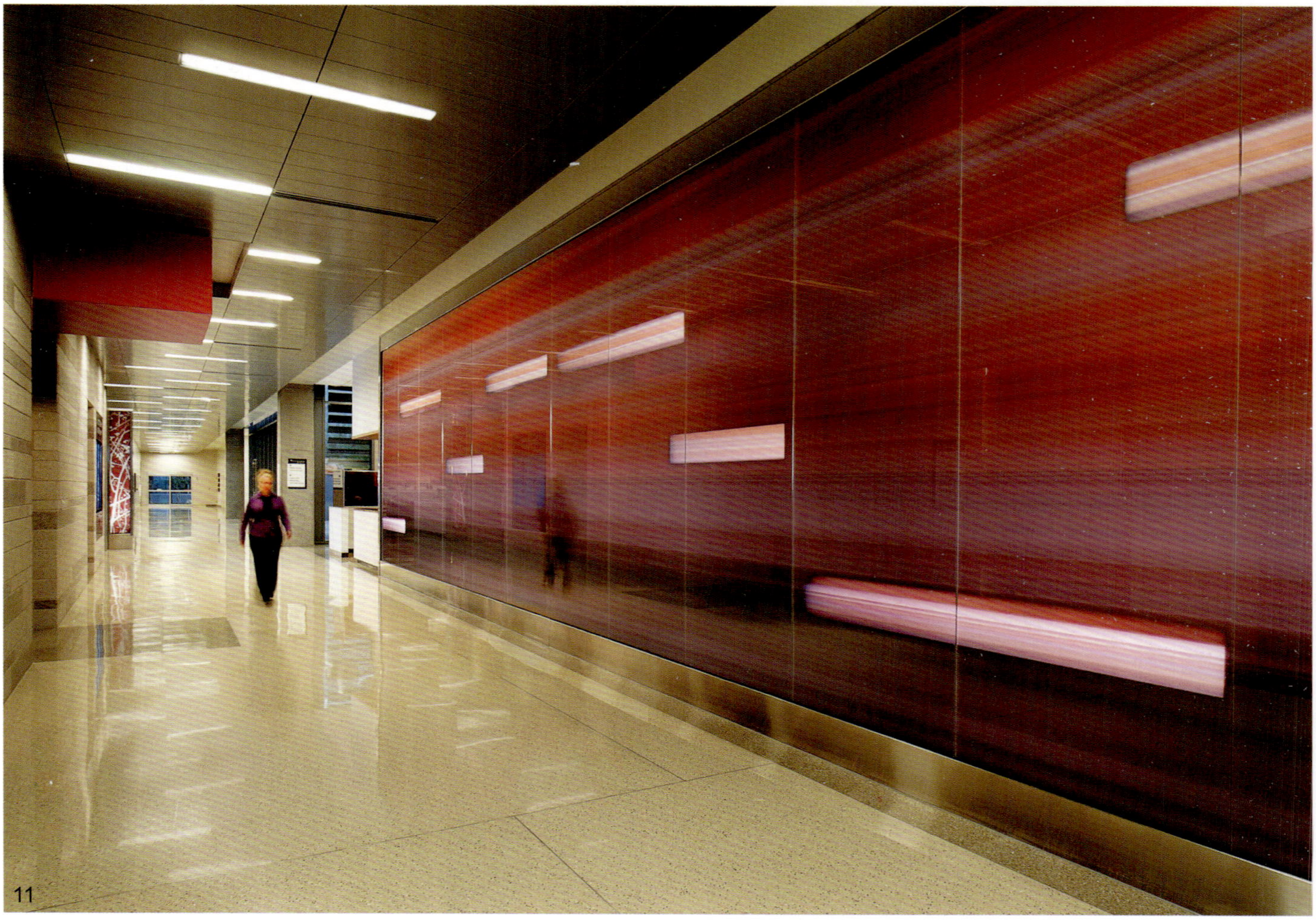

11

Floor Plan – Level 1:
1. Entry
2. Intake centre
3. Welcome Centre
4. Public lifts
5. Info desk
6. Main entry
7. Coffee shop
8. Exterior courtyard
9. Waiting
10. Radiation oncology
11. Service lifts
12. Building support
13. Staff entry
14. Loading dock
15. Staff & transport entry

Floor Plan – Level 2:
1. Canopy below
2. Exterior terrace
3. Public lifts
4. Roof
5. Learning centre
6. Retail
7. Multi-speciality clinics
8. Waiting
9. Diagnostic imaging
10. Service lifts

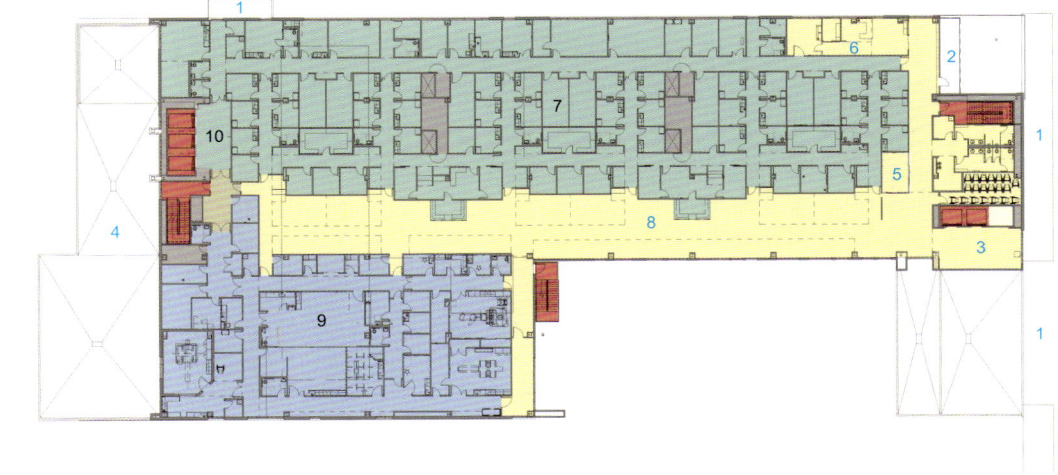

Floor Plan – Level 3:
1. Exterior terrace
2. Public lifts
3. Exterior balcony
4. Waiting
5. Infusion centre
6. Infusion pharmacy
7. CRYOLAB
8. Service lifts
9. Roof

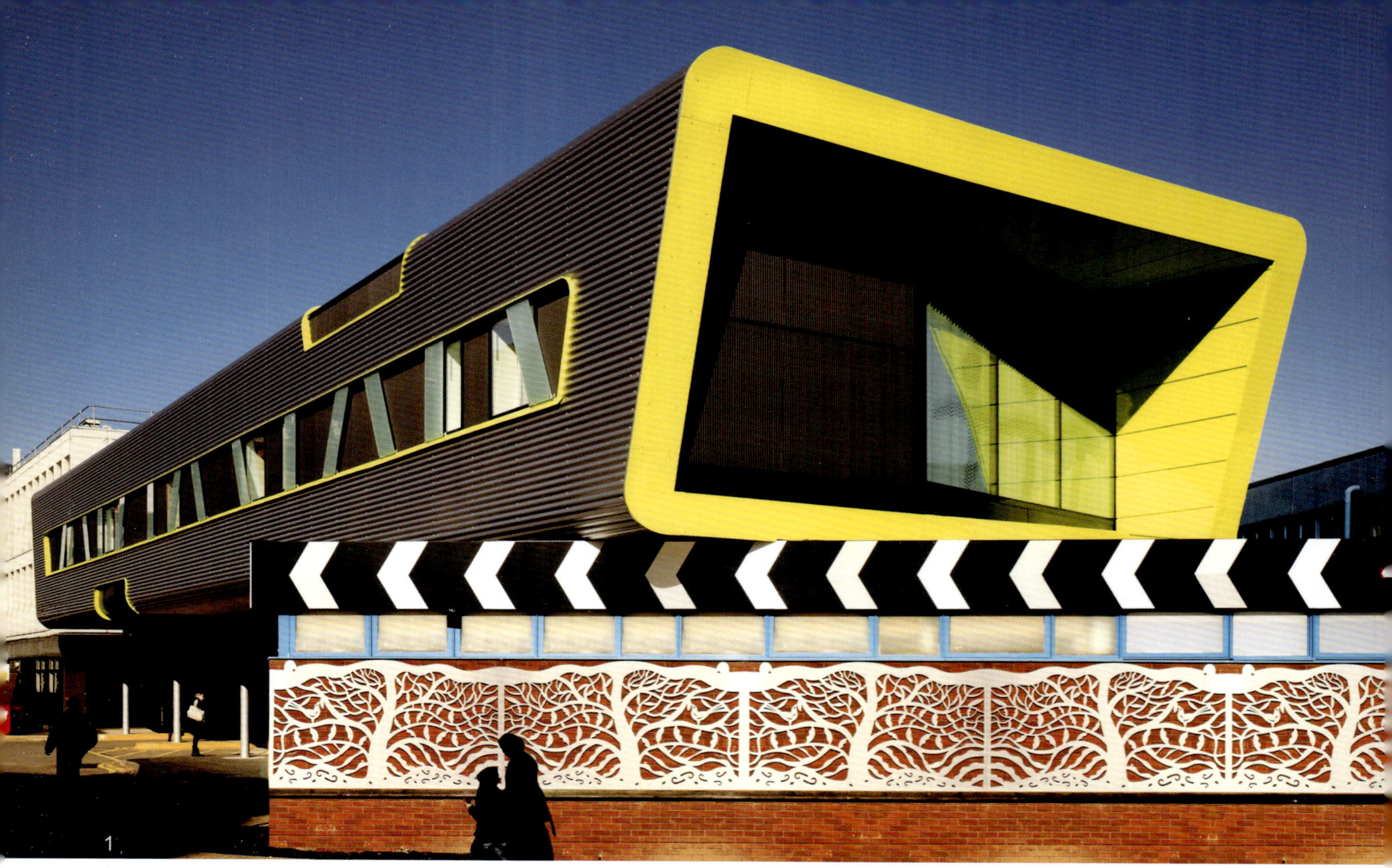

1

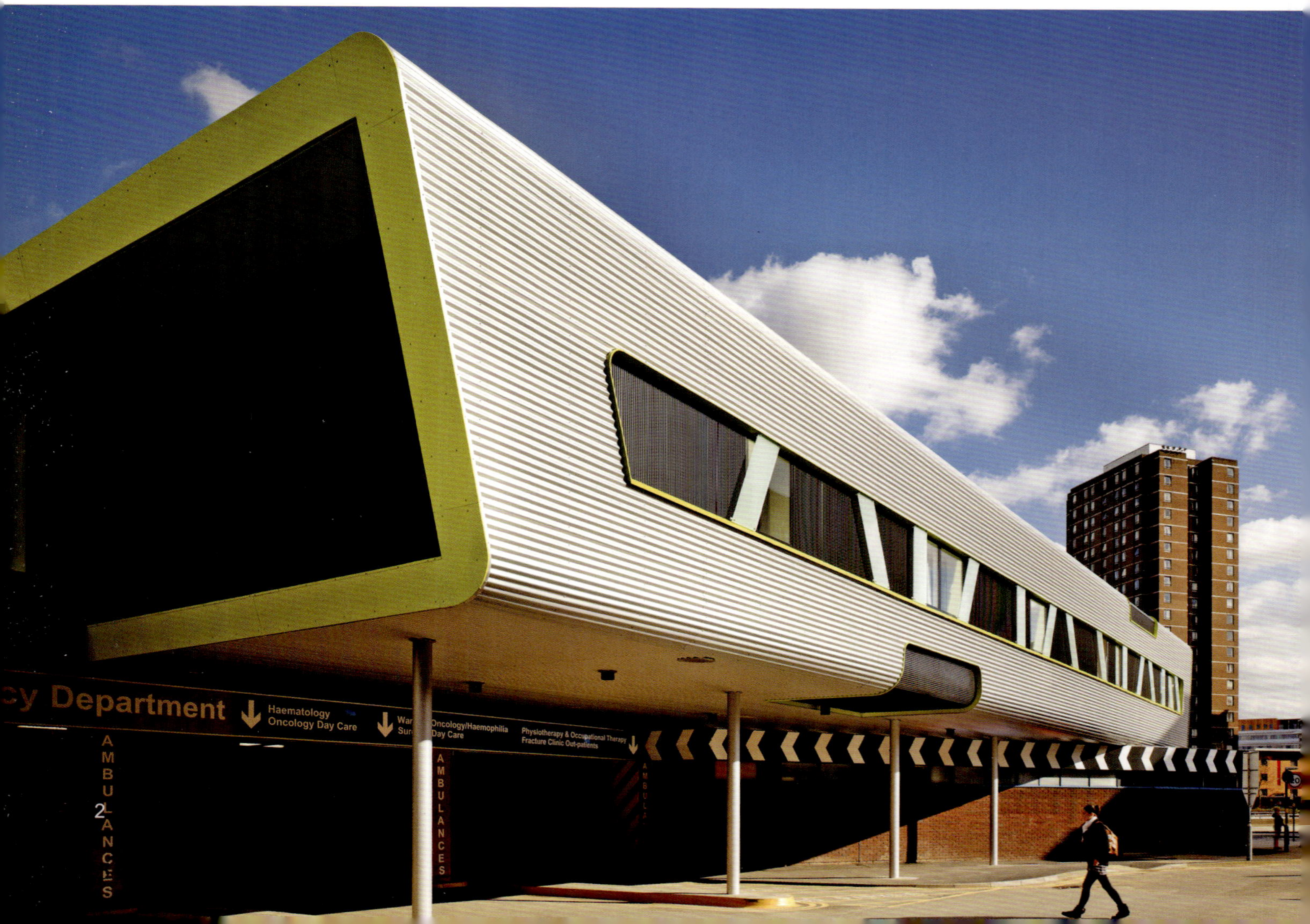
cy Department
Haematology
Oncology Day Care
Oncology/Haemophilia
Day Care
Physiotherapy & Occupational Therapy
Fracture Clinic Out-patients
AMBULANCES
AMBULANCES

2

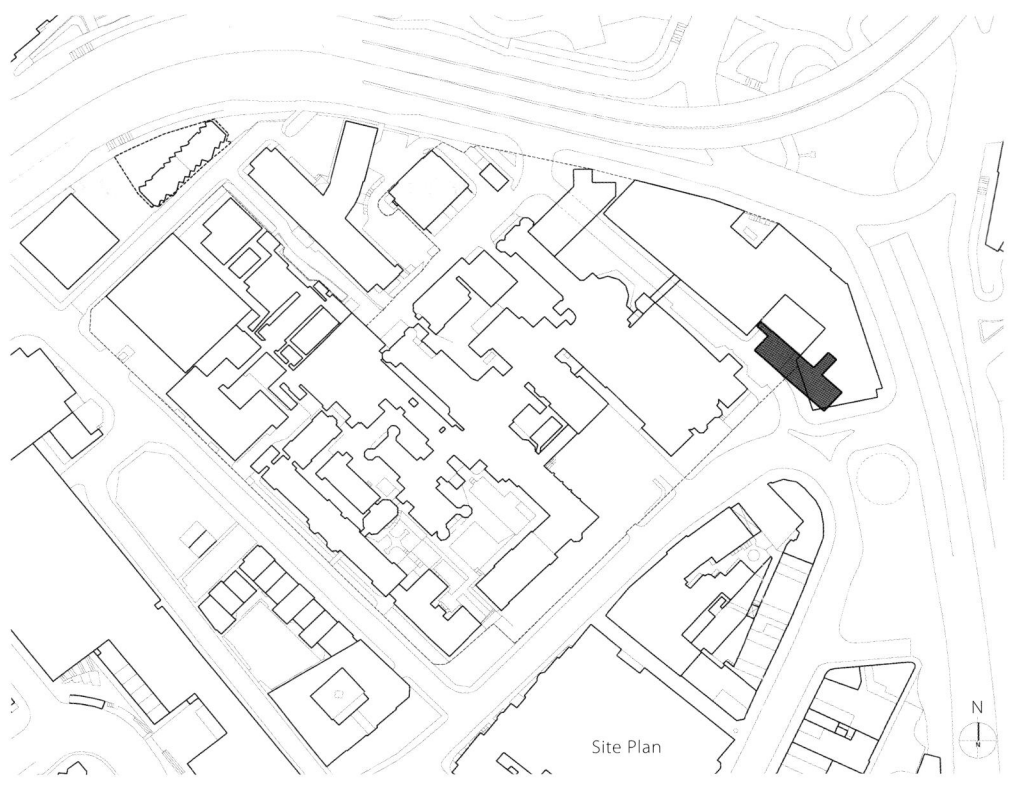
Site Plan

Teenage Cancer Trust Ward

Architects:
Lifschutz Davidson Sandilands
Location:
Birmingham, UK
Project year:
2010
Photographs:
© Chris Gascoigne

Lifschutz Davidson Sandilands' innovative ward for young cancer patients opens in Birmingham. A striking addition to the historic Birmingham townscape, a new Teenage Cancer Trust six-bed ward has officially opened. Trust patron Roger Daltrey opened the ward, set to provide a tailored and welcoming environment for young cancer sufferers and their visitors, while providing the very best in clinical care.

Unlike conventional NHS wards, the design of this six-bed ward extension to the existing oncology department of Birmingham Children's Hospital encourages patient interaction, overnight visiting and the continuation of study for young people undergoing treatment for cancer.

The unit was designed to appear as a distinct new addition to the cluster of existing institutional and civic buildings, floating above the ambulance drop-off and entrance to the A&E department to form a prominent entrance canopy over one of the main hospital entrances. A bridge links the ward to the first floor allowing for shared resources with the existing oncology department.

The interiors of the unit itself are a departure from the institutional formality of the adjoining hospital. The heart of the ward is focused around a large social space with views out over Birmingham. The building is arranged so that all of the patient bedspaces are along the southwest façade giving each patient their own

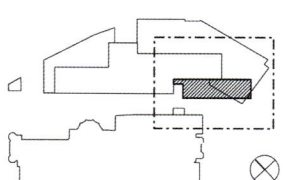
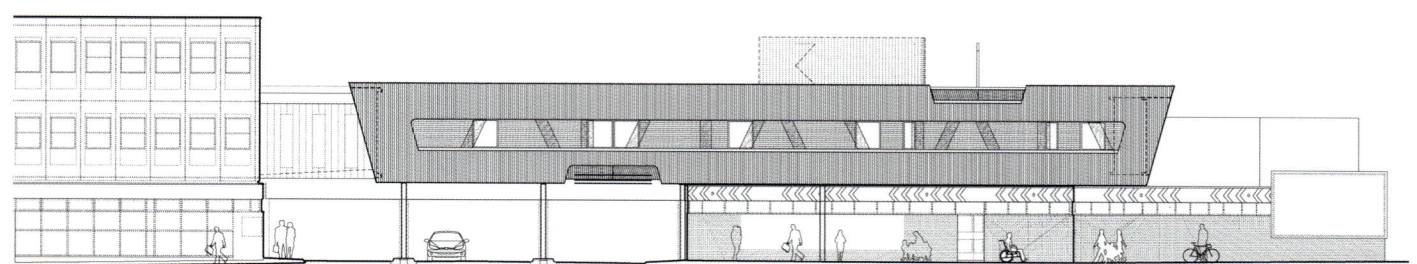

Elevation

window. The main entrance into the ward is activated by a vibrant inhabitable wall providing intimate, private and study areas for patients in comfortable and adaptable niches. A colourful mural leads to the nurses' station and large social area at the heart of the ward. Flooded in natural light with extensive views out of the "pod", this gathering place encourages patients, visitors, parents and medical staff to interact in relaxed and non-clinical surrounds.

The bed spaces are domestic in feel, with clinical services discretely located out of sight. The ceiling height has been lowered to make the bedspace feel more homely. The patients will spend the majority of time in bed making the ceilingscape an unusually important consideration in the design. Each bedspace has its own skylight above allowing views out to the sky. Within these is a colour-changing LED light fitting which will flood the curved form of the ceiling with the colour of the patient's choice. Desks provided at each bedside allow patients space for personal possessions and enable ongoing education, but fold away to reveal a guest bed for overnight visitors. High quality audio-visual facilities, with on-demand video, music and access to the internet provide a valuable learning and recreational resource for patients.

The new unit will provide a total of six-bed spaces in two single rooms and a four-bed ward. The careful specification and detailing of finishes was key to achieving the warm and welcoming feel in what needs to function as a robust clinical ward. Roger Daltry described the ward as "a home away from home for the young people treated in it".

1. The building viewed from the street
2. Main entrance
3~4. The building with the surroundings

5. Reception
6. Corridor with lounge area

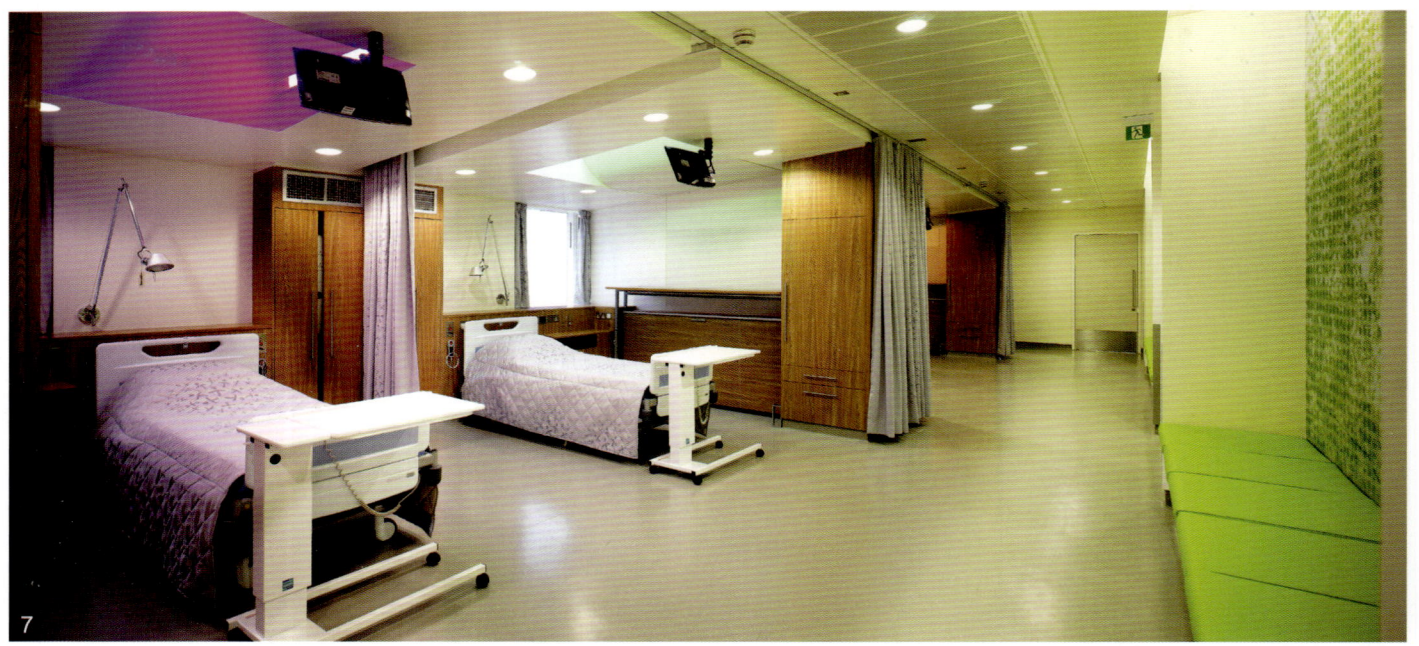

7. Patient bedroom
8. Playing, lounge

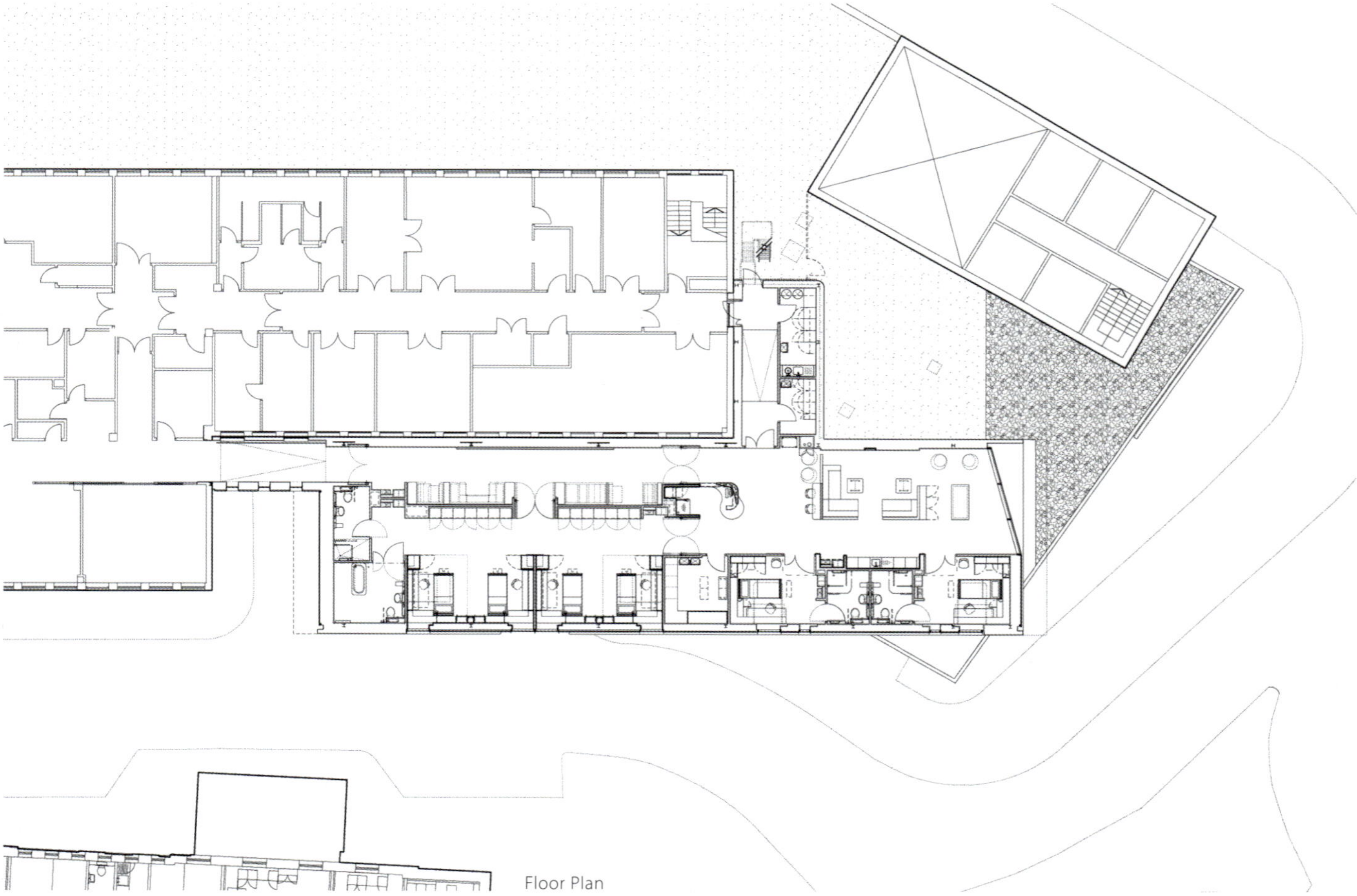

Floor Plan

1

2

Institute Verbeeten Hospital

Architects:
Dutch Health Architects
Location:
's-Hertogenbosch,
the Netherlands
Building Area:
1,920m²
Project year:
2011
Photographs:
© Courtesy of EGM architecten

Verbeeten Institute is a specialist hospital where clinical care is delivered in the field of Radiation Therapy Oncology and Nuclear Medicine. In order to provide better service to its patients, the Institute has added a new wing to the Jeroen Bosch Hospital in Den Bosch. The institute wished to distinguish itself from its large neighbour, but also to create a building that is centred around the needs and experiences of its patients. Within the Institute, this patient-oriented and open approach is reflected in the interior, logistics and design. Transparency, natural light, colour and space are crucial to the design.

The openness of the Institution is reflected in the open waiting areas, which seem to interconnect with each other. With their appearance, location and varying ceiling heights, each waiting area has its own character. The undulating roof links the waiting areas, offers intimacy and opens the interior to the outdoors. This creates an inviting and accessible building that takes full advantage of the "healing environment" in its direct vicinity. The radiation bunkers form the heart of the building. These are not hidden, but clearly visible as a monolithic numental block. They constitute part of the treatment that offers the chance of a cure.

1. Entrance night view
2~3. Exterior night view
4. Top view of the whole building
5. Façade detail viewed from yard

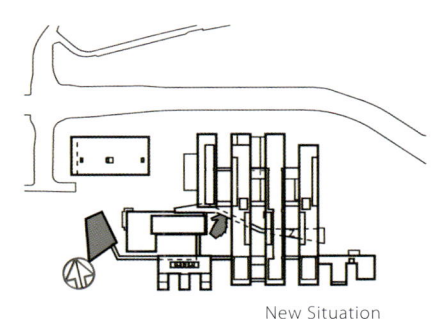
New Situation

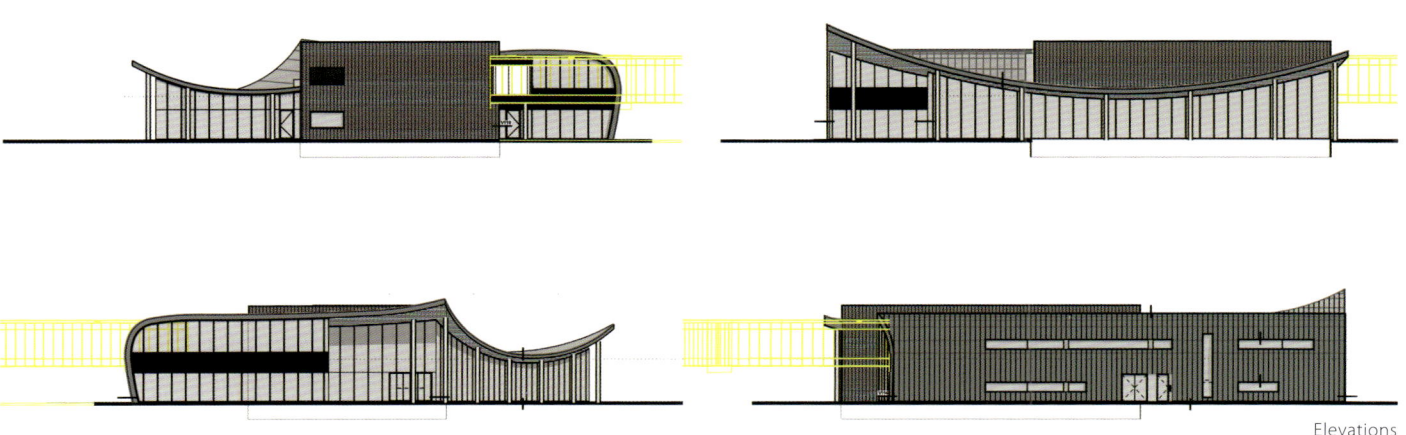
Elevations

6. Lobby and reception
7. Interview area
8. Lobby and waiting

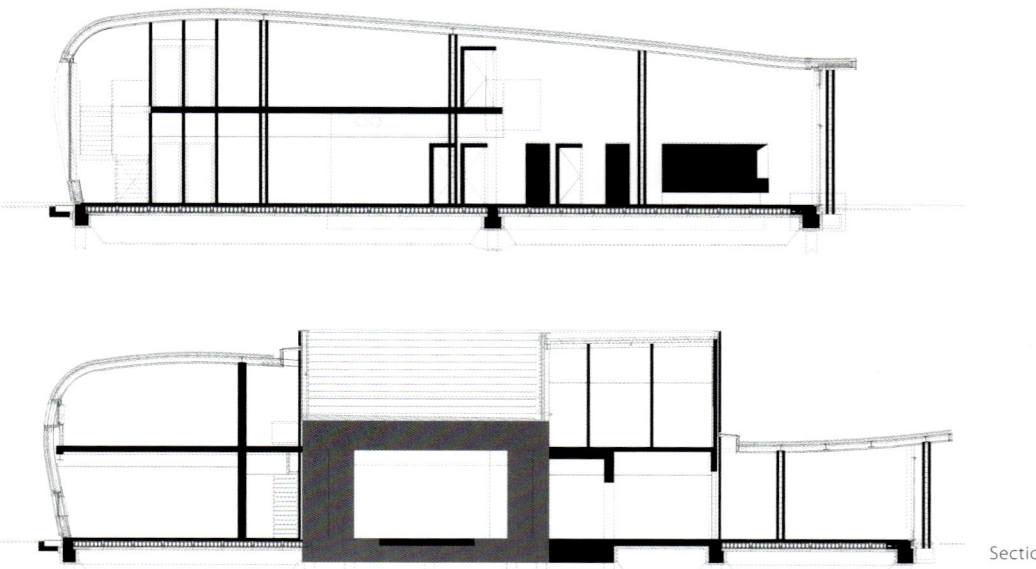

Sections

7

8

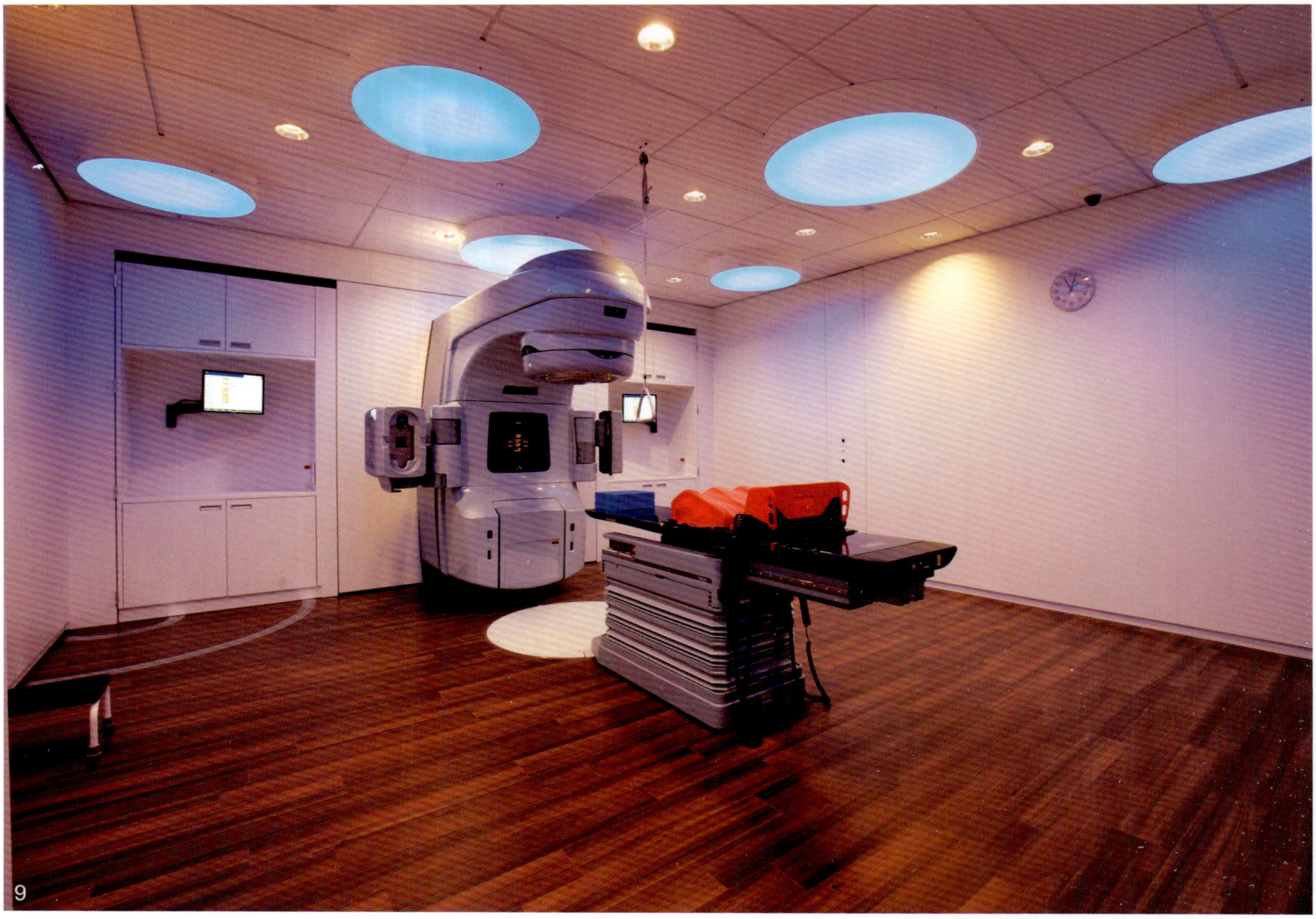

9

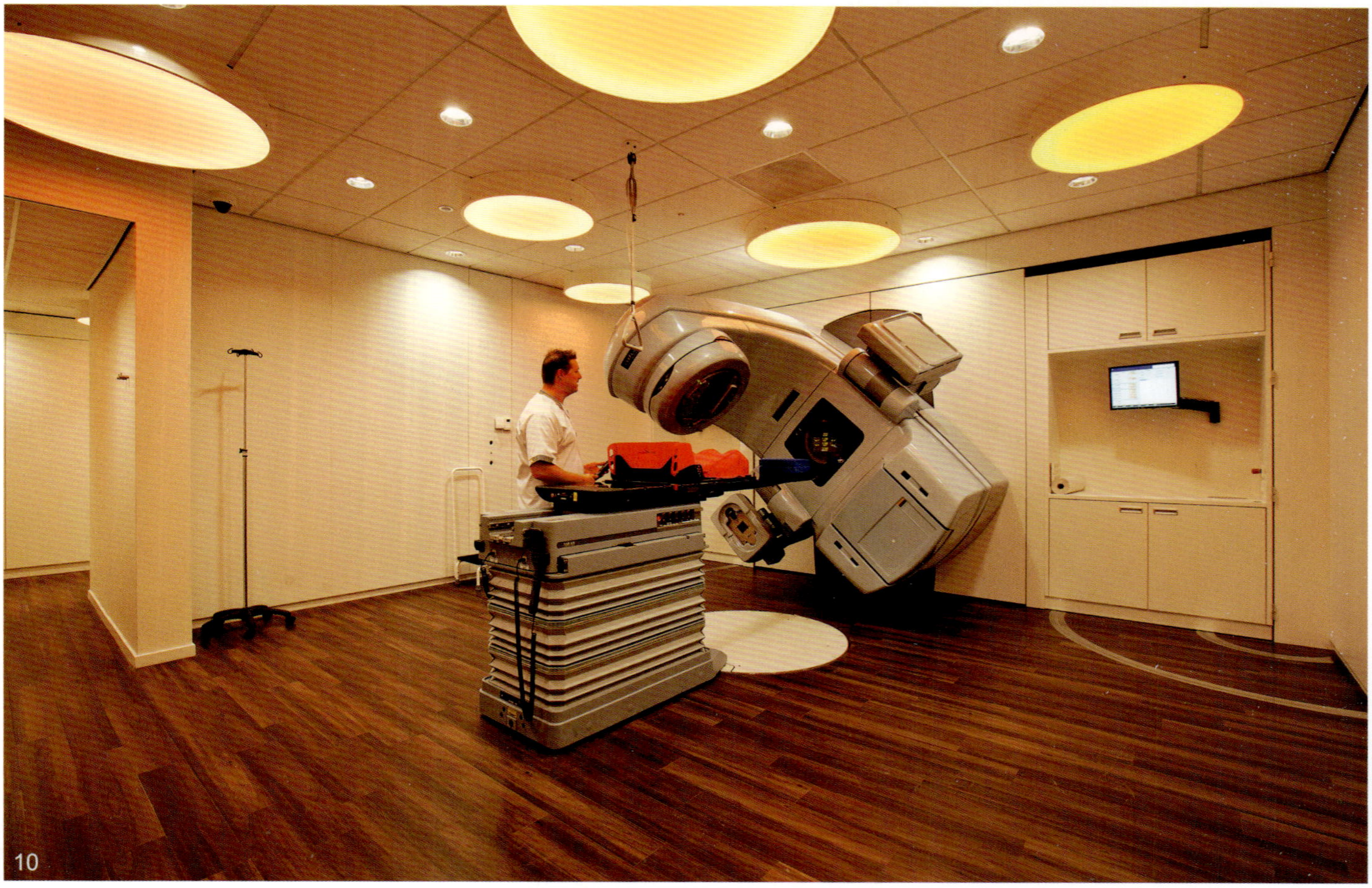

10

9~10. Medical imaging unit

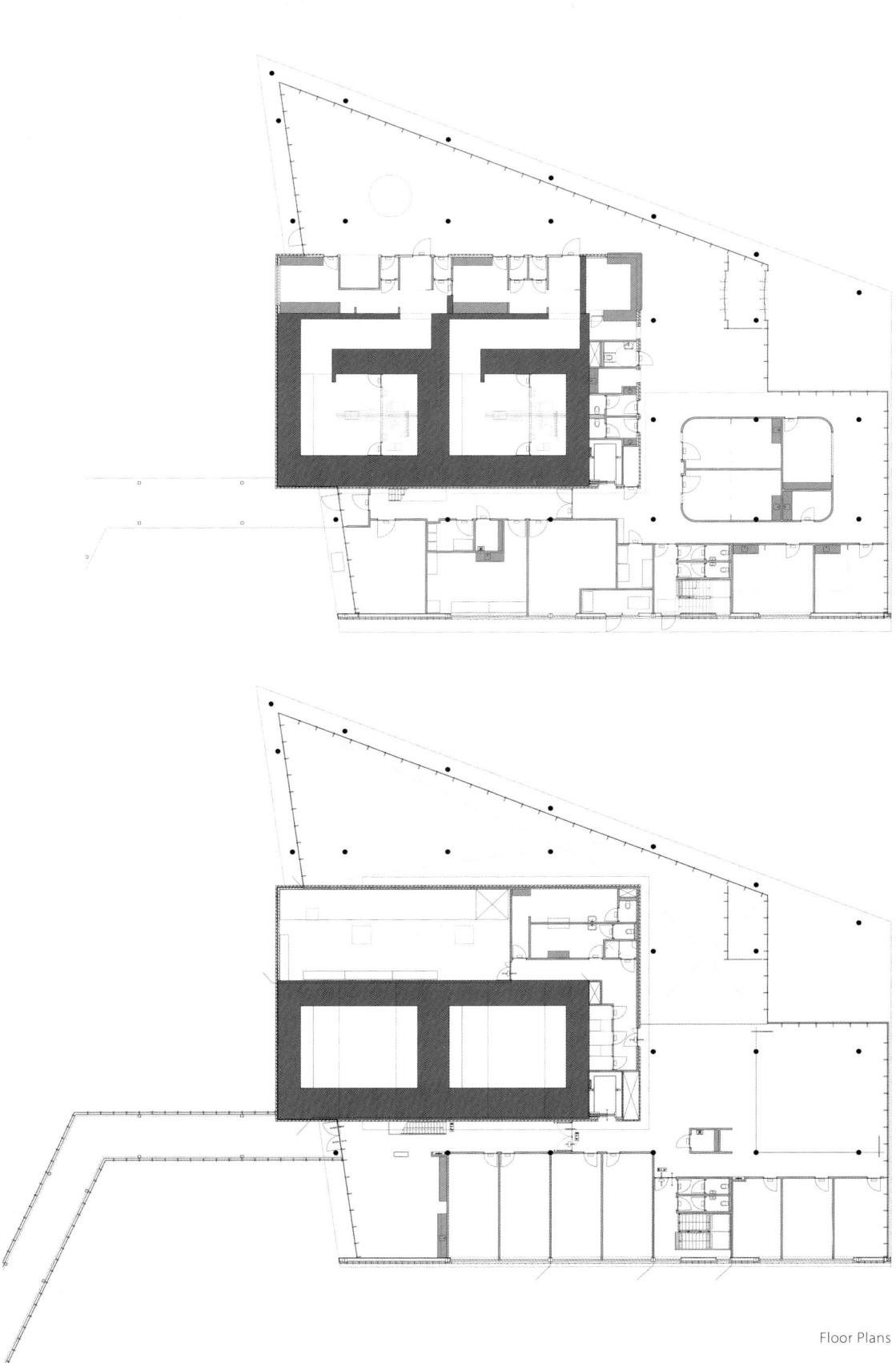

Floor Plans

Healthcare Centre for Cancer Patients

Architects:
Nord Architects
Location:
Copenhgen, Denmark
Building area:
2,250m²
Project year:
2011
Photographs:
© Nord Architects

Getting cancer is like embarking on a journey; you don't know where will end. It requires strength to cope with the disease and take on the new identity as a cancer patient. Research shows that architecture can have a positive effect on people's recovery from sickness. A human scale and a welcoming atmosphere can help people to get better. Despite of this, most hospitals are hardly comfy. Just finding the way from the reception to the canteen can be difficult.

The Healthcare Centre for Cancer Patients in Copenhagen is conceived as an iconic building, which creates awareness of cancer without stigmatising the patients. Designed as a number of small houses combined into one, the centre provides the space needed for a modern health facility, without losing the comforting scale of the individual. The houses are connected by raised roof shaped like a Japanese paper art origami, which gives the building a characteristic signature.

Entering the building you find yourself in a comfy lounge area manned by volunteers. From here you move onto the other parts of the house, which includes a courtyard for contemplation, spaces for exercises, a common kitchen where you can learn to cook healthy food, and meeting rooms for patients groups.

The building is situated close to the city centre of Copenhagen in the same area as Copenhagen University Hospital (Rigshospitalet), so that patients can go to the healthcare centre after their treatment at the hospital. On the other side of the road is the Panum Institute of Medicine.

1. Top view of the whole building at night
2. Exterior night view
3. The building with the surroundings
4. Courtyard and façade detail

Elevations and Sections

5. Lobby
6. Interior view

6

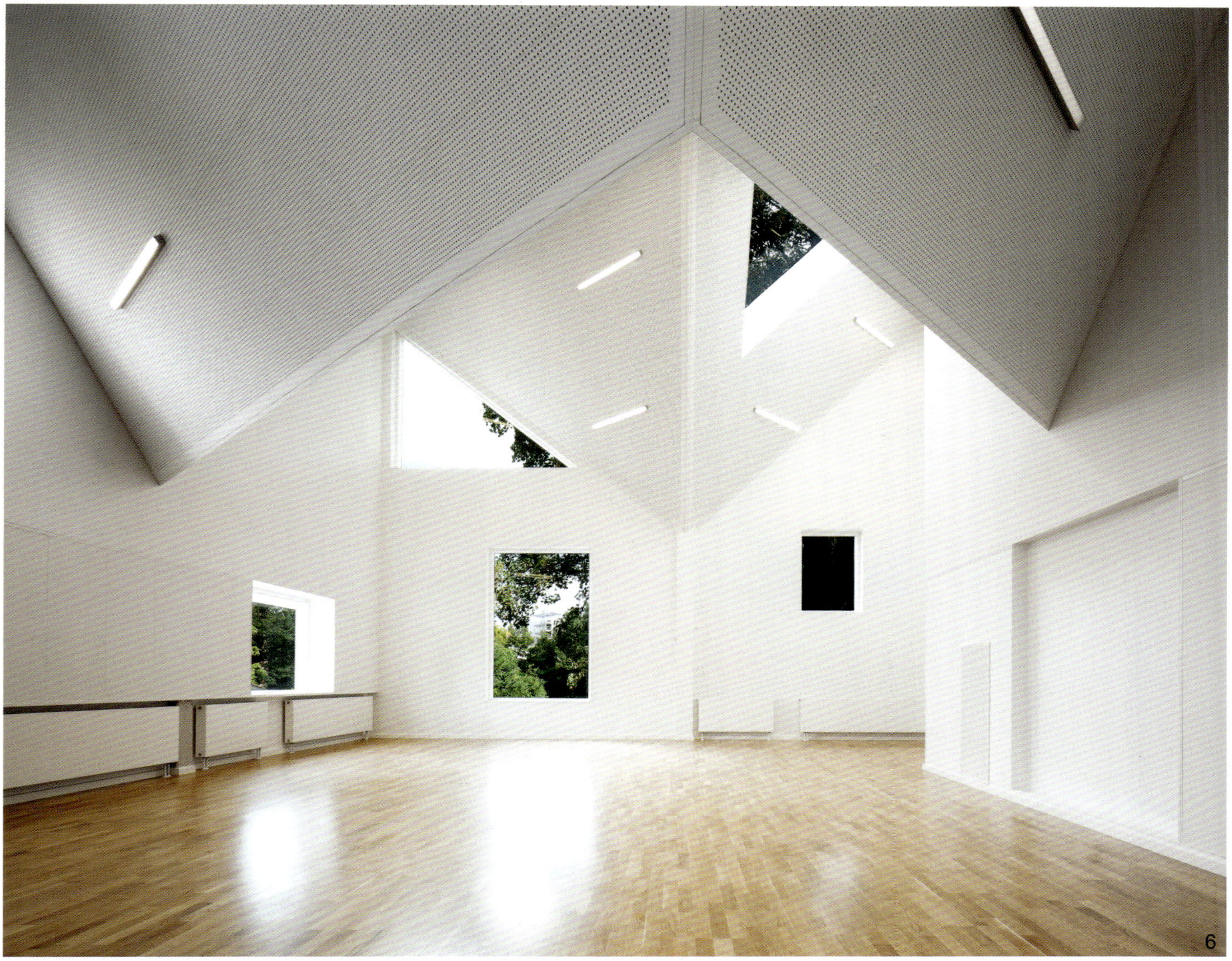

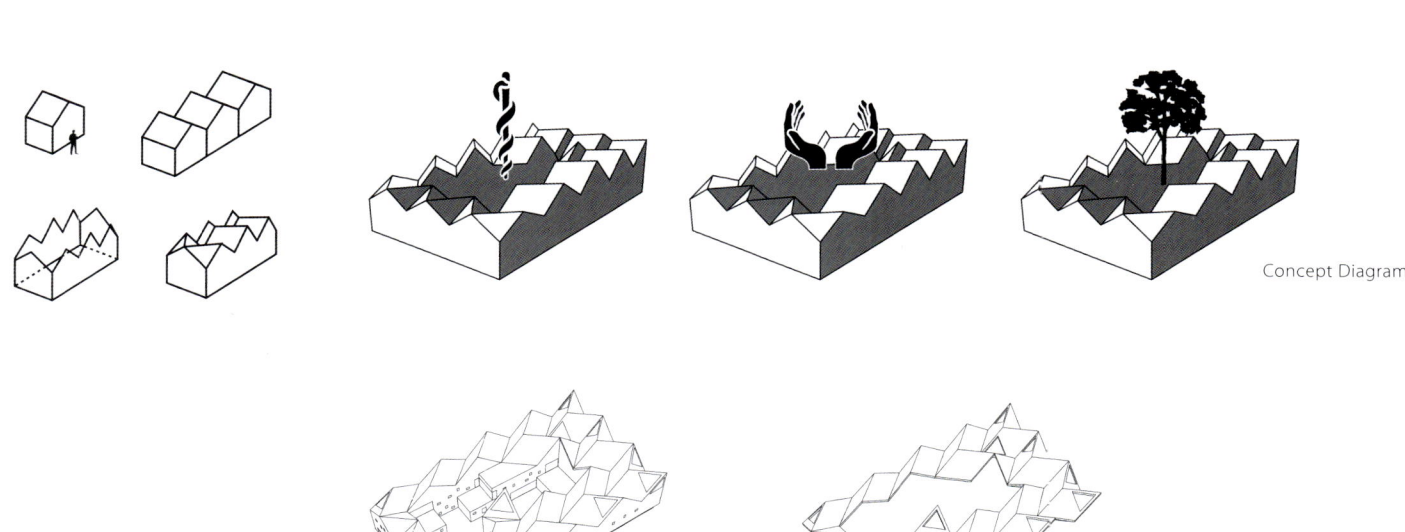

Concept Diagram

Diagram – Roof

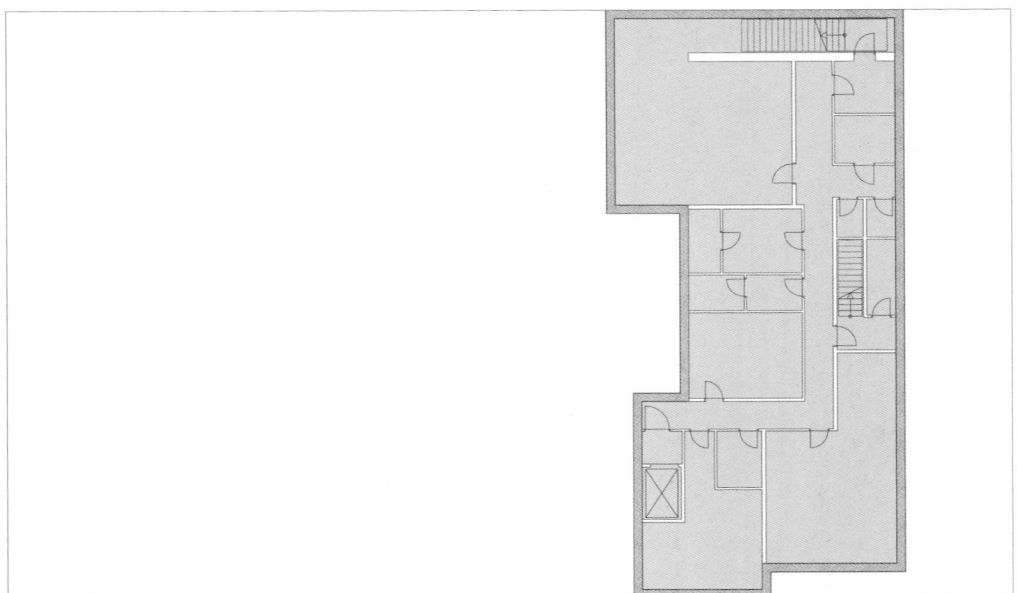

Basement Floor Plan

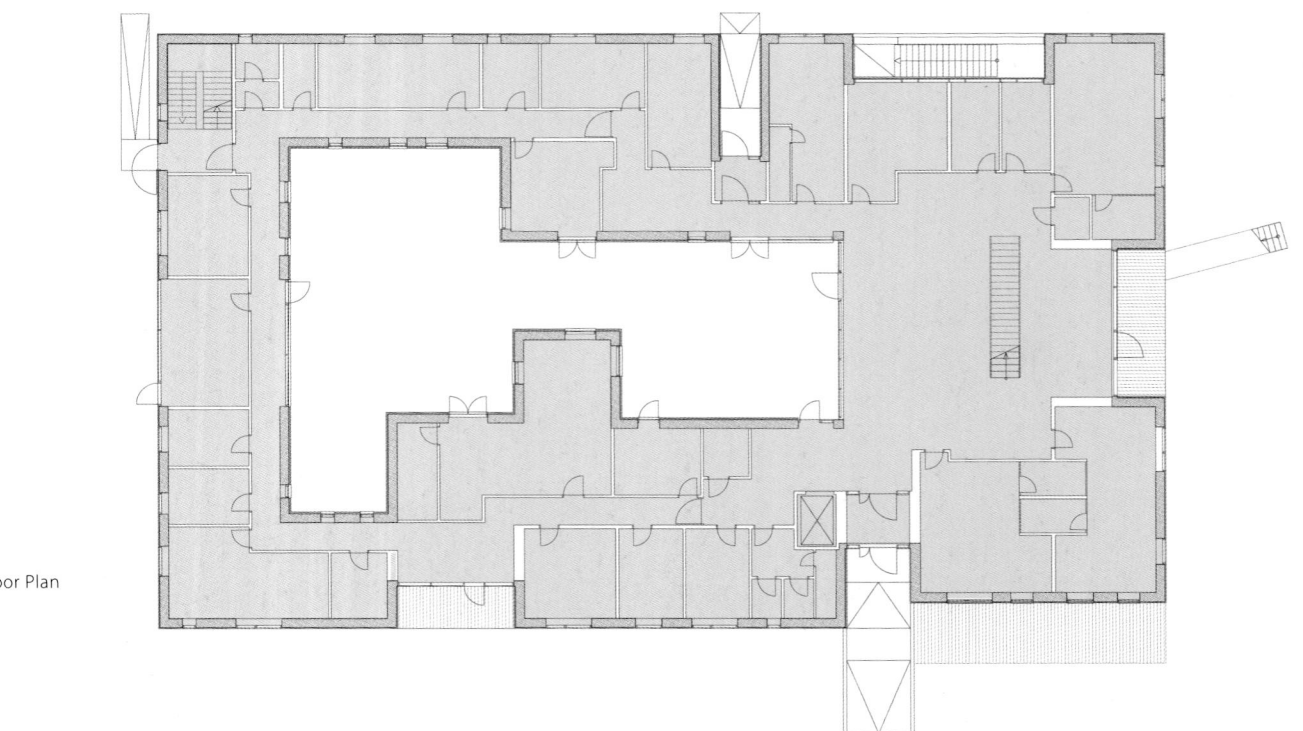

Ground Floor Plan

First Floor Plan

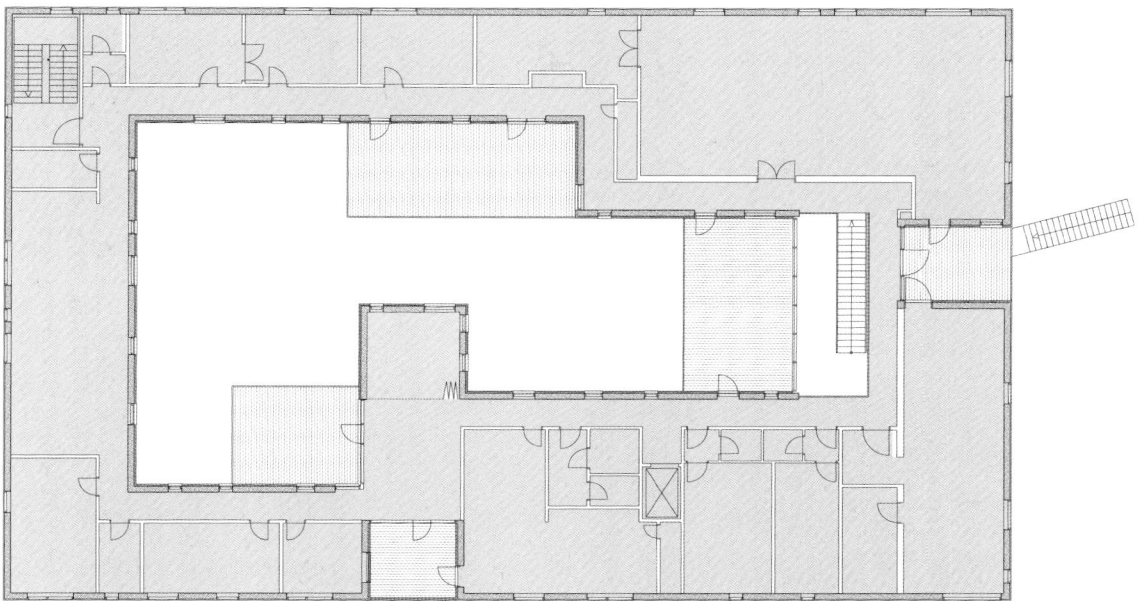

Roof Plan

177

Central DuPage Hospital Cancer Centre and Diagnostic Imaging Centre

Architects:
RTKL
Location:
Chicago, USA
Building area:
4,459m²
Project year:
2010
Photographs:
© Jeffrey Totaro

Central DuPage Hospital in Winfield, Illinois, west of Chicago, commissioned RTKL to design a freestanding cancer and diagnostic imaging centre for a cancer care campus in nearby Warrenville. RTKL's design showcases the high quality of the hospital's brand and its world-class cancer programme by creating a building with a contemporary appearance, simple way finding, and a comforting environment for cancer patients and their families.

The centre's prominent site next to Interstate 88 also influenced the architecture; the elevation was designed for large signage panels visible from the road. The height reflects the scale of the Interstate, but sunshades and columns give the building a more human scale. A landscaped garden makes the building even more intimate and gives patients an opportunity to relax in a natural setting. In addition, a rooftop garden capitalises on the space above the radiation therapy vaults and creates a positive distraction for patients in the private infusion bays that look out to the garden.

The new facility has two components – a cancer centre and an imaging centre. The

1. Covered entry
2. View from west
3. Nurse station
4. Infusion bays

cancer centre houses research, medical oncology, and radiation oncology. The imaging centre includes MRI, CT scan, mammography, and general radiology services. Each centre has its own entrance, but they are connected by an attractive, two-storey, glass-enclosed lobby. The project is one of several RTKL has designed for Central DuPage Hospital.

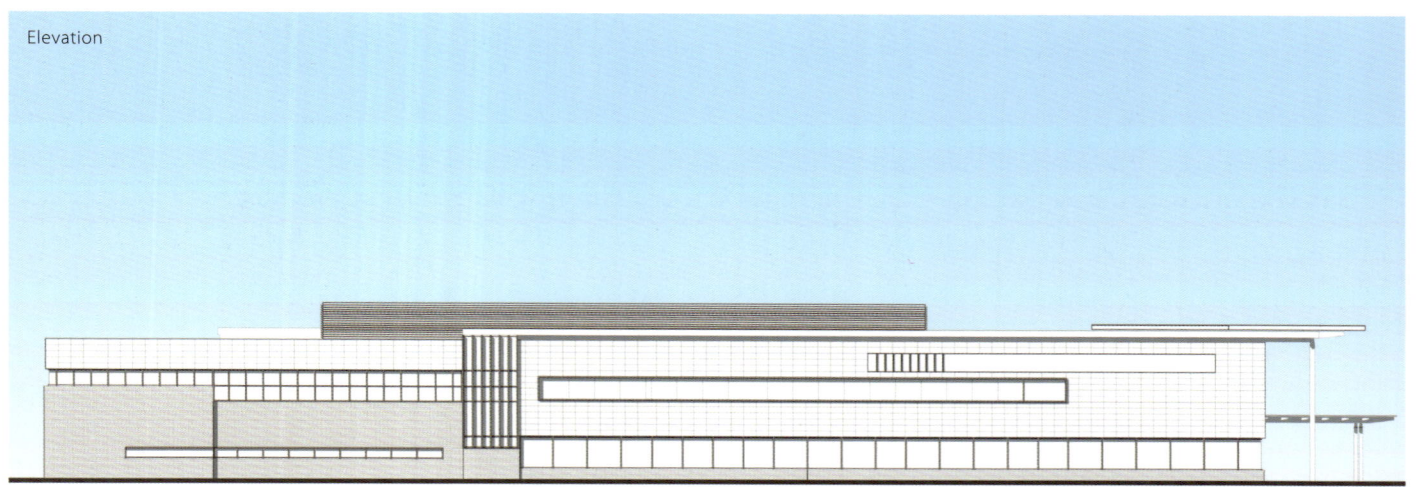

Elevation

5~6. Main stairs in lobby

7. Main lobby and reception desk
8. Linear accelerator

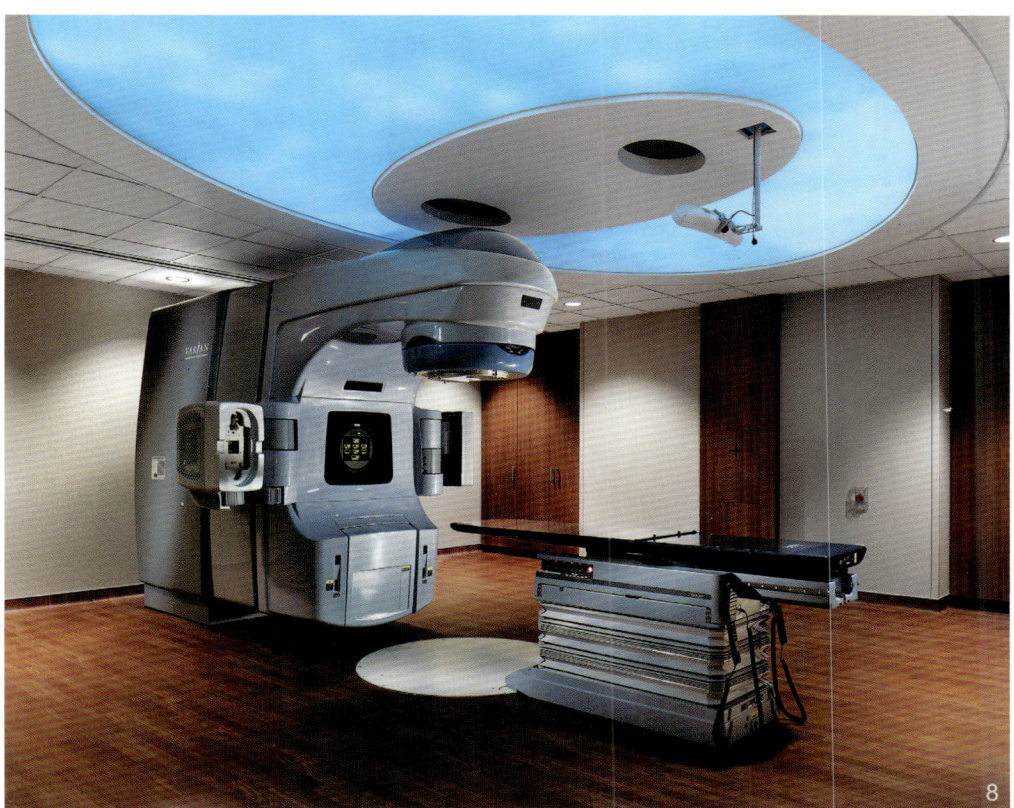

1. Treatment entry
2. Imaging entry
3. Lobby/waiting
4. Treatment areas
5. Administration
6. Radiation therapy
7. Rooftop garden
8. Courtyard
9. Highway

First Floor Plan

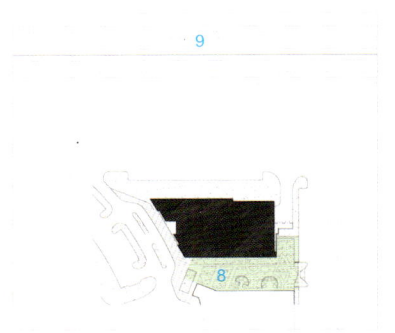

Site Plan

Ground Floor Plan

Obstetrics and Gynecology

MATERNITY UNIT PLANNING AND DESIGN

1. Introduction

The Maternity Unit is a discrete unit providing facilities for the safe antenatal, birthing and postnatal care of mothers and their babies. This Guideline is proposed basing on a nominal 24-bed unit plus birthing rooms capable of accommodating approximately 1,000 deliveries per year. The accommodation is appropriate for the provision of care for mothers and babies with low to moderate risk factors and related complications. It is anticipated that the unit will be managed as one entity including the Nursery. Sub-zones within the unit will provide for the care of mothers with antenatal or postnatal complications requiring acute maternity care, healthy mothers having normal deliveries, healthy newborns requiring minimal care, babies requiring care for complications arising from moderate risk factors and babies with severe complications awaiting transfer to a Neonatal Unit of higher delineation.

The Birthing Unit includes a number of self-contained rooms that accommodate the birthing process of:
- Labour
- Delivery/Birthing
- Recovery
- Postnatal (or Post-Partum)

The model combining Labour, Delivery and Recovery in one room is referred to as LDR. The model combining all four processes is referred to as LDRP. If the LDRP option is selected it will impact on the number of postnatal beds required.

ASSESSMENT OF NUMBER OF BIRTHING ROOMS & BEDROOMS
The level of service and anticipated number of births as determined in the Service Plan, average lengths of stay, number of elective Caesarean sections and model of care will all affect:
- the number of birthing rooms required;
- number of postnatal inpatient beds required.
The anticipated number of elective Caesarean sections booked directly into the operating suite thus bypassing the delivery suite should be deducted from total births when assessing the number of birthing rooms.

The following is based on the LDR model and assumes approximately 1 delivery per room per 24 hours although this may vary from unit to unit:

*1,000 births - 3 birthing rooms plus 1 assessment
*1,500 births - 4 birthing rooms plus 1 assessment
*2,000 births - 5 birthing rooms plus 1 assessment
*3,000 births - 8 birthing rooms plus 1 or 2 assessment rooms

Hospitals adopting the LDRP model will need to reassess these figures depending on Operational Policy and average lengths of stay.

FACTORS AFFECTING PLANNING & DESIGN
The following are not traditional priorities but are a reflection of our changing society and may have an increasing impact on design:
- increasing concerns about infant safety and possible abduction;
- prevalence of domestic violence;
- prevalence of theft;
- continuing change in the composition of the maternity population with a higher percentage of older women and / or women with complex pregnancies - particularly multiple births and prematurity;
- early discharge and community care programmes (that may transfer facilities from the hospital to the community setting);
- increase in elective Caesarean sections as a birthing option;
- increasing emphasis on mental health and well-being.

2. Planning

2.1 Planning Models

LOCATION
In order to provide easy access for ambulances or private vehicles, a ground floor position is the location of choice for the Unit if this can be achieved. Such a location would additionally facilitate access to hospital grounds and

verandas for the mothers and their supporters. If this cannot be achieved, access to a secure courtyard is desirable.

Units should be located to avoid:
- disturbing sounds, both on-site and off-site such as ambulance sirens, traffic and trains
- disturbing views such as cemeteries, mortuaries or their entries etc
- problems associated with prevailing weather conditions. It is preferable for patient accommodation to have a north-east aspect.

The functional needs of the Unit, however, must take priority over other locational needs.

CONFIGURATION
In small centres, if an LDR model, Birthing Rooms and inpatient beds may be combined as an integrated unit. In larger centres, there will be dedicated maternity inpatient beds/units separate from the Birthing Suite. Where a Hospital has no dedicated Special Care Nursery or Neonatal Intensive Care Unit, a small Level 1 nursery will/may be part of the Maternity Ward.

2.2 Functional Areas

FUNCTIONAL ZONES
The Maternity Unit at Level 4 comprises the following functional zones:
- Reception and arrival area including provisions for visitors and administrative activities;
- Birthing Rooms;
- Inpatient Areas – Acute Care (Antenatal & sick post-natal) & Mother Care;
- General & Special Care Nursery;
- Support & Staff areas including facilities that can be shared between zones and other units.

RECEPTION
This zone provides an area where mothers, their supporter/s, visitors and

other members of the public are initially received and directed to the appropriate part of the Unit. There needs to be convenient access to public telephone and toilet facilities particularly for supporters. It may be the preferred location for a Visitors' Lounge that could include Child Play Space.

The office/s for nursing administration and midwifery educators may be located in this vicinity.

The area may be used as a booking facility for expectant mothers or this may occur in the Maternity Ambulatory Care Area.

When designing the Reception, particular consideration needs to be given to security of the area (duress alarm, controlled access, etc.) and also to space for the initial holding of frequent flower/gift deliveries.

BIRTHING AREAS
The entire birth process takes place in this area and involves assessment, early and established labour, vaginal delivery – with or without intervention, the bonding process of mother, partner and family with baby as well as a rest period prior to transfer to a ward bed or discharge if required a community midwifery programme. If the Facility provides LDRP rooms, the patient will occupy the same room for the entire length of stay.

Facilities comprise:
- Birthing Rooms;
- One at least multi-purpose assessment room that can be used for consultations and examinations and as a back-up birthing room;
- Facilities for support persons and other family members throughout the entire birthing process and period immediately following the birth;
- At Level 3, a holding nursery to provide additional facilities for baby resuscitation, space for parking a transport humidicrib and additional bassinettes for multiple births. The nursery should provide facilities for preparing babies for early transfer home directly from the Birthing Unit and for the laying out of stillborn babies.

NURSERY AREAS

Provided at Level 3/4 Maternity as a possible adjunct to a Maternity Inpatient Unit, the General (Level 1) Nursery will provide facilities for the care of well babies away from their mother's bed area and for the following functions:
- baby weighing, bathing and changing;
- Feeding of babies in comfortable chairs;
- Parent and staff education;
- Phototherapy;
- Sleeping of babies in daytime using partial blackout curtains;
- Short-term accommodation, with assisted ventilation if required, for the care of babies with unexpected severe complications while awaiting transfer to a centre with a Neonatal Intensive Care Unit.

The Nursery must have a minimum floor area of $2.8m^2$ per bassinet and a minimum of 1-metre clear and unobstructed passageway between each bassinet. Number of cot bays will depend on rooming-in policies and the number of mothers unable or reluctant to do so. The Special Care (Level 2) Nursery will in addition to the above have sick and recovering premature infants requiring care in humidicribs and bassinettes due to problems related to their prematurity and/or low weight.

INPATIENT ACCOMMODATION

The Inpatient Area provides suitable accommodation for antenatal and postnatal mothers.

The Schedule of Accommodation assumes a 24-bed unit comprising a mix of one- and two-bed rooms for acute care mothers and for mothercare but bed numbers are nominal only and will need to be adjusted to suit the specific project – and geography and patient demographics. The bed mix should be designed for use by a variable mix of mothers, e.g. a higher than normal antenatal population. Acute care may include antenatal patients and mothers recovering from Caesarean sections, etc. Mothercare areas are for well mothers and well babies. The bed rooms should be arranged in functional groups according to degree of dependency. Acute care rooms should be well positioned in relation to the staff station and utility areas to facilitate effective patient observation by staff. The bed rooms for the mothercare group may be located towards the periphery of the Unit and should convey a relaxed domestic environment. Four-bed rooms are not recommended for Maternity Units due to the roomingin policy in many hospitals, as four babies in one room can cause excessive disruption to mothers requiring rest.

It is suggested that at least 1 pair of adjoining one-bed rooms be designated for standard isolation with a handwash and PPE bays outside. Provision of Class N Isolation Rooms (negative pressure plus ante room) will depend on level of service and even geographical location with regard to likelihood of diseases such as TB.

SHARED AREAS

The opportunity to share space, equipment and staffing should be maximised, both between the various zones of the Unit and between the Maternity Unit and other units where appropriate. Within the Unit it will be possible to share areas such as staff station, utilities, waiting and lounge space between zones. By judicious planning it should be feasible to share areas such as tutorial and toilet facilities with adjacent units. The size of shared spaces may need to be larger than "standard" to accommodate the greater number of staff or visitors occupying them.

OFFICE ACCOMMODATION

With the exception of the office for the NUM that is included in the Schedule of Accommodation, the staff establishment will determine the number of offices/workstations required.

2.3 Functional Relationships

EXTERNAL

The Unit should be located to maximise or provide quietness and an outlook and access to the outside during long periods of labour. This latter is of particular importance for units in rural areas with high aboriginal populations who are not used to being confined indoors. However, privacy must be maintained. The Maternity Unit, and in particular the Birthing module, should be located with easy access to the Operating Suite.

INTERNAL
The Maternity Unit should be designed to prohibit non-related traffic through the Unit. Within the Unit, the Reception should be located at the entrance to the unit and should provide direct access to each of the Birthing, Inpatient and Nursery areas. The area should accommodate waiting space and provide ready access to assessment & consultation/examination facilities. Refer to Functional Relationship Chart on page 197.

3. Design

3.1 Access

EXTERNAL
The Unit requires 24-hour access. If the Unit does not have its dedicated entry, specific arrangements will need to be made for after-hours access.
Access during normal hours will be via the Reception Area. After-hours access for expectant mothers and their supporters will be via the Birthing Area. After-hours policy may allow restricted access to partners/support persons of mothers in the Inpatient Area and parents of neonates in the Neonatal Special Care Area.

The Unit should be located close to:
- ambulance transport bay – particularly for the NETS retrieval team;
- helipad if provided – also for retrieval teams;
- short-term car parking for partners bringing women to the Birthing Unit and for flower deliveries although the latter must not obstruct the patient drop-off area;
- hospital car park;
- public transport facilities.

3.2 Infection Control

HANDWASHING
There will be a scrub basin Type A (Refer Standard Component) in each Birthing Room. Hand basin in each bed room and outside each pair of designated Isolation Rooms if provided. At entry to Nursery for parents & staff. At least one hand basin per six cots in the Nursery. Staff to be no further than six metres from a basin.

PLACENTA DISPOSAL
Placental material will usually be considered contaminated waste and dealt with as per the individual hospital/Area Health Service Waste Management policies. The use of placental macerators is not recommended. Units may need to consider providing dedicated refrigerator or freezer for storage whilst awaiting disposal or collection by families for cultural reasons.

3.3 Environmental Considerations

GENERAL
The Birthing Rooms should have individually-controlled air-conditioning systems. If the thermostats are located inside the Birthing Room, the controls should be located out of the reach of children and under the control of staff only. The rooms need to be able to quickly obtain a temperature range of 25-27°C when the baby is born. The Nursery also requires similar temperature control.

ACOUSTICS
Acoustic treatment is essential in the Birthing Rooms to allow the mother to vocalise as desired during labour without disturbing other mothers in labour. Babies crying at night are a major source of noise and for those mothers recovering from surgery or other conditions, e.g. pre-eclampsia, noise may be detrimental to their condition. One of the prime considerations in the Nursery is the amount of noise created by babies crying, monitors, suction pumps, ventilators, etc. Methods of sound dampening should be carefully considered, but should not interfere with observation and ease of access between the Nursery and staff/support areas.

LIGHTING
Colour-corrected dimmable lighting is essential in all patient areas where high dependency care is provided – birthing/assessment rooms and birthing room en-suites and bathrooms, all nurseries and baby bathing/examination/resuscitation areas.

NATURAL LIGHT
Essential in all bed rooms, birthing rooms and nursery.

PRIVACY
The design of the Assessment and Birthing Rooms should ensure that the foot of the bed does not face the door. Viewing panels in the Birthing Room door should be avoided.

INTERIOR DESIGN
Particular care needs to be given to the Nursery and to the Birthing Rooms to achieve a non-clinical ambiance. Medical services may be encased in joinery panels and equipment stored in an adjoining area or behind folding doors or screens. Care must be taken with the reflective quality of colours, e.g. the effect of yellow on jaundiced babies.

3.4 Security

SECURITY
Security issues are of major importance in design of what is a highly emotional environment due to the prevalence of domestic violence, theft and the seemingly increase in infant abduction or other illegal acts by estranged parents or disturbed members of the public. Fridges and freezers used for storage of breast milk should either be locked or the Formula Room restricted to Staff access only or mothers under staff supervision to ensure that the correct milk is issued to the right infant.

Minimising entry and exit points, incorporating an Access Control System, by means of a reed switch, electric strike and card readers to all Unit perimeter

Functional Relationship Chart – Maternity Unit

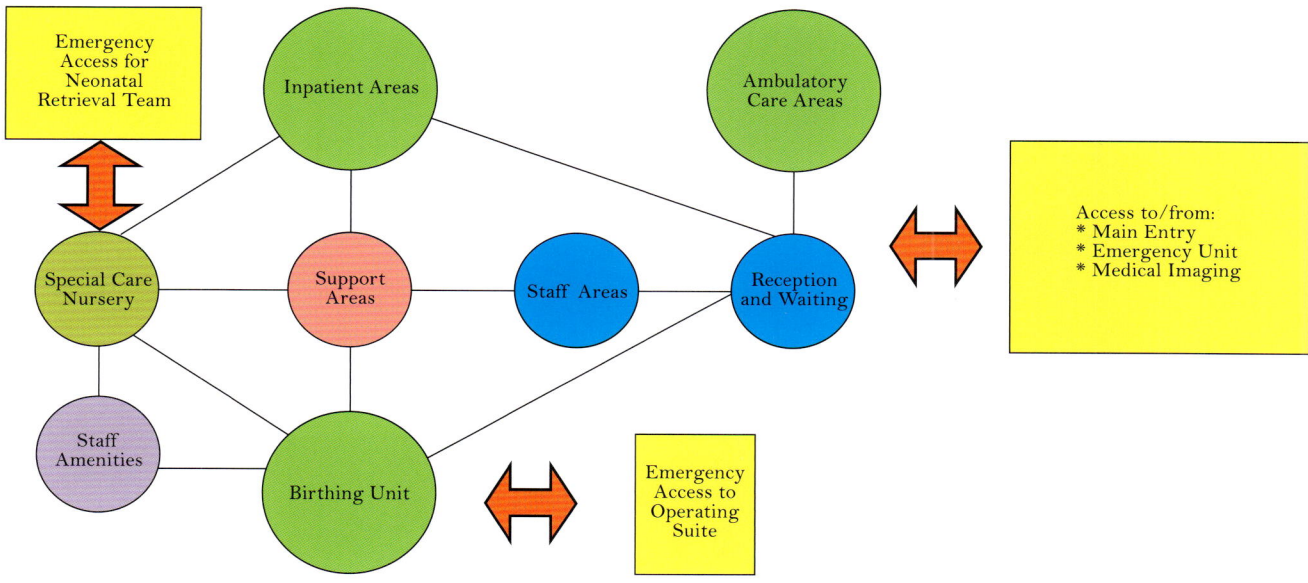

doors, can avoid the use of an unsophisticated – and costly – infant tagging system. Card readers need to be provided on the internal as well as the external approach to all egress doors, including fire egress doors. No unsecured exit from the Maternity.

Unit should be available, except in a fire or other emergency situation.

Provision of one entrance for patients and visitors to enter the Birthing Area will aid security. To maximise control by the staff there should be direct observation of all persons entering the Unit including video intercoms for after-hours remote access.

ELECTRONIC INFANT TAGGING
Electronic infant tagging involves a tag being put around a baby's ankle which responds to sensor panels located at Unit/hospital exits. If the baby is taken through the sensor an alarm goes off and the hospital's security team is alerted. Infant tagging is costly and has proved problematic where it has been implemented as neonates loose weight in the first days of life; the tag bracelets therefore become too large and slip off easily.

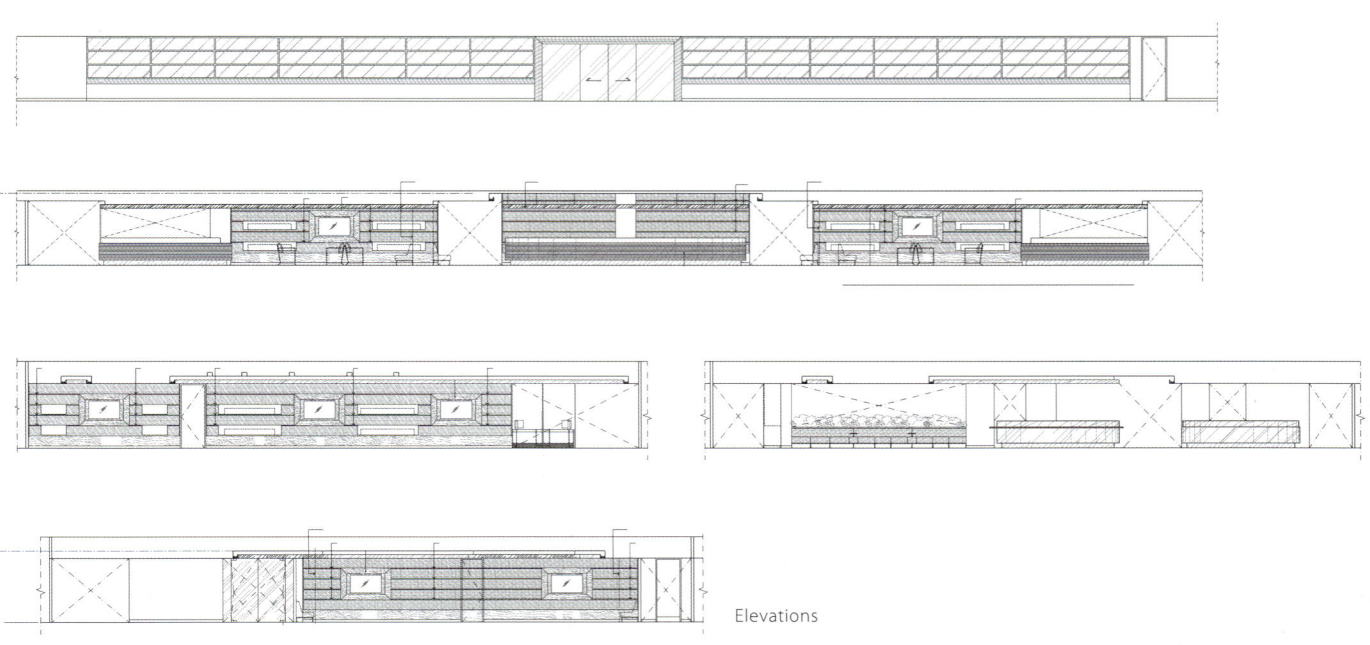

Elevations

Bumrungrad International Hospital, Women's Centre

Architects:
dwp
Location:
Bangkok, Thailand
Building area:
3,600m²
Project year:
2010
Photographs:
© Weerapo Singnoi

dwp undertook its most recent commission for the full renovation and upgrade of Bumrungrad International Hospital in the interior and FF&E design of the Women's Centre, completed in March 2010.

The brief was to create a fresh and contemporary identity for the centre, while complimenting other areas and ongoing refurbishment works in the community. The functional and spatial requirements of the brief meant the layout needed to be very efficient but also be generous and practical in providing user comfort to the patients, visitors and the staff. The interior scheme drew from an underlying "Zen" warm contemporary Asian theme, which, depicted in the common area, links the space through the visual language. The area introduces a new and rich colour palette, as well as soft materials and intimate screened seating areas that create a unique identity. To maximise comfort and efficiency, lounge-style seating areas are located adjacent to the examination rooms and are linked by streamlined cross-over circulation spaces thus allowing for staged waiting sequence and improving traffic flows.

dwp's design responds to the client's service-oriented approach and addresses the specific needs of individual patients and visitors. In addition to making the waiting lounge and examination rooms

1. Overall view of nurse station/register and waiting area
2~5. Waiting area

experience as comfortable as possible, care and attention to addressing the staff's clinical needs, including integrating existing solutions, was a primary concern. For example, spacing specialised exam rooms and equipments at intervals within the space, rather than grouped, customised document storage units to suit file management, and highly efficient detailed room layouts enabling a greater number of smaller examination rooms. As a designer, dwp is convinced that this attention to detail is essential to assisting the client in enhancing their best practice approach, and in achieving the most efficient, fluid, and reliable service to patients and visitors.

6. Front view of reception
7. Circulation and waiting
8. Perspective view of corridor

9. Exam room viewed from corridor
10. Doctor office

Floor Plan:
1. Main lobby
2. Waiting area
3. A.H.U
4. N' Station
5. Main corridor
6. Lift lobby
7. Service lift lobby
8. Corridor
9. Staff corridor
10. Register
11. Casher express
12. O.B GYN. Dept.
13. Inner corridor
14. Sub. station
15. Scope waiting area
16. Register counter
17. DDC & Scope DEPT.
18. Reg. waiting area
19. Recovery room

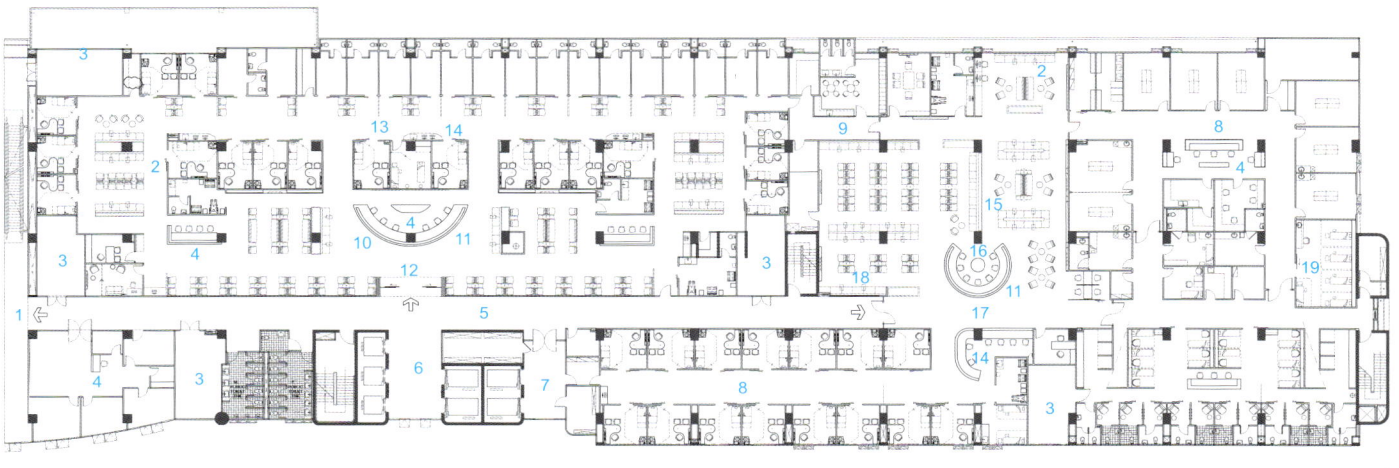

Prentice Women's Hospital and Maternity Centre of Northwestern Memorial Hospital

Architects:
VOA, as a joint venture with OWP/P.
Location:
Chicago, USA
Project year:
2008
Photographs:
© Jeff Milles, Craig Dugan, Nick Merrick

Prentice Women's Hospital and Maternity Centre of Northwestern Memorial Hospital, located at 250 E. Superior Street in Chicago, offers a comprehensive, patient-centred programme for women's and infants' health. Prentice is also the primary teaching facility for Northwestern University's Feinberg School of Medicine, providing graduate and undergraduate education in women's healthcare and newborn pediatric care.

The hospital has 58 postpartum and antepartum beds and 27 beds for gynecologic care. The labour-delivery-recovery (LDR) area has 20 LDR rooms with 4 operative rooms. The Prentice operative room has 6 suites for gynecology, breast, and plastic surgeries. The Level III Reneé Schine Crown Special Care Nursery accommodates 46 newborns and is staffed at all times by neonatologists. The nursery, which receives transports through the Northwestern Perinatal Network as well as infants born at Northwestern Memorial, provides care for up to 500 premature or seriously ill newborns each year.

1. Exterior viewed from street
2. The hospital with the surroundings
3. Exterior view
4. Lobby

The Prentice Women's Hospital for Northwestern Memorial Healthcare continues to enhance and promote the hospital's "Patients First" mission and philosophy. Completed in 2008, the 18-storey hospital accommodates 13,600 annual births and provides cutting-edge, women-specific healthcare that demonstrates nationally benchmarked excellence in patient services and clinical outcomes. Patient care, research, and a state-of-the-art teaching facility attracts and retains renowned physicians and allied healthcare providers.

The design incorporates hospitality industry standards and amenities into the state-of-the-art healthcare environment, and capitalises on the beautiful views of water and greenways available from the site, one block from Lake Michigan in metropolitan Chicago. Labour/delivery/recovery rooms are organised into clusters that break down the scale of the space to create intimate waiting areas. Family-friendly rooms are equipped with dining areas and window seats that convert to beds.

The design also includes a Breast Health Centre, a women's cancer treatment centre, a full surgical unit, space for 100 private physician offices, a women's health and education centre, and full-service retail amenities including a florist, maternity shop, bookstore, and coffee shop.

At the time of its designation, Prentice was the first LEED-NC Silver certified inpatient hospital in Illinois and the largest in the country.

Elevations

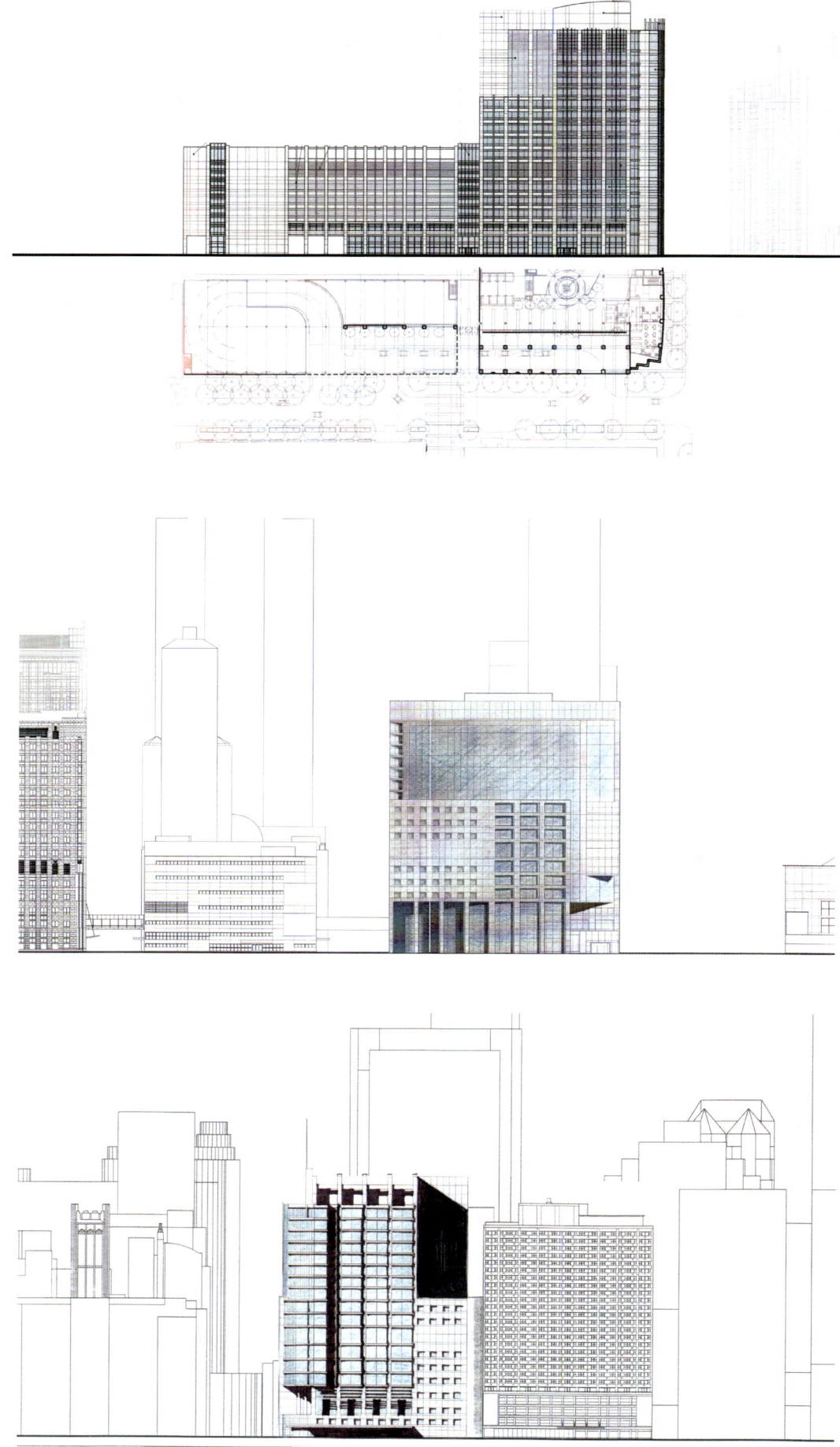

5. Reception viewed from waiting area

Programme and Stacking:
1. Building services
2. Women's care unit (36 beds)
3. Post-partum (36 beds)
4. Physician offices
5. Special care nursery (86 bassinets)
6. Antepartum/post-partum (26 beds)
7. Labour and delivery (32 beds)
8. Building systems
9. Women's surgery (10 operating rooms)
10. Pre-administration, test/imaging/ultrasound
11. Comprehensive breast centre
12. Conference centre/ classrooms/chapel
13. Business office/ cafeteria/retail
14. Lobby/admitting/ women's health centre
15. MAT. MGMT. dietary support services
16. Breast centre, RAD. ONC.
17. Building systems
18. Parking garage (1,140 cars)

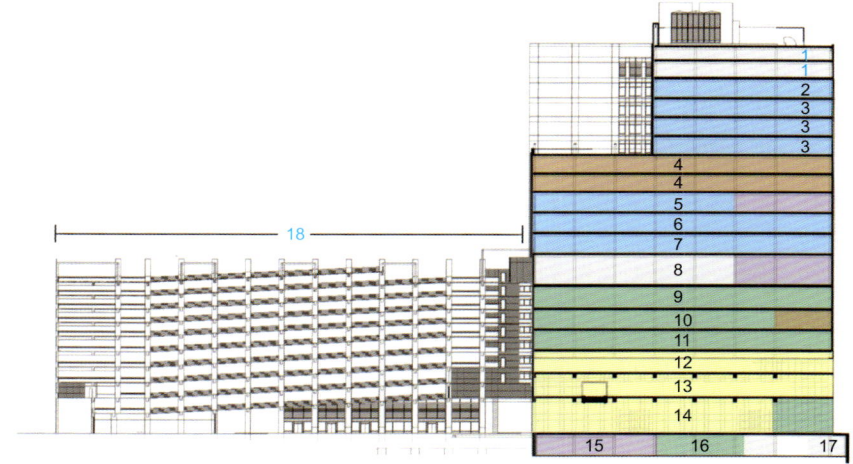

Stacking and Ground Floor:
B. Service/support
1. Lobby
2. Admin/public/retail
3. Women's spa/amenities
4. Physician offices
5. Physician offices
6. Mechanical
7. Support
8. DIAG/treatment
9. DIAG/treatment
10. DIAG/treatment
11. Women's inpatient unit
12. Women's inpatient unit
13. Women's inpatient unit
14. MED/SURG inpatient
15. MED/SURG inpatient
16. Mechanical
17. Service tunnel
18. Bridge
19. Access drive
20. Concourse level
21. Future extension of MIES
22. Spa/child care
23. Retail/concourse
24. Parking
25. PSYCH outpatient
26. PSYCH inpatient
27. PSYCH inpatient

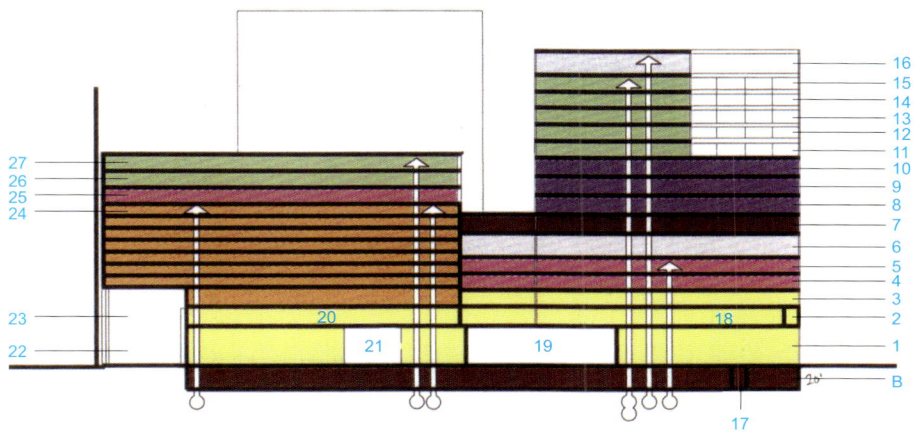

① Public
② Patient
③ Service
④ Psychiatric inpatients
⑤ Physician offices
⑥ Parking

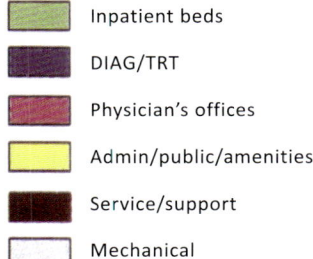
Inpatient beds
DIAG/TRT
Physician's offices
Admin/public/amenities
Service/support
Mechanical
Parking

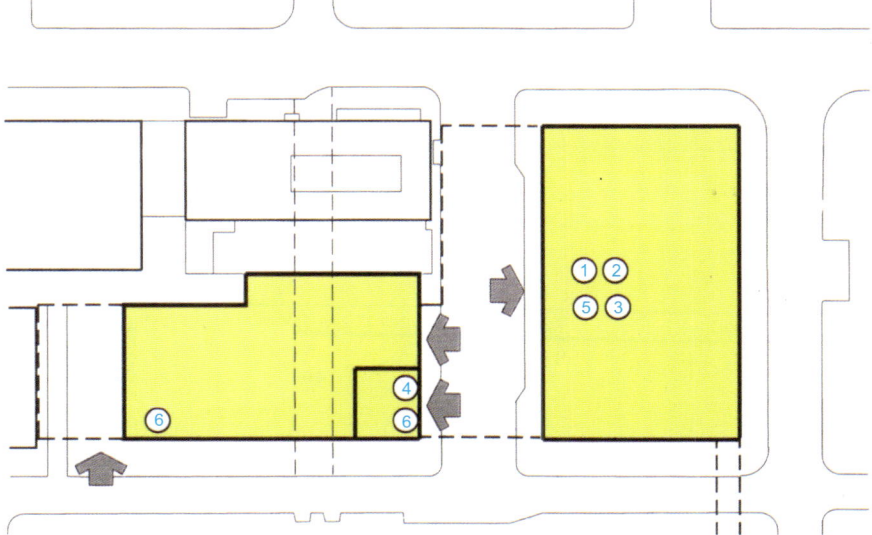

211

6

7

6~7. Lobby
8. Lounge/waiting

9. Family waiting
10. Cashier

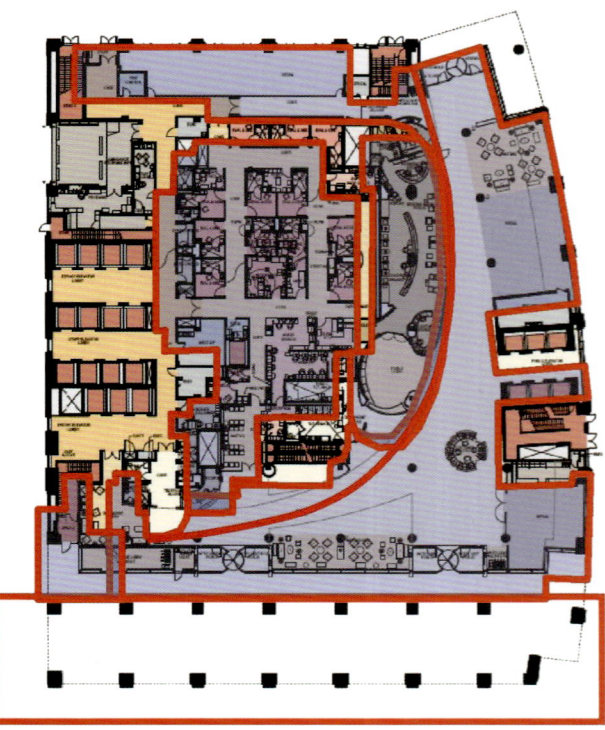

Ground Floor Plan
(Women's health learning centre
and Obstetrical triage unit)

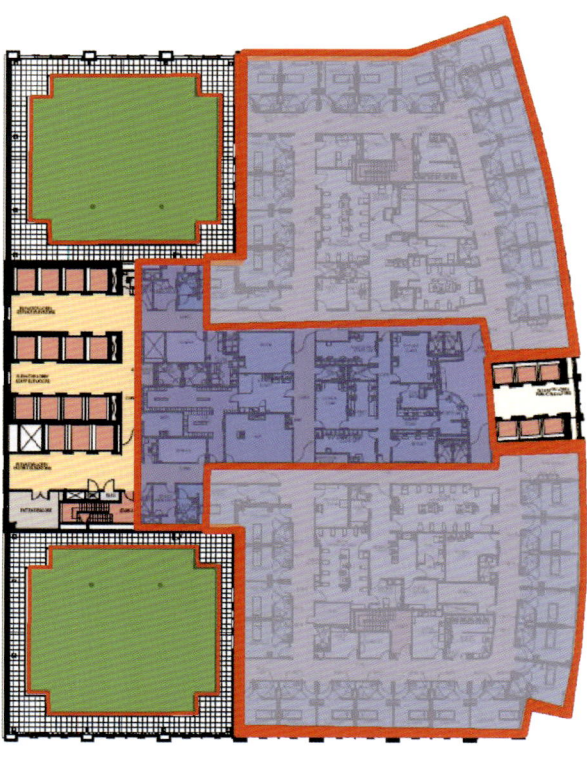

12th & 13th Floor Plan – Post Partum
(2-18 bed pods each with normal nurseries
and all private rooms)

11~12. Cafeteria

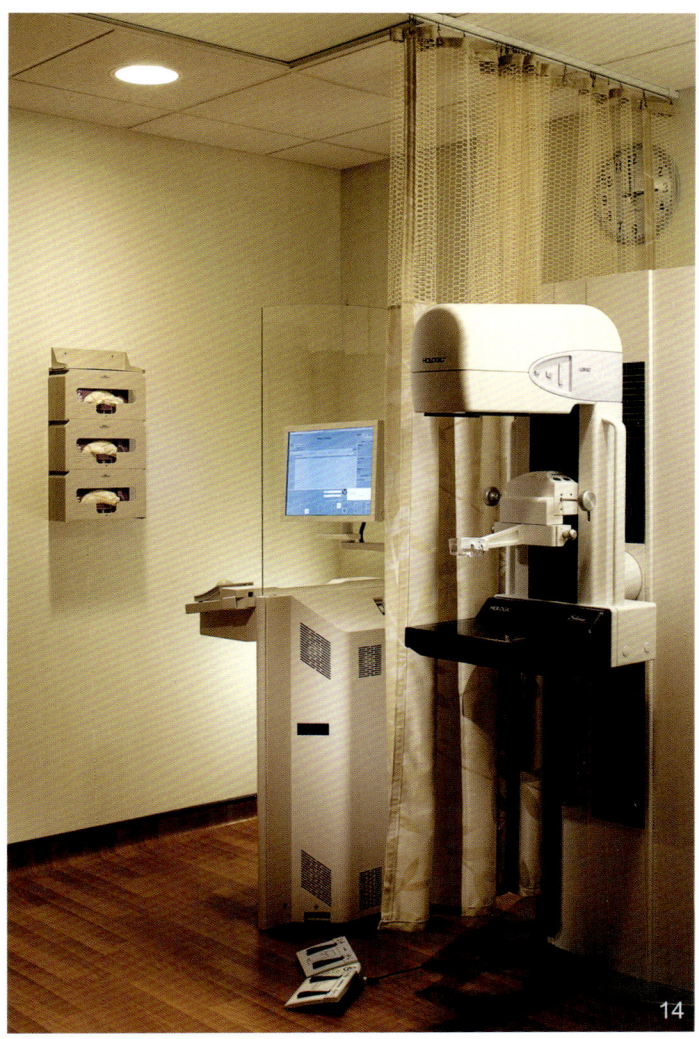

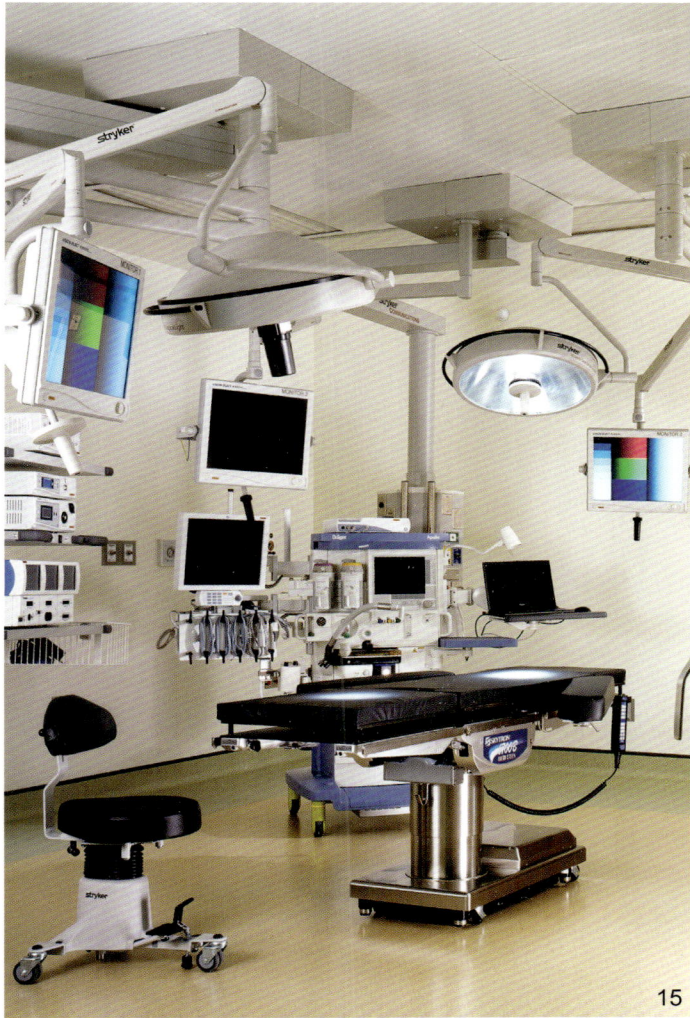

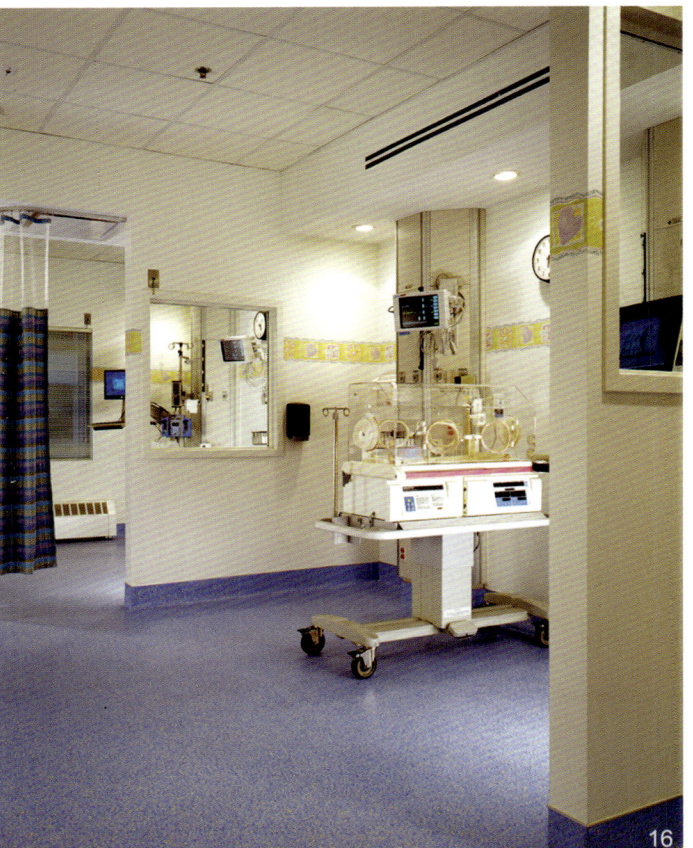

13. Patient room viewed from corridor
14. Exam room
15. Operating room
16. NICU
17. Corridor and nurse station
18. Neonate nursery
19~20. NICU

17

18

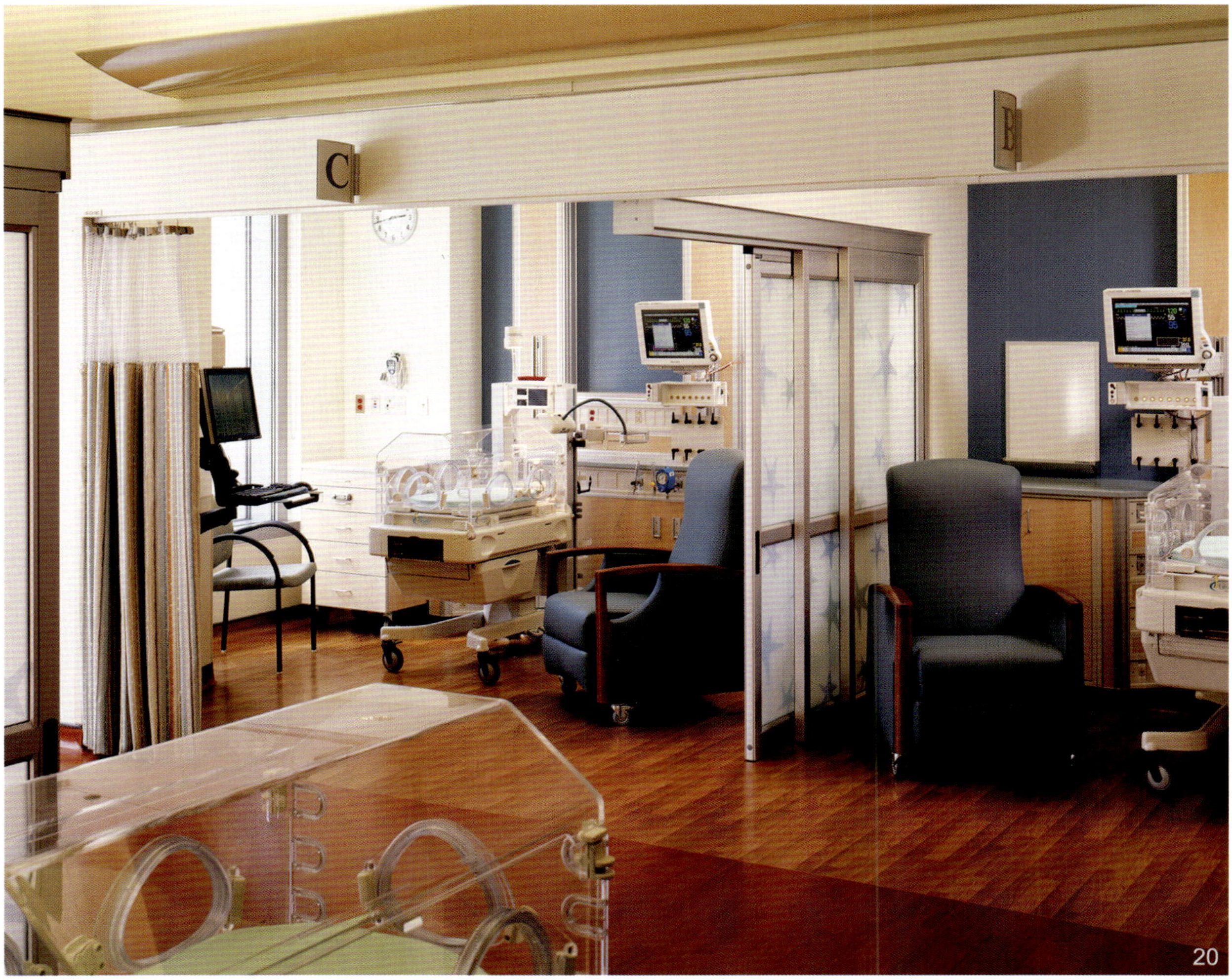

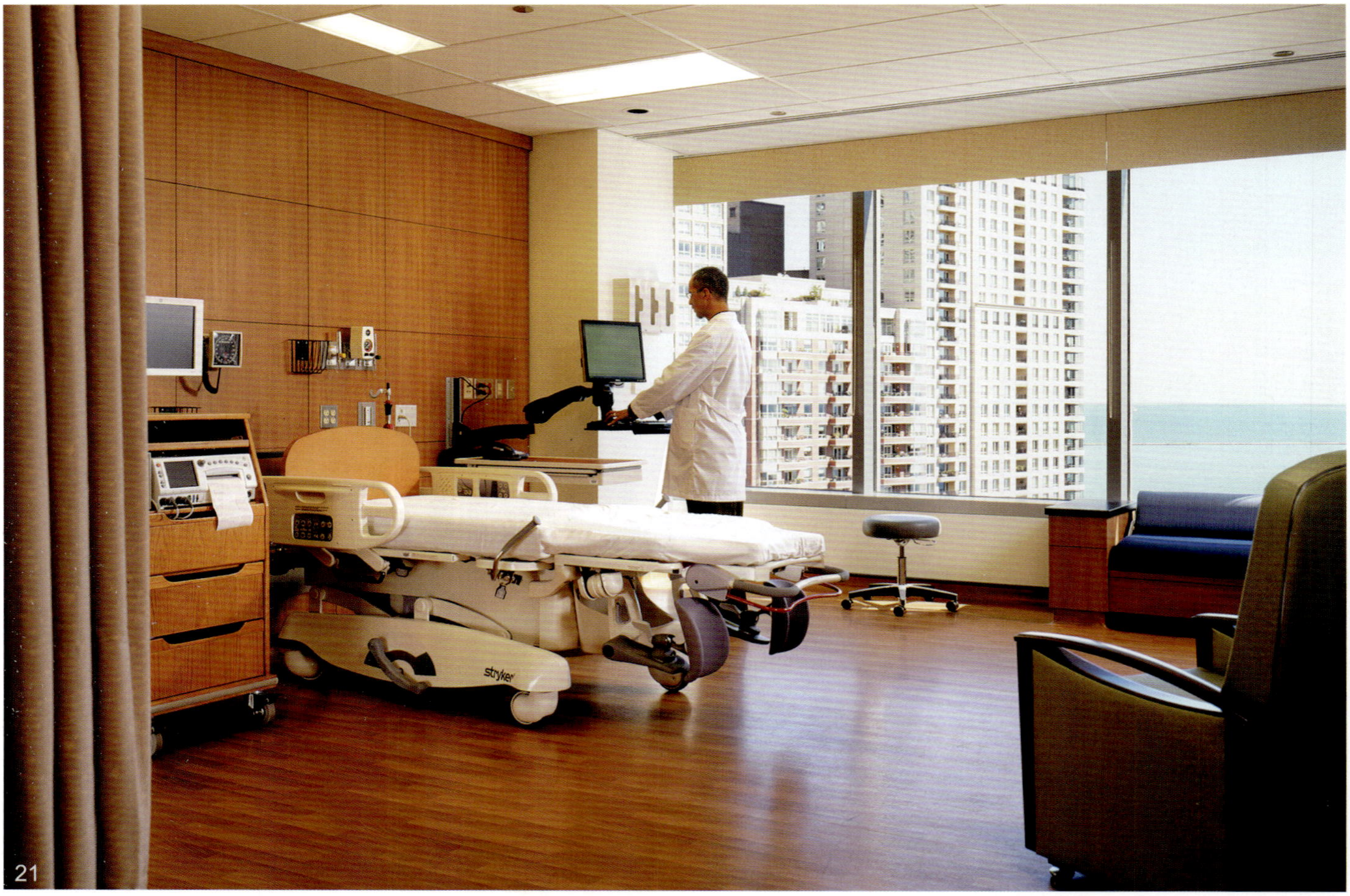
21
stryker

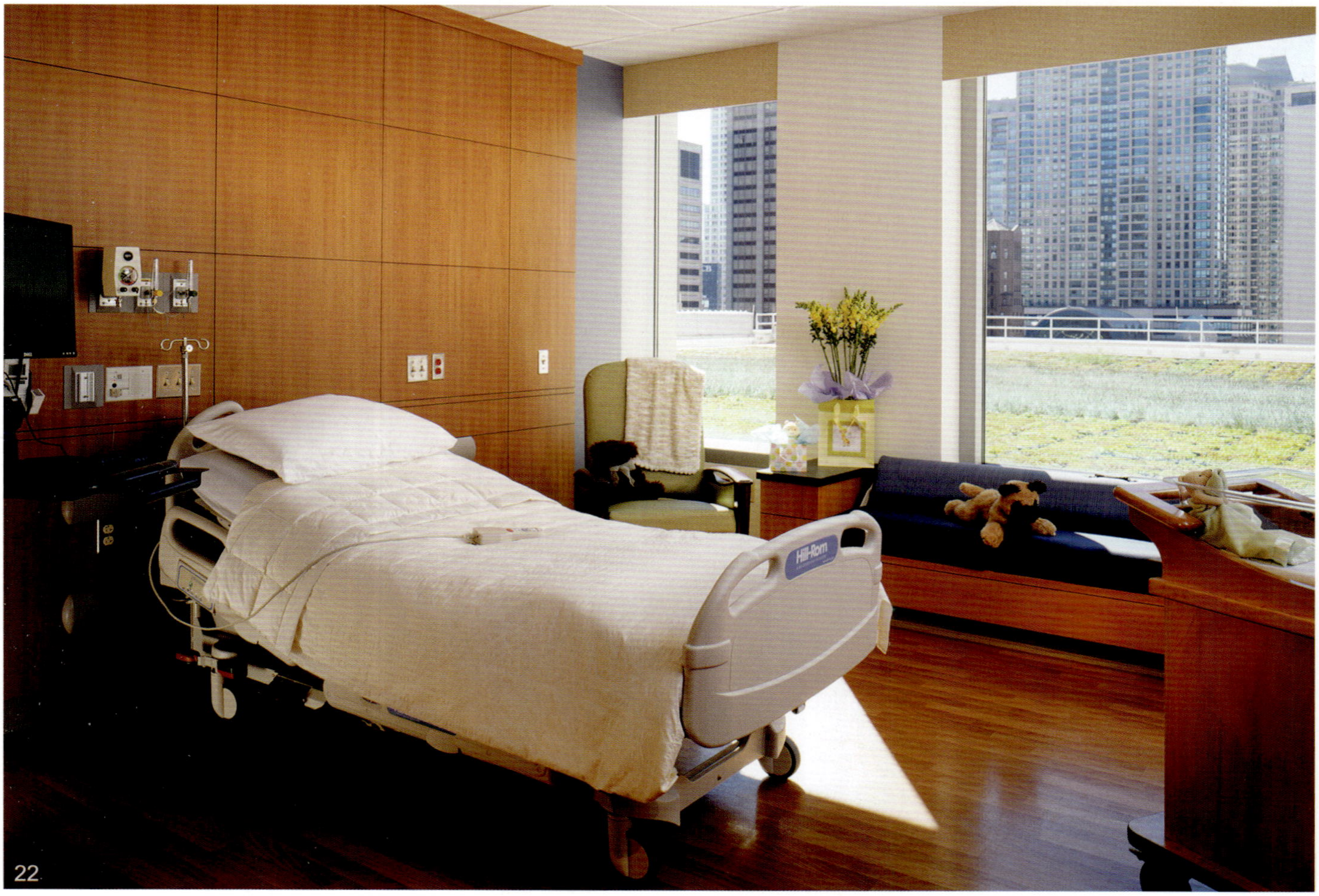
22
Hill-Rom

21. ICU
22~23. Single patient room

Mental Health

ADULT MENTAL HEALTH INPATIENT UNIT PLANNING AND DESIGN

The Acult Acute Mental Health Inpatient Unit provides assessment, admission and inpatient accommodation in a safe and therapeutic environment suitable for adult mental health patients and staff.

This section is applicable to:
- A stand-alone Adult Acute Mental Health Inpatient Unit or group of units;
- A dedicated Adult Acute Mental Health Inpatient Unit within a general hospital;
- A number of dedicated Patient Bedrooms as an annexe to an Acute Inpatient Unit.

The Operational Policy shall determine the size and function of the Adult Acute Mental Health Inpatient Unit. An Adult Acute Mental Health Inpatient Unit shall comply with the requirements outlined for Inpatient Accommodation, but with the noted modifications or additions in this section.

1. Planning

1.1 Planning Models

Some patients may at times exhibit disturbed or high risk behaviour. Appropriate planning and use of materials (for example safety glass and low maintenance/resilient surface) can achieve an environment where all patients can co-exist with minimal disruption to each other. The building should be able to accommodate patients of all levels of disturbance without taking on the characteristics of a jail.

Externally the principal concept of planning should be to integrate the new facility with its surrounds, and with the other buildings. Planning of external spaces must take into account the requirement for provision of a secure garden associated with the High Dependency area, and an open garden area for general use. The area should be based on $10m^2$ per person.

The design of external spaces, as for the building, should be domestic in nature, rather than formal or monumental. They should have the following features:
- The building should consciously have a front and a back;
- It should provide opportunities for privacy, recreation and self expression;
- It should provide opportunities for movement/ambulation both indoors and outdoors with unobtrusive environmental boundaries and with appropriate safety provisions;
- Single rooms are recommended.

Rooms may be grouped into clusters that can be defined for distinct patient groups; each cluster of rooms should include a recreational space to allow for patient therapy and flexibility for a variety of patient categories.

Additional considerations include:
- Flexibility of space usage through consideration of a range of patient needs for personal and shared space;
- Clearly defined patient residential areas readily identifiable by patients who may be disoriented or disturbed;
- An effective balance between opportunities for patients' privacy and the need for staff to observe patient behaviours.

1.2 Functional Areas

The Adult Acute Mental Health Inpatient Unit will consist of a number of functional areas or zones as follows:
- Main Entry/Reception / Clerical area;
- Assessment/Procedural area;
- Staff Offices/Administrative and management area;
- Staff Amenities area;
- Inpatient Area including outdoor areas;
- Secure Area including secured courtyard.

ADMINISTRATION AND OFFICE AREAS

The Unit Manager's Office should be located in, or directly adjacent to the patient area and in particular, the Staff Station. There should be the capacity to control patient's access to administrative and office areas. There may be a requirement for a communication system between interview areas and the Staff Station to signal the need for assistance. There should be provision for a Secure Store as part of the Group/View Room to house audio-visual equipment.

ADMISSIONS AREA
The Admissions Area will comprise an Admission Office, general purpose Interview Room and Examination Room and will be used by nursing, allied health and medical staff to interview relatives/patients. Examination and consultation of patients will be carried out in these areas. Duress alarms are required in all these areas.

The Admissions Area should be directly screened from Waiting Area. Noise transmission between these rooms and waiting area should be reduced to a minimum so that conversations are not overheard.

DAY ROOMS
At least two separate social spaces shall be provided, one for quiet activities and one appropriate for noisy activities.

DRUG DISPENSING/STORAGE
The Drug Distribution Station shall include extra provision for security against unauthorised access.

ECT FACILITIES
ECT (Electroconvulsive Therapy) procedures should be undertaken in the Day Procedures Unit, ECT Suite or Operating Unit.

EN-SUITES
Each bed room in the open unit is to have its own en-suite. There are a number of configurations – inboard, outboard and between rooms. The latter option is preferred as it maximises bed room use and patient observation.

The inboard option provides privacy and dignity but should be used with caution for the following reasons:
- a narrow passage may be created at the entrance to the bed room that may limit observation through the door vision panel;
- blind spots may be created inside the bed room, facilitate barricading;
- staff attending any emergencies in the room must enter in single file.

The door to en-suites should open in a way to avoid creating a blind spot when open or – with inboard ensuites – enable the en-suite door and bed room door to be tied together to create a barricade. En-suite doors are to be lockable by staff when needed and have a privacy latch that can be opened by staff in an emergency.

ENTRY AREAS
The Entrance provides direct access to the Unit for patients referred for admission arriving either with relatives, via police or ambulance and alternative access to the Unit for patients arriving via the Emergency Unit of the main hospital. Provision should be made for a gun safe that allows Police to deposit firearms when they are in attendance at the Inpatient Unit.

The Emergency Entrance should be capable of direct approach by ambulance/police vehicles and should have sufficient shelter to allow transfer of patients in shelter from the elements. The Entrance should have an airlock capable of accepting an ambulance trolley with ease.

There should be provision for an intercom between the Emergency Entrance and the Staff Station. The Entrance Area zone of the building should attempt to break down the "threshold" feeling of many institutional buildings, while maintaining a sense of direction to the approach.

GROUP THERAPY AREA
Space for group therapy shall be provided. This may be combined with the quiet Day Room provided that an additional 0.7m²/patient is added and a minimum room area of 21m², enclosed for privacy, is available for therapy activities.

SECURE AREA – HIGH DEPENDENCY/SECLUSION/INTENSIVE CARE
The High Dependency/Intensive Care bed rooms must be lockable and able to be opened from the corridor should a patient attempt to blockade themselves in the room. Doors require a viewing panel, positioned to ensure that should the glass be broken or removed, a patient cannot put an arm through and operate the door lock.

High Dependency bed rooms may be accessible to both the low dependency and high dependency sections of the Unit. The High Dependency/Intensive Care Areas will require access to a Seclusion Room.

These zones should be capable of secure separation from the remainder of the Unit. There should be defined areas for male and female patients.

The High Dependency Unit, for client and staff safety purposes, should back onto the Staff Station to ensure easy visibility of the interior of the High Dependency Unit and rapid response in times of patient emergency. Patients in this area will require access to a secured courtyard.

INPATIENT AREAS
- Single-Bed Rooms:
An external outlook coupled with high ceilings adds to the perception of light and space and is a positive contribution to treatment. There should be no "blind spots" in the rooms particularly any created by open doors and the rooms should be key-lockable from the outside. Doors should be able to be opened from the corridor should a patient attempt to blockade him/herself in the room. Door viewing panels are optional in open unit bed rooms and will be dependent on the Unit's Operational Policy. Low wattage night light over the bed space for use by staff when carrying out night time observations of patients should be considered. Acoustic treatment to bed rooms is required to minimise transference of noise between adjoining bed rooms. Whilst domestic-style beds may be preferred for ambiance, consideration should be given to occupational health and safety issues of staff attending to low height beds.

- Two-Bed Rooms:
Two-bed rooms may be included in the General Inpatient Zone providing an option for sharing, or provide accommodation of a mother and child. They can, however, be restrictive, resulting in the disruptive movement of patients to other rooms in order to accommodate new admissions and are generally not recommended.

OCCUPATIONAL THERAPY AREA
Each Adult Acute Mental health Inpatient Unit shall contain $1.5m^2$ of separate space per patient for Occupational Therapy with a minimum total area of $20m^2$. The space shall include provisions for:
- Hand-washing;
- Workbenches;
- Storage;
- Displays.

Occupational Therapy Areas may serve more than one Inpatient Unit.

1.3 Functional Relationships

The Adult Acute Mental health Inpatient Unit should be located with ready access to the Emergency Unit, Main Entry and service and support areas including Catering Unit, Cleaning/ Housekeeping, Linen Handling, Waste Management and Supply Unit.

2. Design

2.1 Environmental Considerations

ACOUSTICS
Acoustic treatment should be applied to the following areas:
- Day Areas such as patient living, dining and activities areas;
- Patient Bed Rooms including high dependency, intensive care and seclusion rooms;

- Consulting Rooms;
- Admission Areas.

In acoustically treated rooms, return air grilles should be acoustically treated to avoid transfer of conversations to adjacent areas. Door grilles to these areas should be avoided.

WINDOWS AND GLAZING
Wherever possible, the use of natural light is to be maximised. For glazing, graduate the impact resistance of the glass from toughest at lower level to weakest at high level. In areas where damage to glass may be expected, avoid larger pane sizes. Smaller panes are inherently stronger for a given thickness than larger panes. Where toughened glass is used it should be treated with a protective film to ensure glass is held together when broken. Laminated/toughened glass of various thicknesses should be installed dependent upon the likelihood of patient injury or building damage. All windows and observation panels shall be glazed with safety glass. Polycarbonate is not recommended due to surface scratching which will reduce visibility over time. Where windows are openable, effective security features such as narrow windows that will not allow patient escape, shall be provided. Locks, under the control of staff, shall be fitted.

2.2 Space Standards and Components

SIZE OF UNIT
The schedule of accommodation has been developed for typical 20- and 30-Bed Adult Acute Mental Health Inpatient Units.

For alternative configurations, allocate space for key areas according to the following guide:
- Lounge/dining/activity areas – Secure Observation - 7.5m^2 per person;
- Lounge/dining/activity areas – General - 5.5m^2 per person;
- Outdoor areas (courtyards and terraces) – Secure - 10m^2 per person;
- Outdoor areas (courtyards and terraces) – General - 5m^2 per person;

- Courtyard and Terrace – minimum area - 20m^2;
- Consultation rooms – 1 per 5 beds;
- Examination/assessment rooms – 1-2 per unit.

2.3 Safety and Security

Security within the facility and the surrounding outdoor area, related to patient movement requires careful consideration and may include use of video surveillance and motion sensors. The security of access for staff, community and domestic service deliveries should also be considered.

The design should assist staff to carry out their duties safely and to supervise patients by allowing or restricting access to areas in a manner which is consistent with patient needs/skills. Staff should be able to view patient movements and activities as naturally as possible, whenever necessary.

Controlled and/or concealed access will be required as an option in a number of functional areas. Functionally the only difference between an open and a closed (locked) area in their design should be the provision of controls over the flow to, from and throughout the facility. Such controls should be as unobtrusive as possible. A communication system which enables staff to signal for assistance from other staff should be included.

2.4 Finishes

The aesthetics are to be warm and user-friendly wherever possible.

2.5 Fixtures and Fittings

Fixtures and fittings should be safe and durable. Generally, all fixings should be heavy duty, concealed, and where exposed, tamperproof.

Fittings, including hooks, curtain tracks, bathroom fittings, should be plastic where possible, and have a breaking strain of not more than 15kgs.

Fittings should avoid the potential to be used either as a weapon or to inflict personal damage. Paintings, mirrors and signage should be rigidly fixed to walls with tamperproof fixings.
Mirrors shall be of safety glass or other appropriate impact-resistant and shatterproof construction. They shall be fully glued to a backing to prevent availability of loose fragments of broken glass.

Holland blinds, Venetian blinds and curtains should be avoided in patient areas. Curtain tracks, pelmets and other fittings that provide potential for patients to hang themselves should be avoided or designed so that the potential is removed.

2.6 Building Services

Avoid exposed services, for example, sink wastes which may be easily damaged.

Light fittings, smoke detectors, thermal detectors and air-conditioning vents to higher dependent areas, particularly Seclusion Rooms, should be vandal-proof and incapable of supporting a patient's weight.

3. Functional Relationship Diagram

Adult Mental Health Inpatient Unit Functional Relationship Diagram (Facing Image).

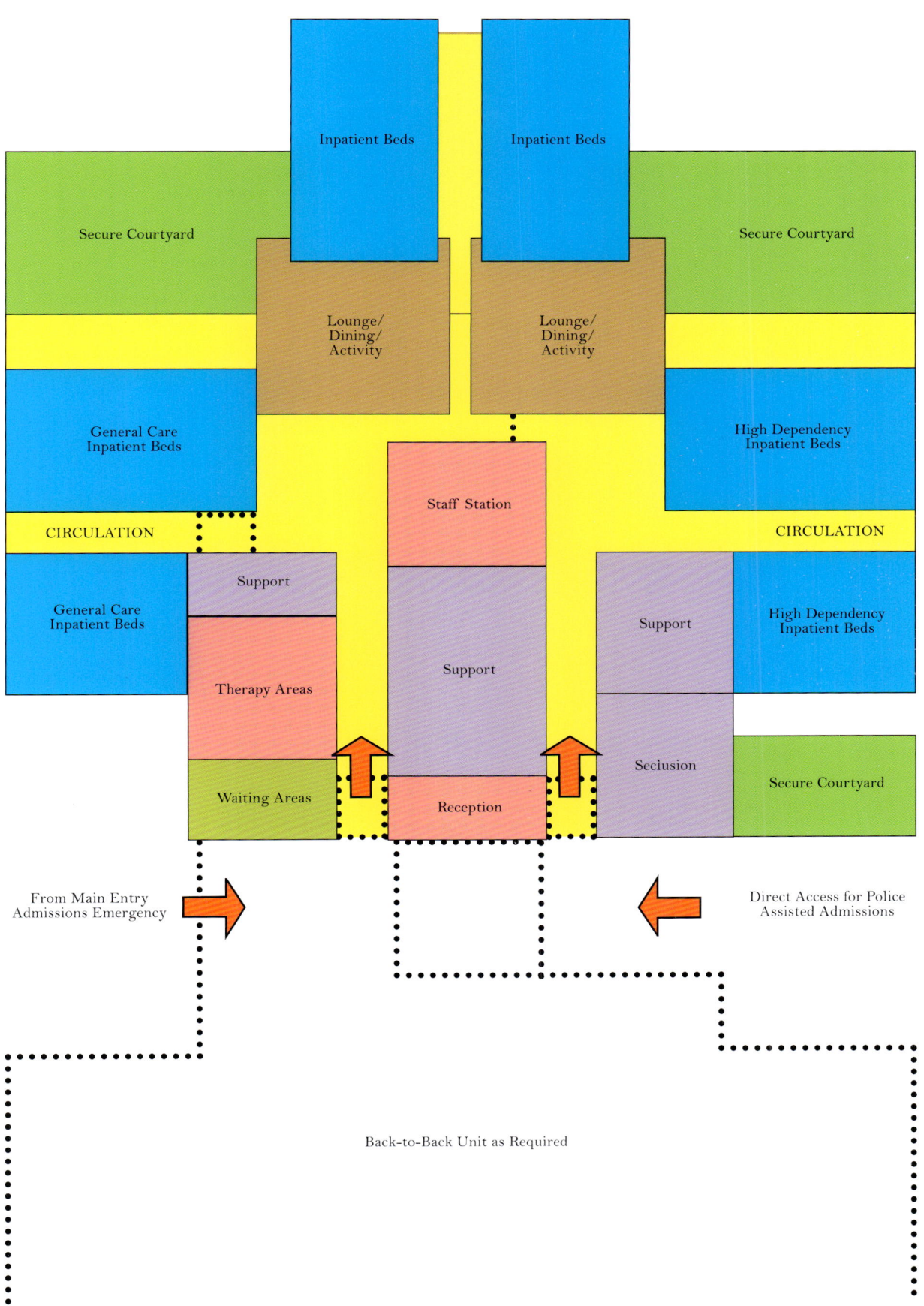

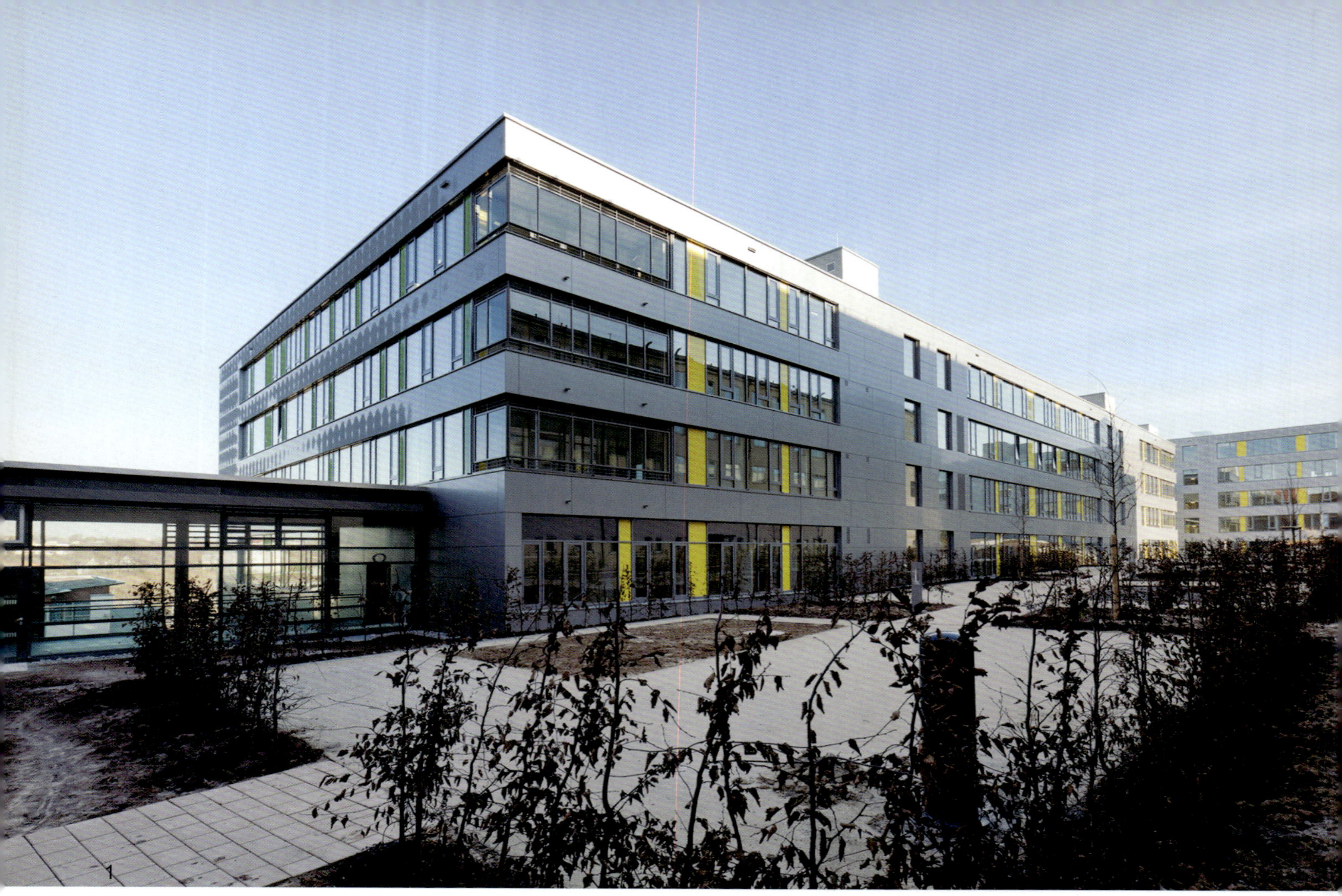

1

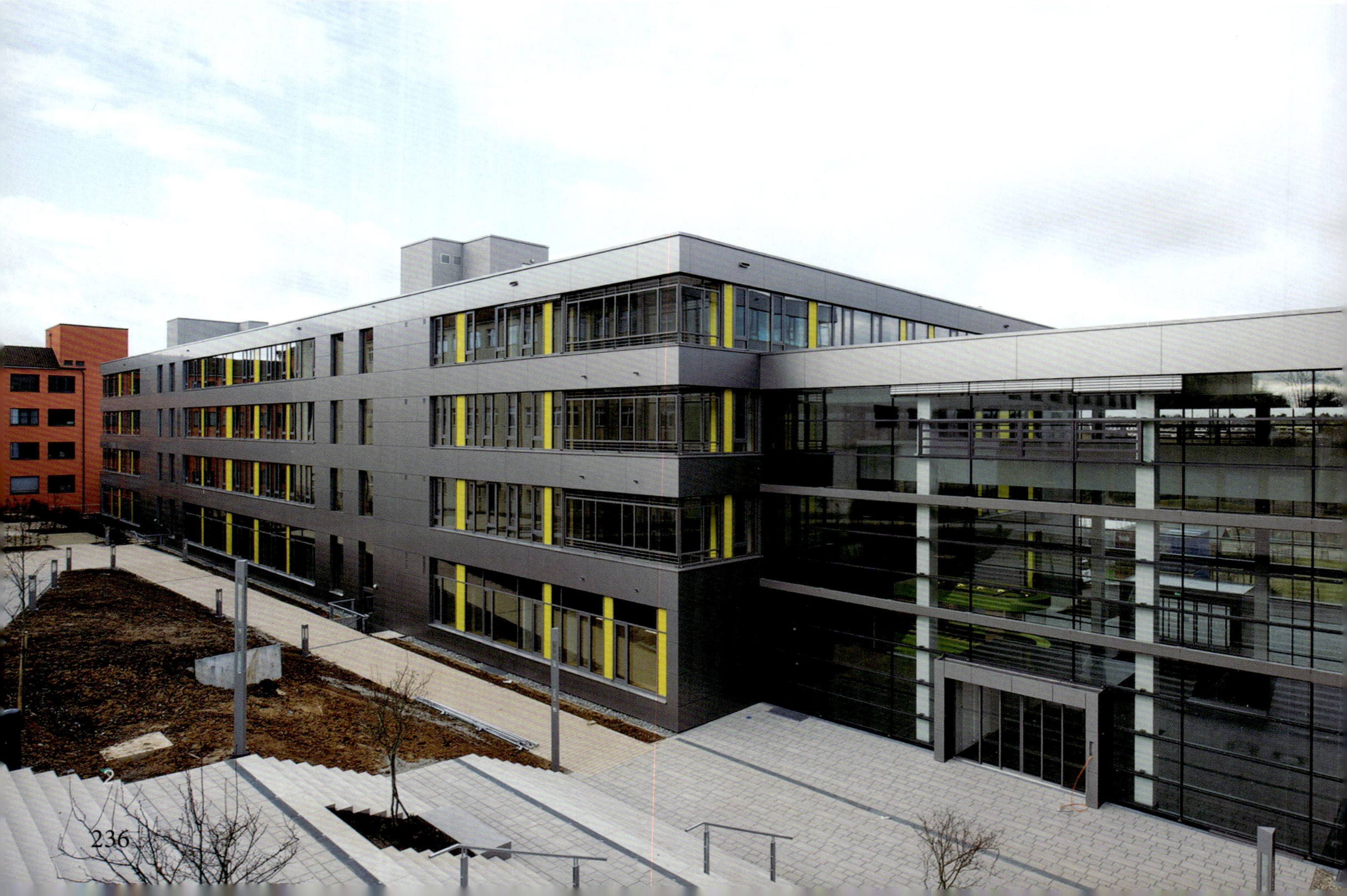

2

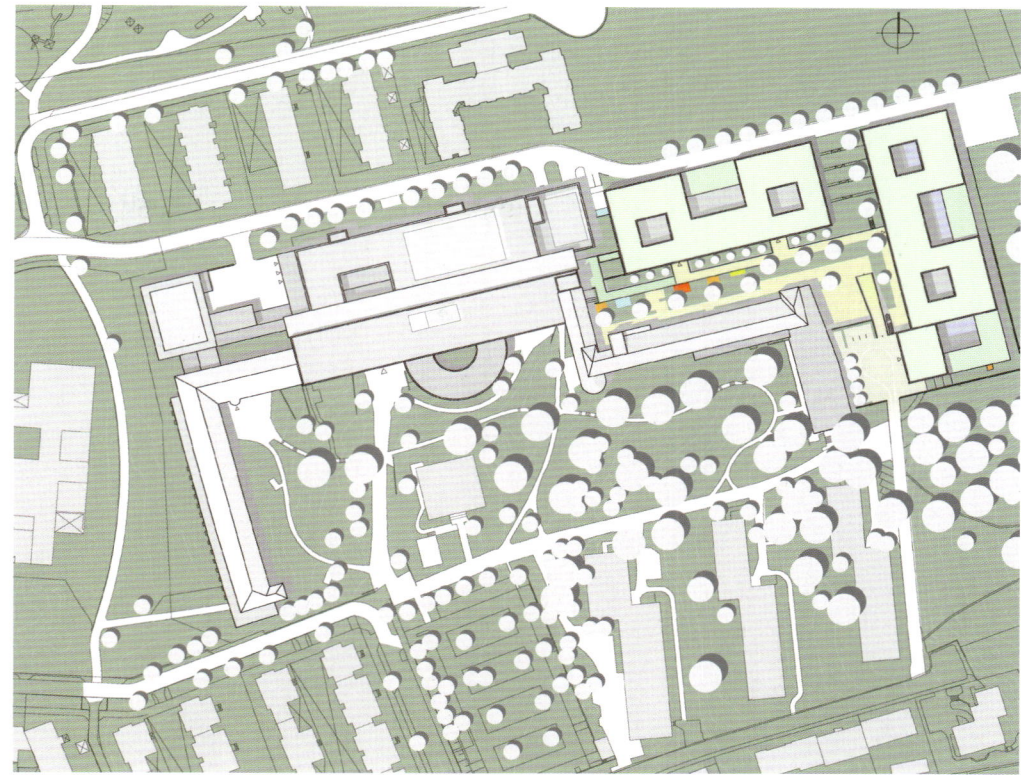

Site Plan

Centre for Mental Health in Stuttgart

Architects:
weinbrenner.single.arabzadeh,
architektenwerkgemeinschaft
Location: Stuttgart, Germany
Site area:
10,130m²
Construction area:
6,000m²
Project year: 2011
Photographs:
© Courtesy of architect

Two compact buildings with inner courtyards complement the existing building and realign the site to the north and the east. The narrowness of the site is compensated by the adjacent open fields with panoramic view and landscape in the north and the east.

The selected arrangement of the two building structures allows a "free flow" of the landscape. One can sense the existing topography through the entrance hall with the natural terrain from the south to the north. The division of the building mass leads to a centrepiece that is based on the existing structure.

Two angularly arranged cubic compact structures form the new centre for mental health. The chosen form fulfills the complex functional requirements through the double-station with the sharing of common areas.

All double-stations function independently and can also be conducted as closed stations as needed with the user-friendly and well-oriented accessibility of the circulation systems.

The exterior of the hospital should match with the existing site on the one hand and on the other hand it should be distinguishable as an individual and separate building. The centre houses 242 beds, a school for patients, a 24-bed outpatient clinic at the department of child and adolescent psychiatry and 20 places in the rehabilitation centre.

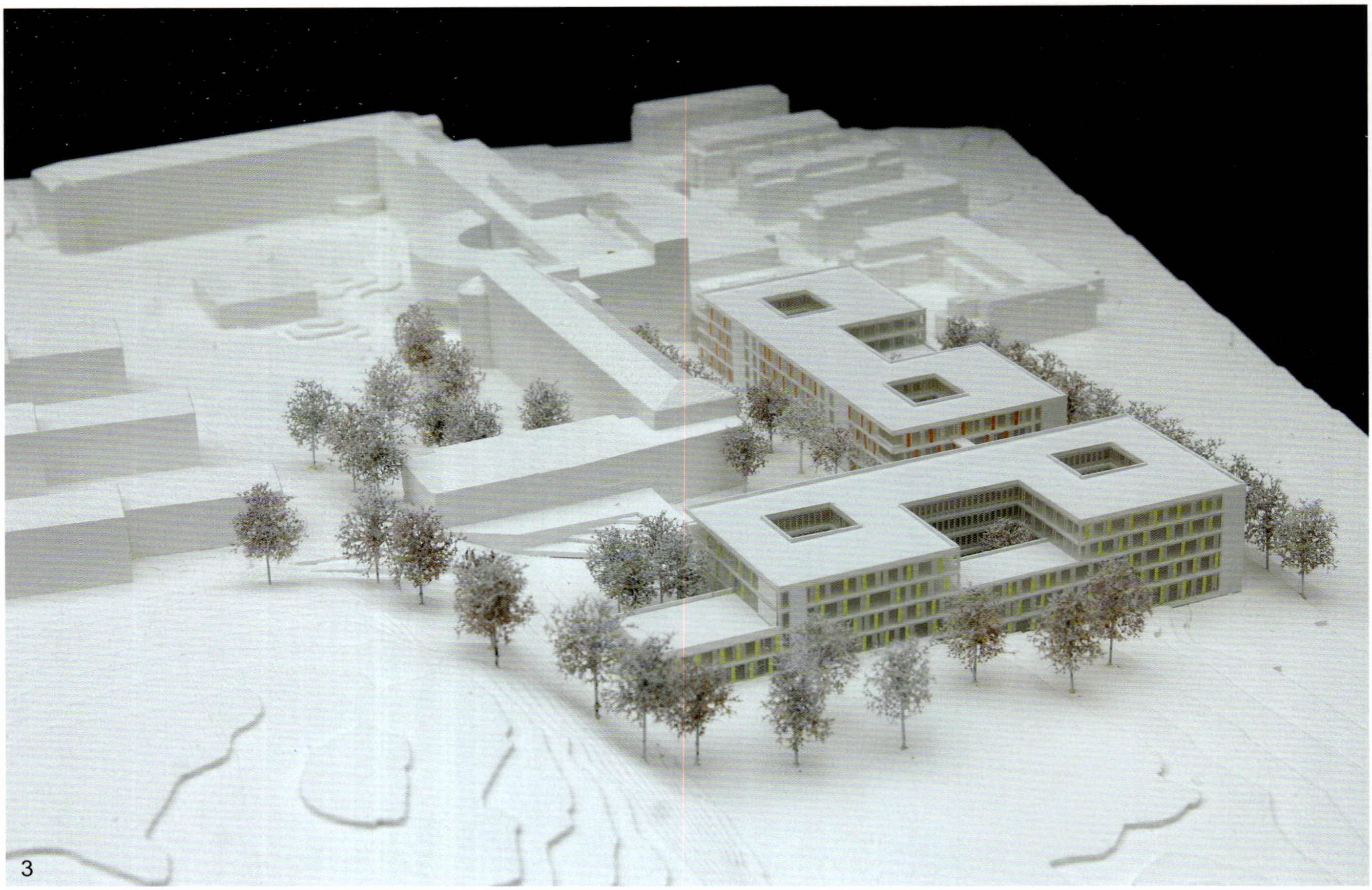

3

Elevations

238

1~2. Exterior view of building
3. Model rendering
4. Façade detail and inner courtyard

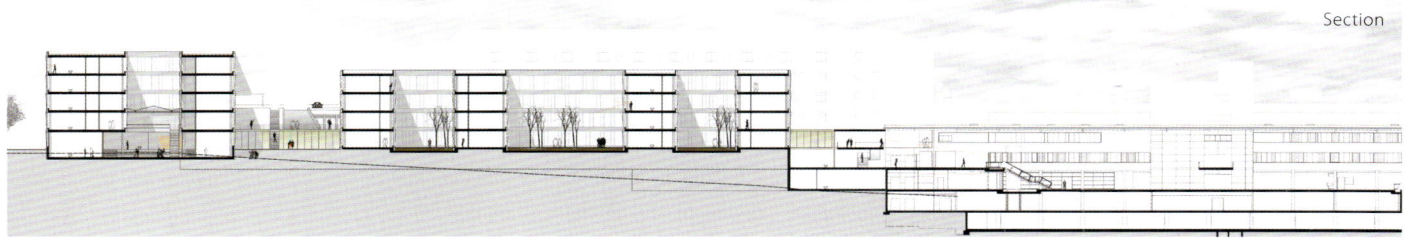

Section

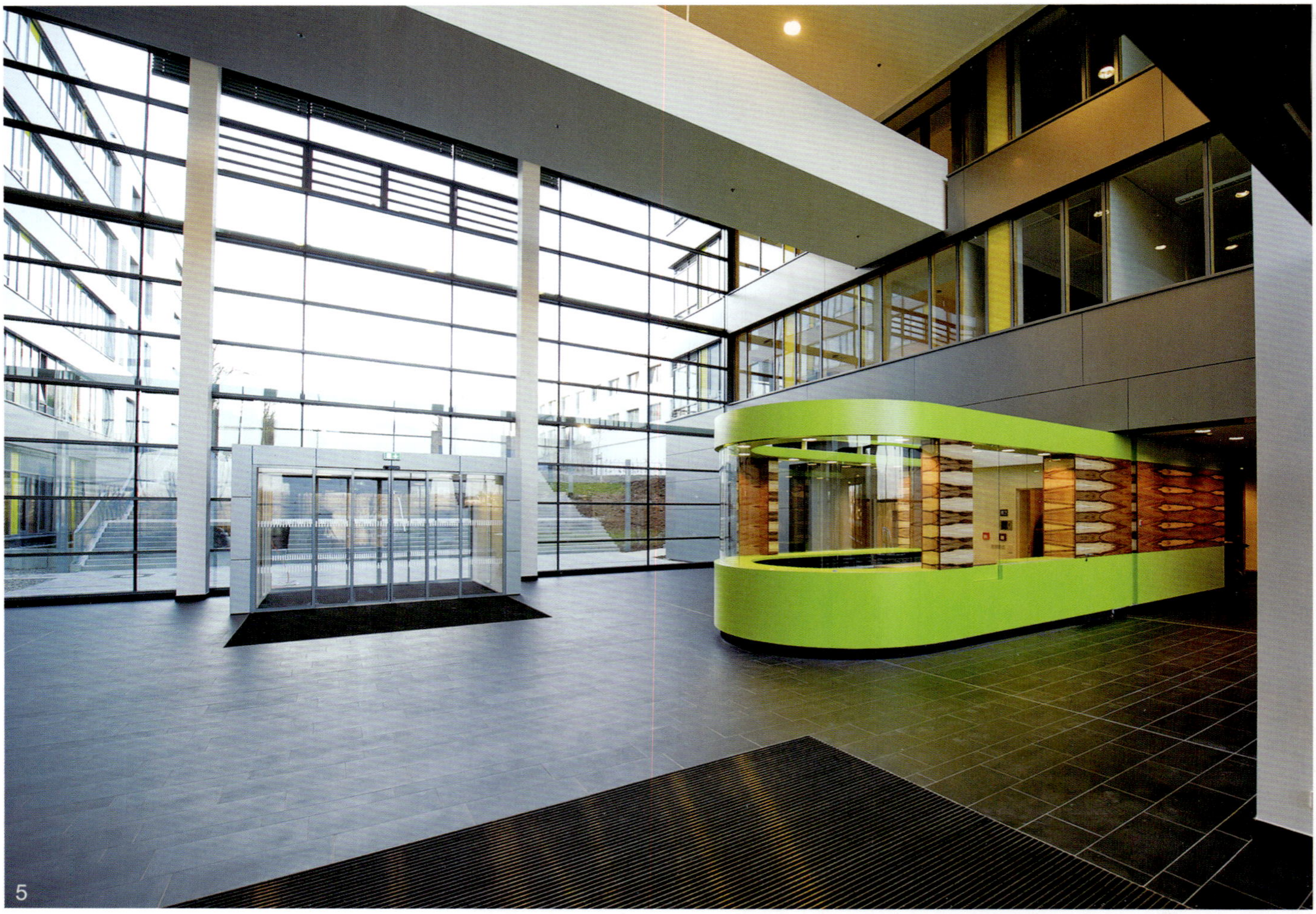
5

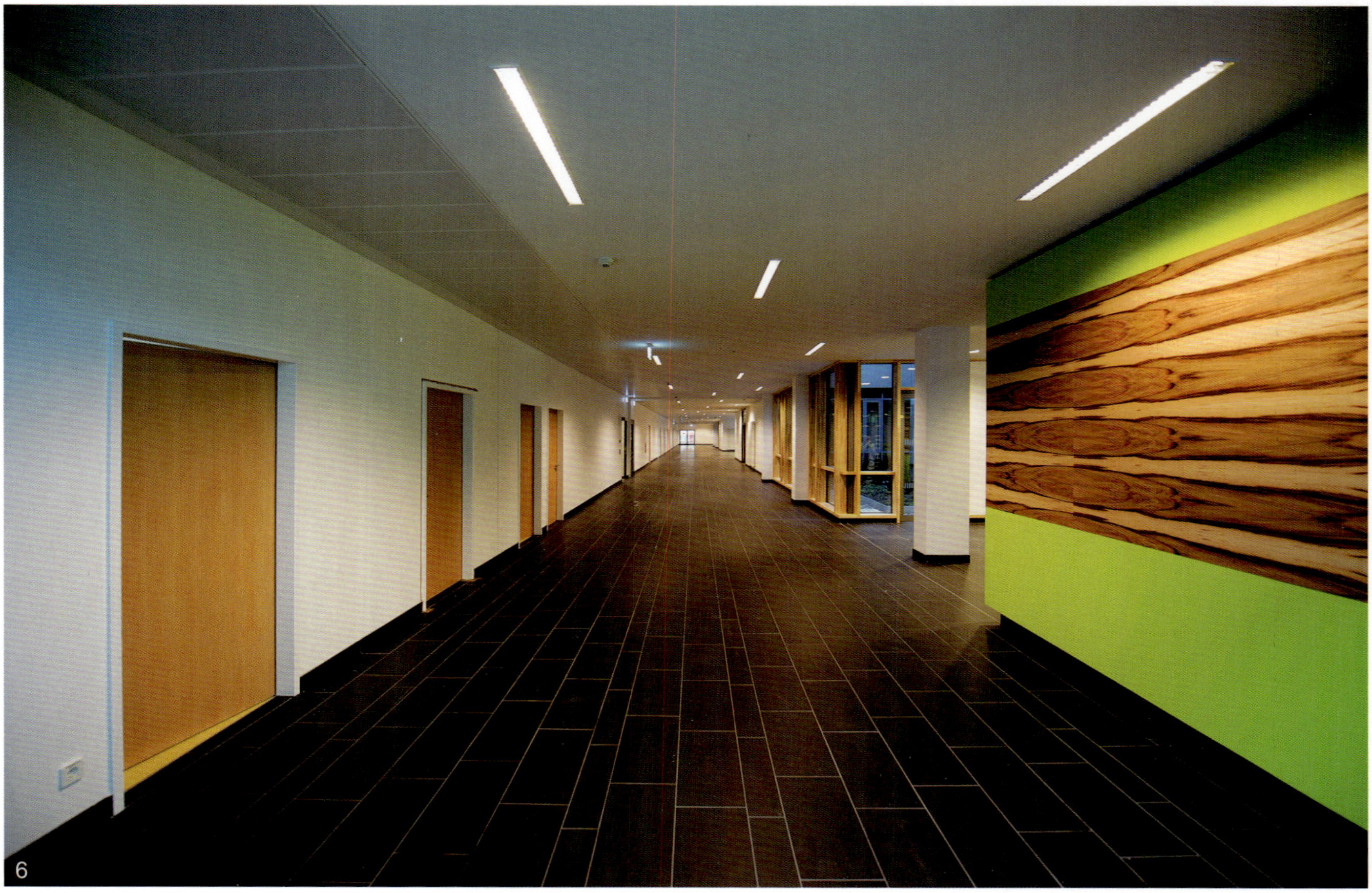
6

5. Entrance lobby
6~7. Corridor

Floor Plan

7

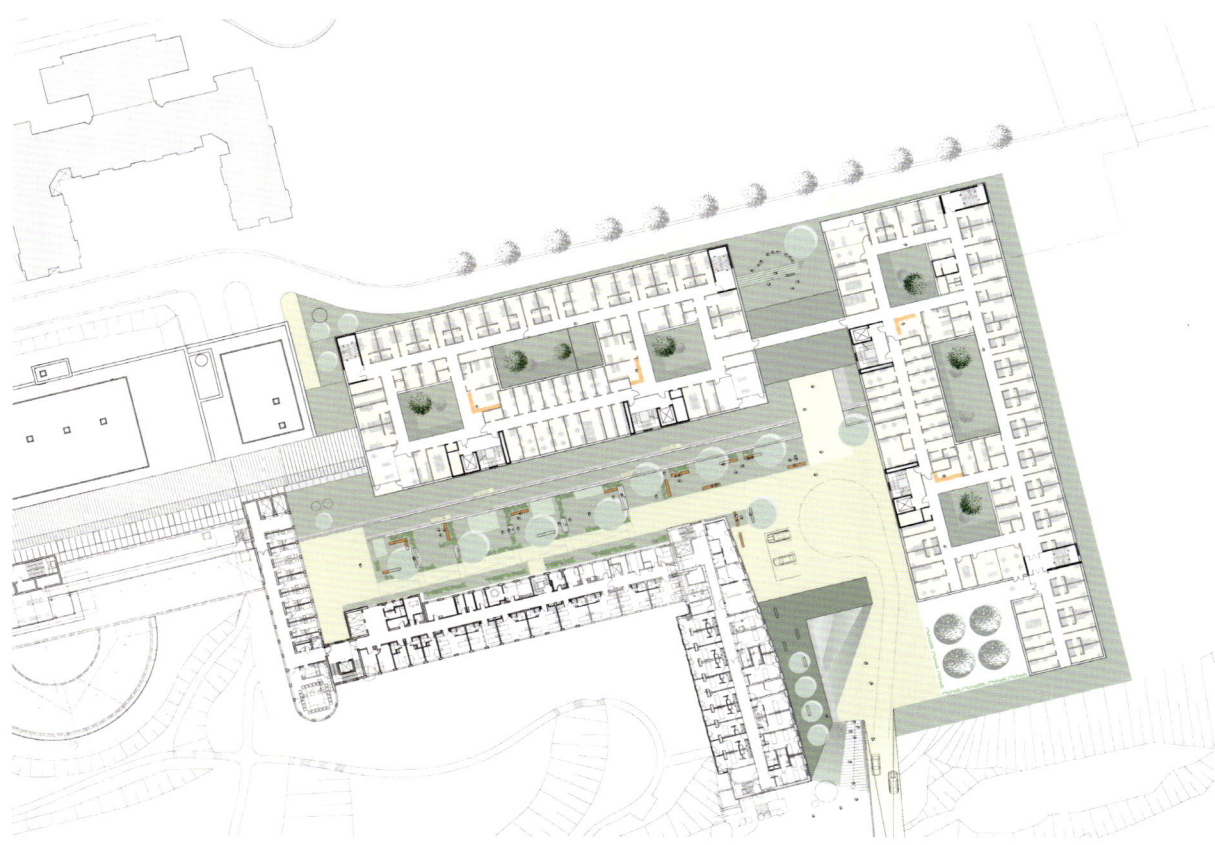

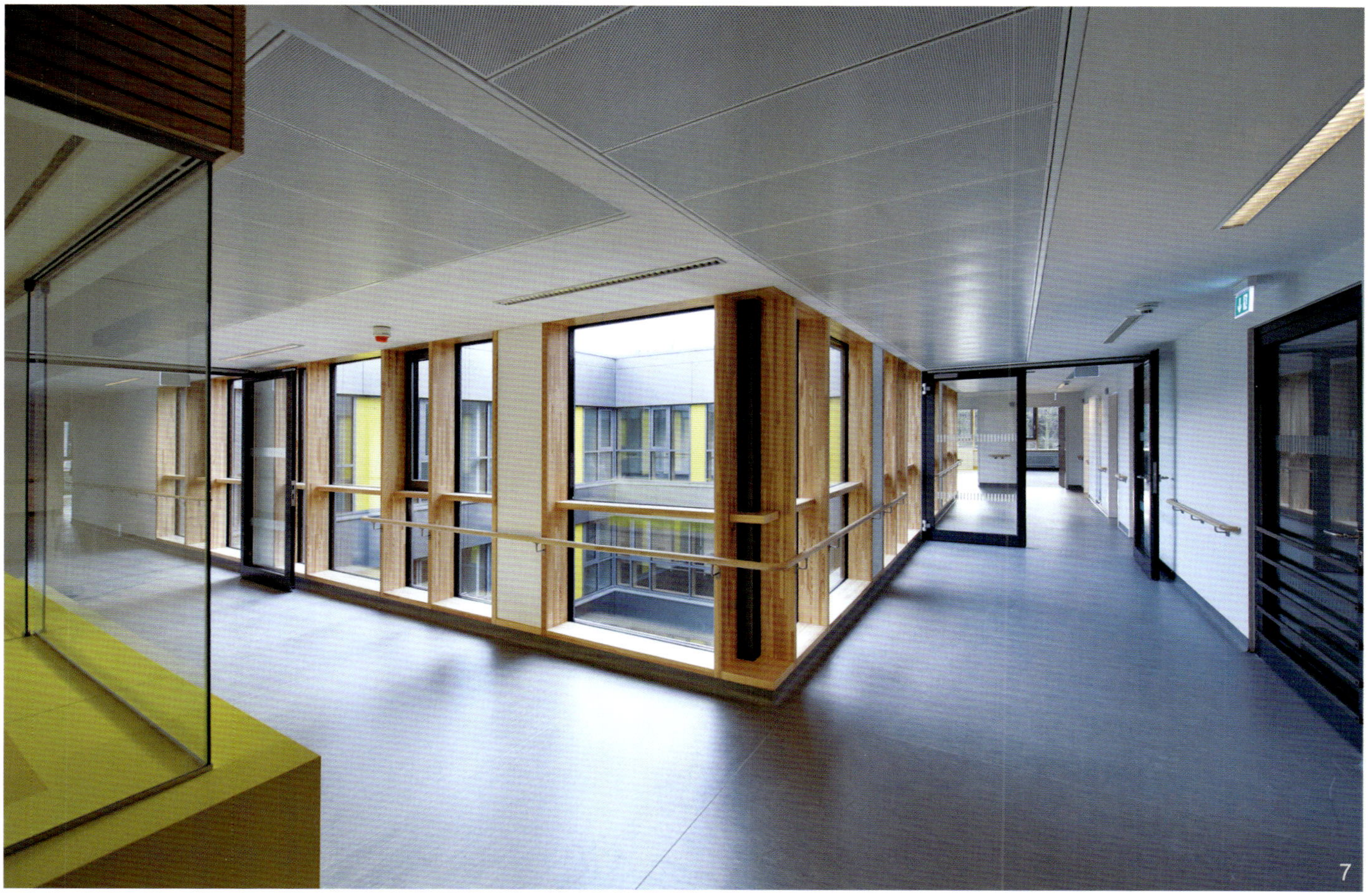

8. Staff station
9. Interior view of staff's working area
10. Bed room

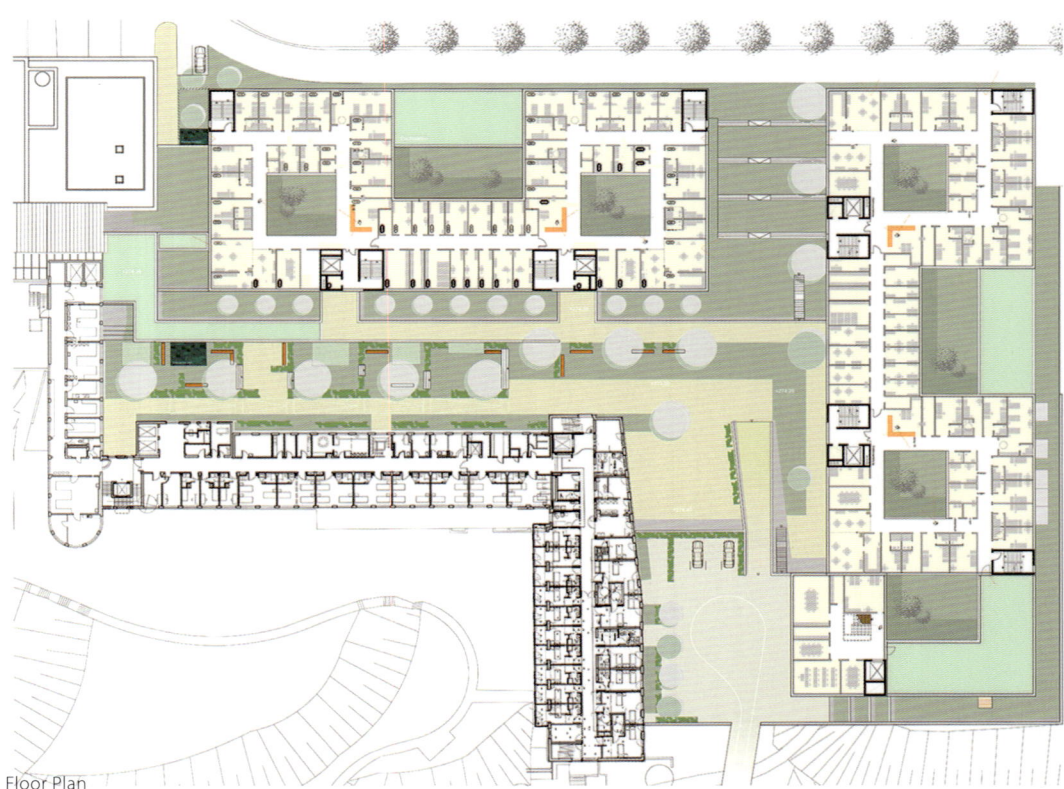

Floor Plan

243

1

2

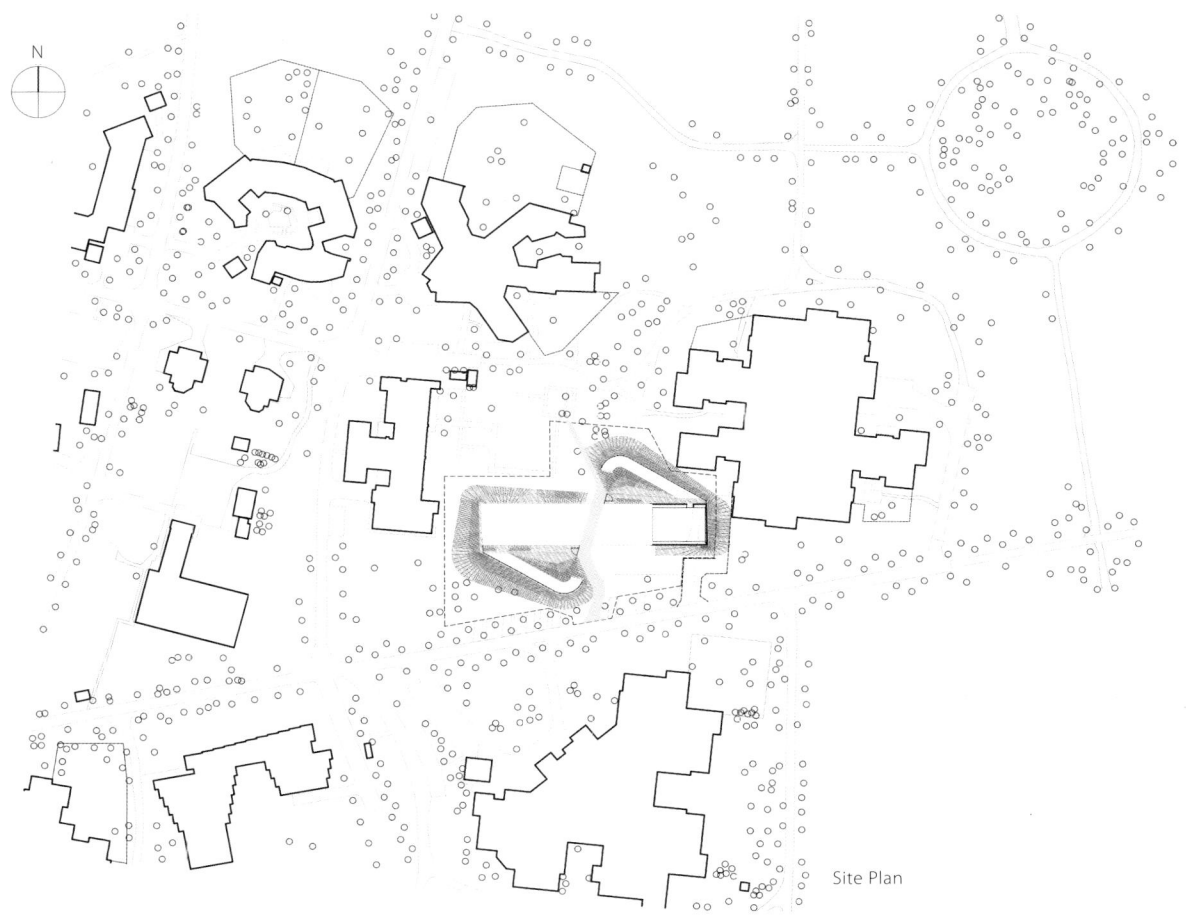

Site Plan

Wier 2

Stichting Altrecht has commissioned VMX Architects to design the accommodation for 24 delinquent, lightly mentally handicapped persons with heavy behavioural disturbances (sglvg+). The project is a part of a series of five similar institutions that will be built in separate locations throughout the country in the coming years, under a scheme headed "De Borg".

Wier 2 is to be built on the wooded grounds of Altrecht in Den Dolder. The project aims to create a quiet accommodation for this target group, with a close relation to the surrounding nature. An existing therapy complex, "Boerhaave" has already been built nearby and likewise makes use of the harmonious setting.

The intention is to realise a volume that is as compact as possible, in order to limit impact on the surrounding woodland. In this way, it has been resolved as an extruded four-storey baton, lying adjacent and parallel to the road.

On the two upper floors circulation runs centrally along its length, allowing accommodation to be arranged along the outer walls. On the lower floor, a public route through the building leads to the covered main entrance, and on the first floor, a ramp passes through the volume, providing access for the inhabitants into two secured gardens either side of the building.

Architects:
VMX Architects
Location:
Den Dolder, Germany
Building area:
3,600m²
Project year:
2010
Photographs:
© Courtesy of VMX Architects

1~2. The building hides between landscapes
3~4. Façade detail

The patients' rooms are situated in four living units on the first and second floor with a view to the forest. The ground floor contains office spaces, the sous-terrain therapy rooms and a gym.

An important requirement from the client was that damage-resistant materials must be used, given the patients' sometimes aggressive behaviour. The façades of the building will be covered with sprayed concrete, which will provide the durable finish. It will furthermore facilitate the chiselled shape, whilst creating a solid, homogeneous volume which will have the appearance, with time, of a mossy rock lying in the forest.

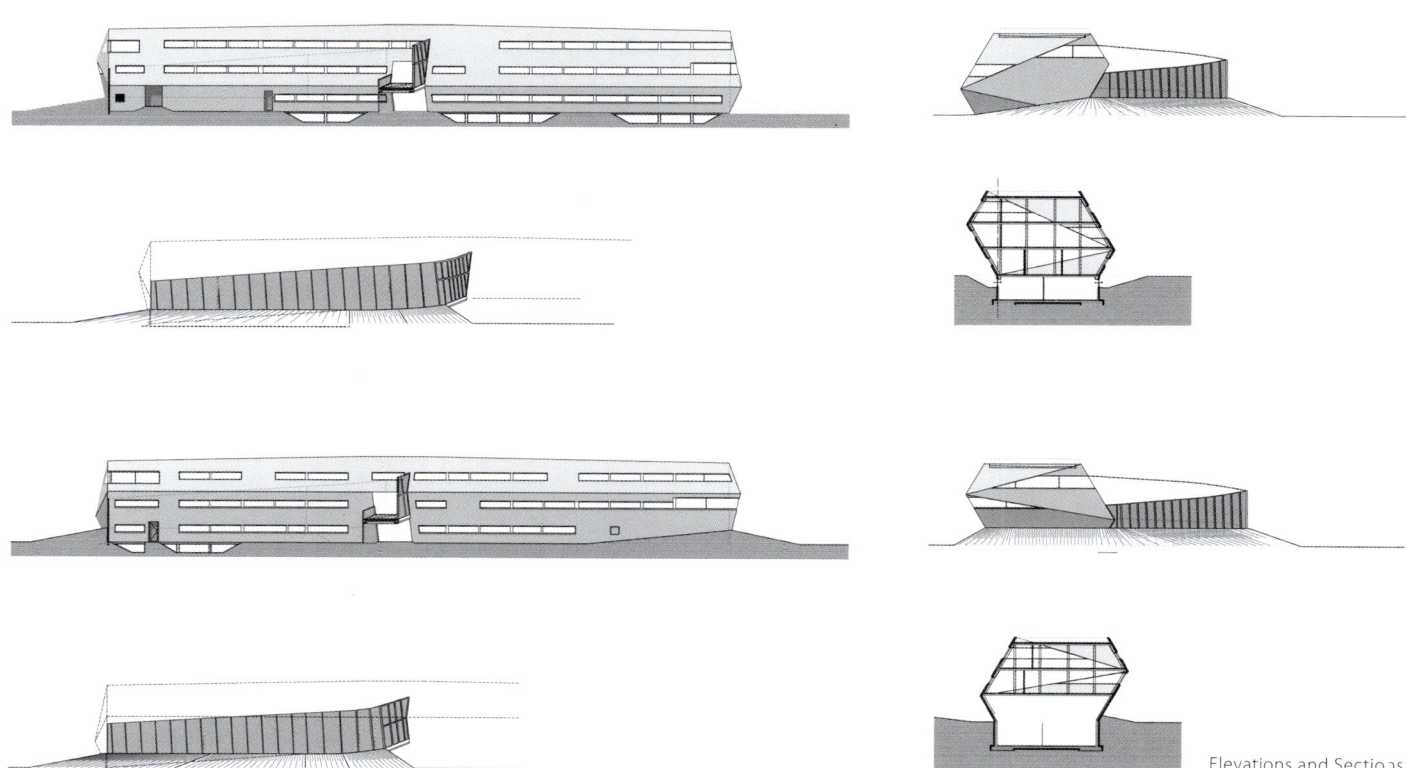

Elevations and Sections

247

5. Lounge room
6~7. Corridor and connection door

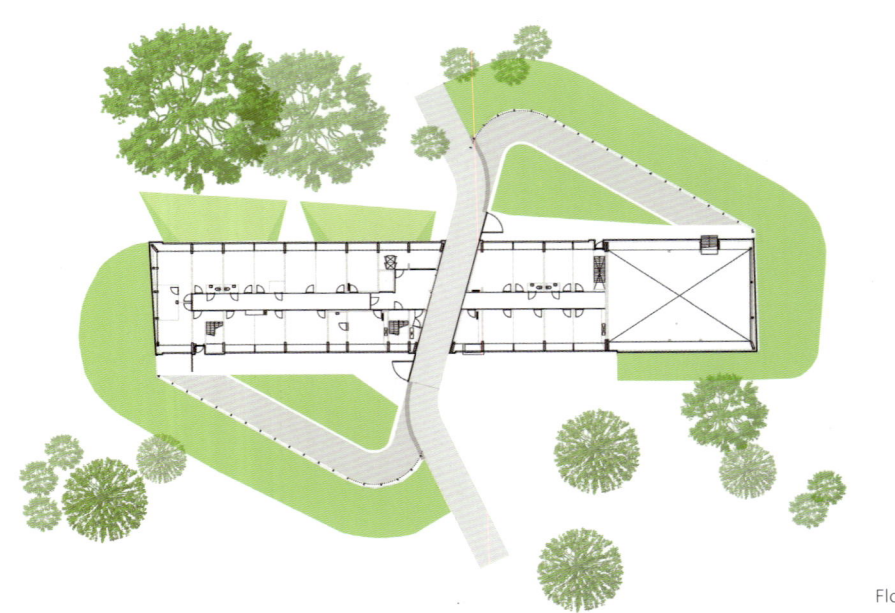

Floor Plan

249

State Reference Centre for the Mental Care

Architects:
Peñín Architects
Location:
Valencia, Spain
Building area:
12,362m²
Project year:
2010
Photographs:
© Diego Opazo

The urban conditions of the site are at the origin of the proposal of an autonomous system tilted towards the strict north orientation, the protection against noise and direct views. The compactness of the building gets smoothed with its porosity, luminosity and interior fluidity, and also with its relation with the surrounding garden that becomes a second ground floor thanks to the manipulation of the levels. The institutional and reference character of the centre is underlined by the precision of the structural system, metric (60cm for pavements, concrete forms, wood panels...) and the limited use of materials.

The building has apart from the own services, a care area for 20 persons and day centre, and a research area with labs, classrooms, administration and auditorium.

The recovery of the "mat building" mechanism allows embracing the complexity of the assistance and education programme in a self-dependent organism and to respond to the topographic and urban requirements. Its entailment to a rigorous constructive system, made out of white concrete 2.40-metre modules, controls the cost and contributes to the institutional character of the centre. As in the mat building, its compactness is attenuated by the interior spatiality, the shaping of the voids, and in this case by the presence of nature and the conviviality between the common and exterior spaces.

3

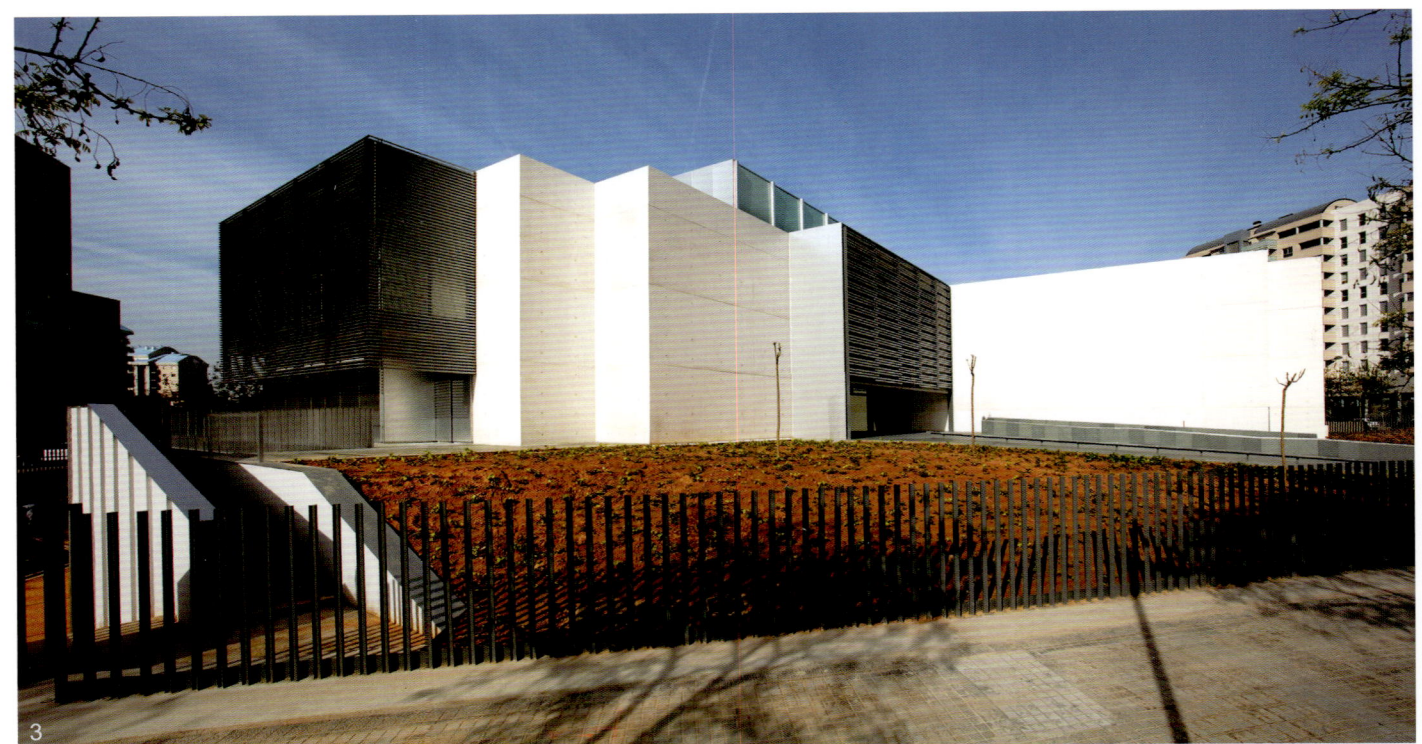

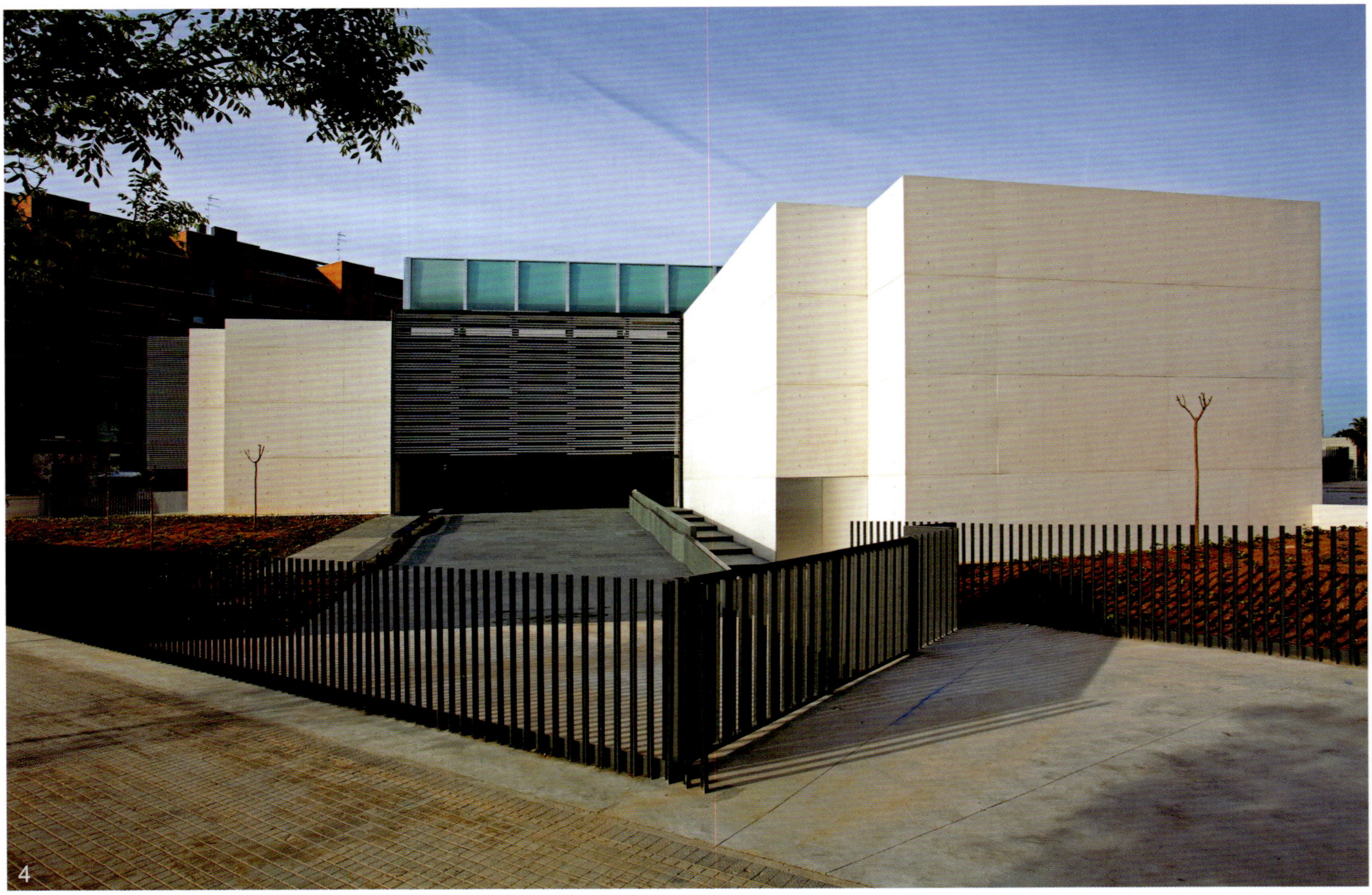
4

1~2. The building and courtyard
3~4. The building viewed from street

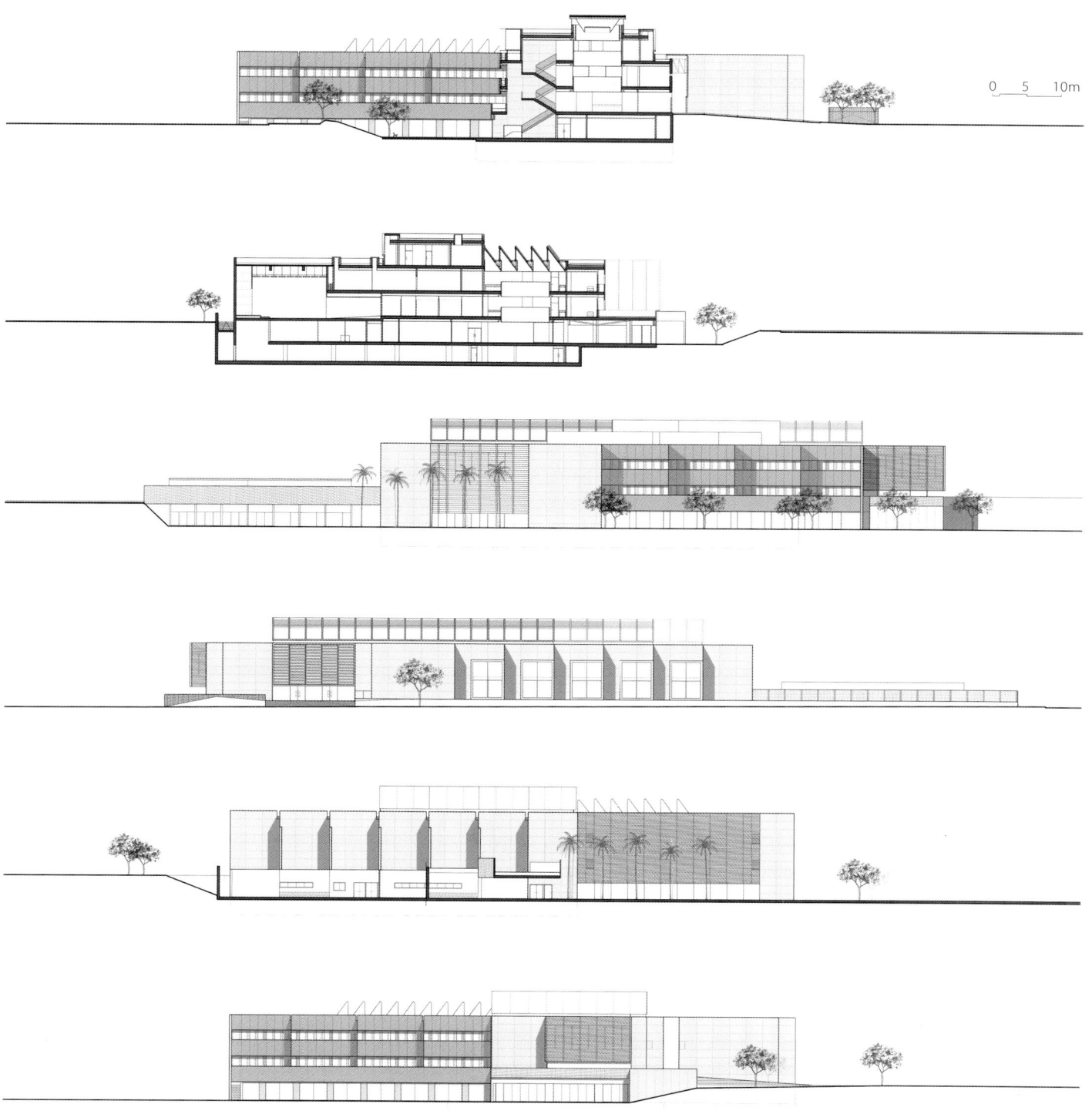

Elevations and Sections

253

Construction Details:
1. Steel beam formed by tubular profiles. Steel plates to perimeter beams
2. Painted iron metalwork
3. Solar panels
4. Thermal insulation and waterproofing membrane
5. Gutter
6. Prefabricated plasterboard linear light
7. Perimeter concrete beam
8. Trafficable roof
9. Metal structure and plates for framework modules spacing
10. Casement metalwork
11. 20cm thick soil layer over drainage and waterproof system
12. Painted metal sheet
13. Structural profiles. UPN 180+1/2 IPE360 – polished wielding/fire resistant paint in interior
14. 35cm thick waffle grid in-situ cast reinforced concrete floor
15. Tube framing forming lintel
16. Acoustic plasterboard following ruled surfaces
17. Metal framework. Sliding and hinged doors
18. Similar laminated flooring
19. U-profile holding soil
20. Soil. Slope 1.5%
21. Compact soil – granular material – waterproof membrane – concrete. Sole-drainage system
22. Metal profile. Substructure over anchorage plate and concrete brick wall
23. Laminated glass with acid-treated layer
24. Prefabricated plasterboard. Linear light
25. Sandwich panel on T profiles. Ventilation grille for laboratory gas evavulation
26. Skylight
27. Inverted roof over light structure
28. Light structure
29. Wood ceiling. DM18 fire-resistant board. Maple-veneered.
30. Installation cavity. Embedded shown nozzles
31. Slope forming. Fireproof board over aluminium. Similar laminated flooring
32. Frame formed by 60mm tube profiles with anchorage plates to the floor slab. Maple wood panelling
33. Vinyl coating. 3mm aluminium sheet
34. Prefabricated plasterboard housing indirect lighting system 30x60cm
35. Lacquered door. Continuous flashing
36. Security railing after disability regulations
37. Special in-situ reinforced concrete columns. Ruled-surface formworks

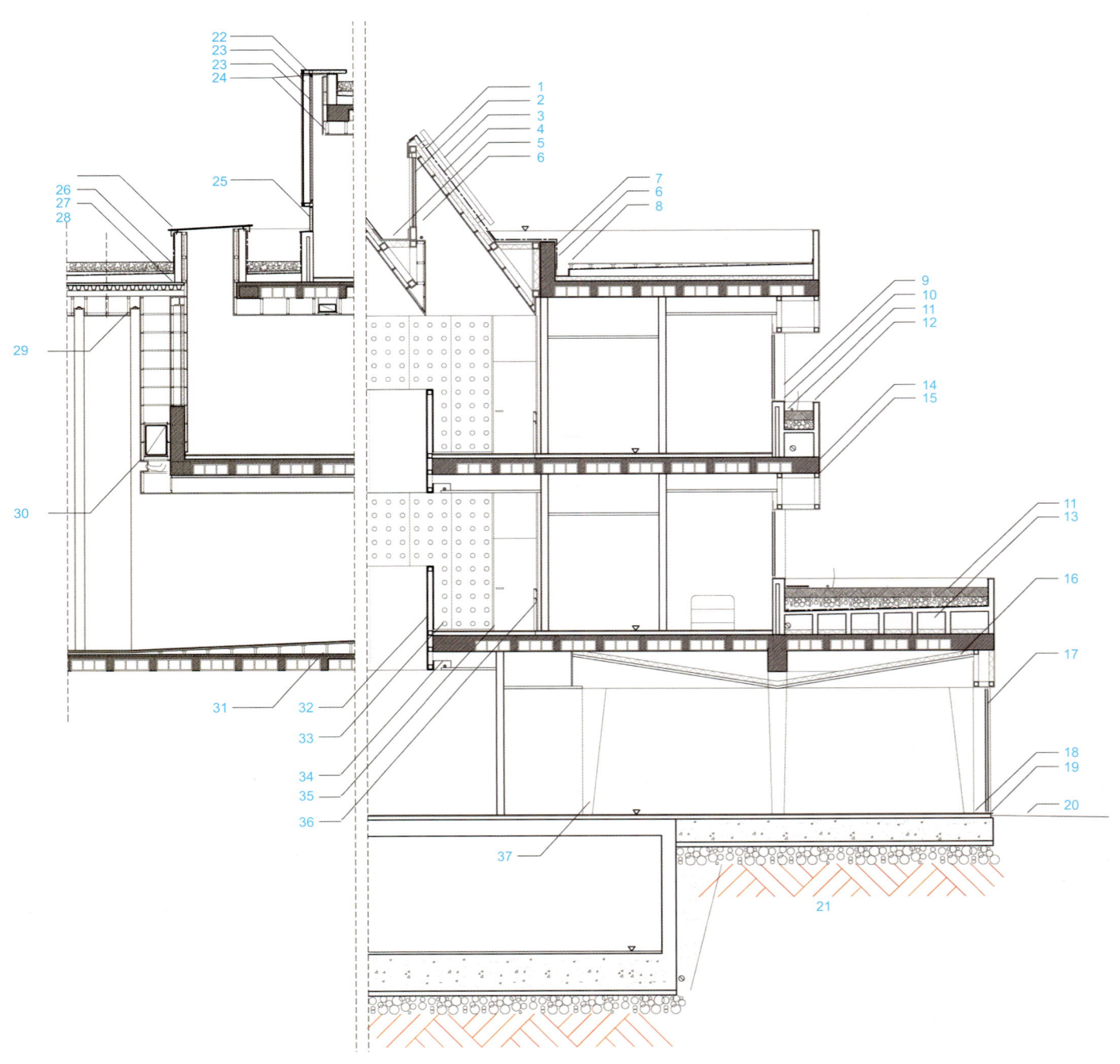

5. Roof terrace detail
6. Entrance of the building

7. Façade detail
8. Patient room
9. Classroom

10

11

258

10. Lobby
11. Corridor
12~14. Patio

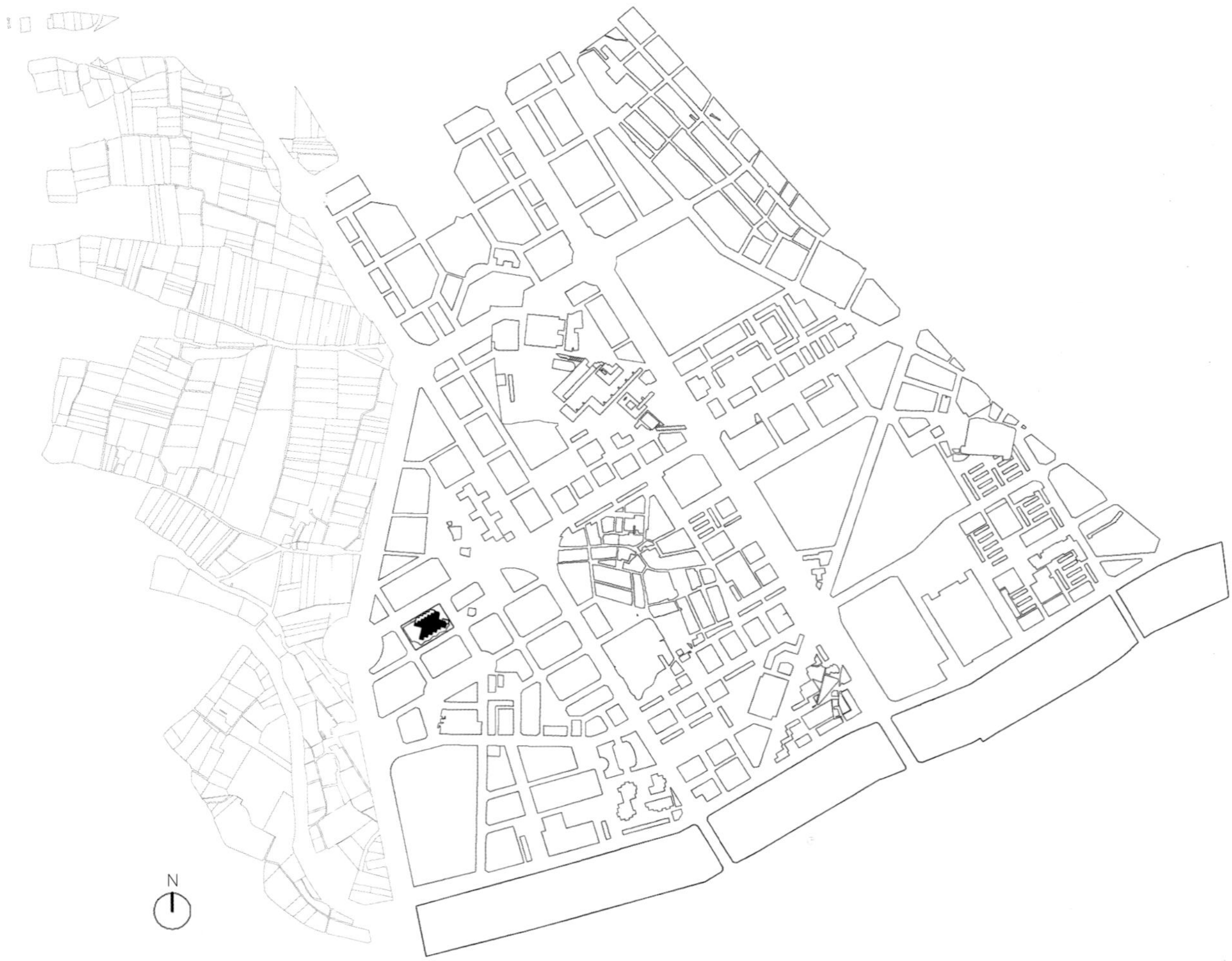

Site Plan

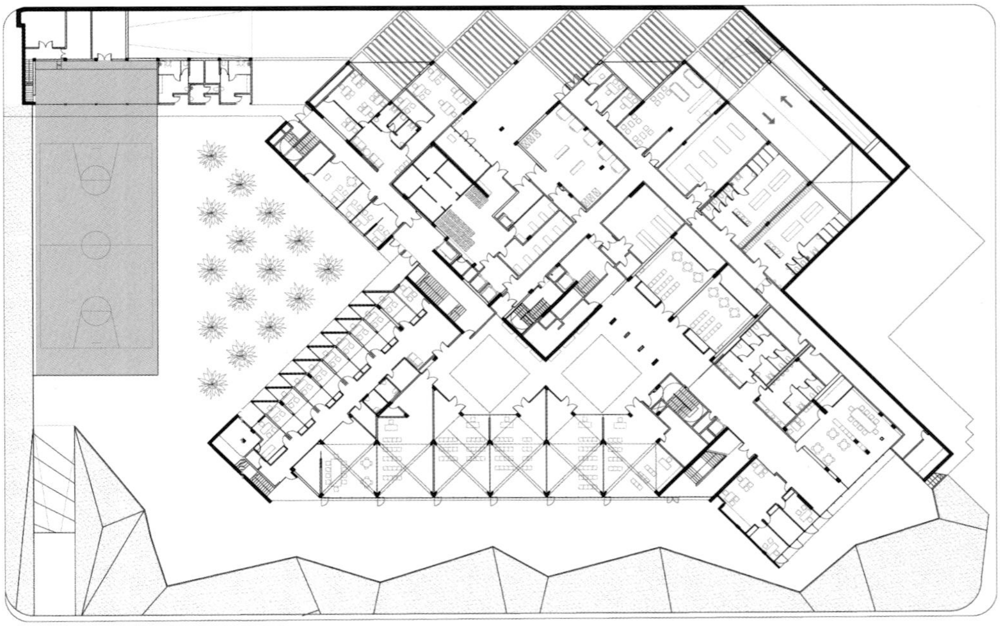

Floor Plan

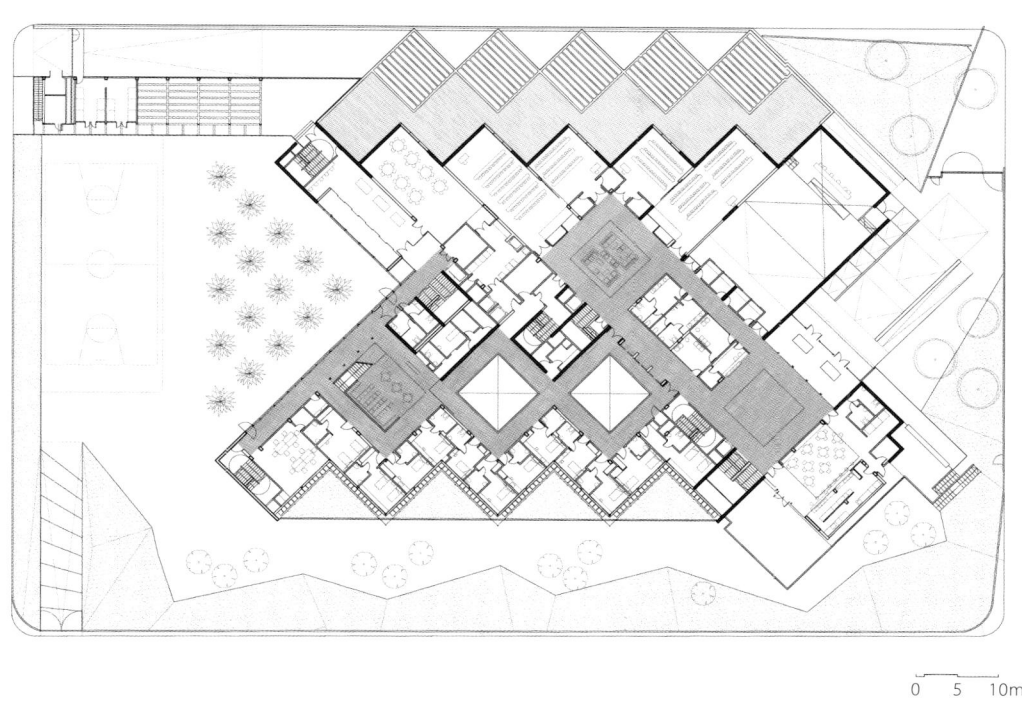

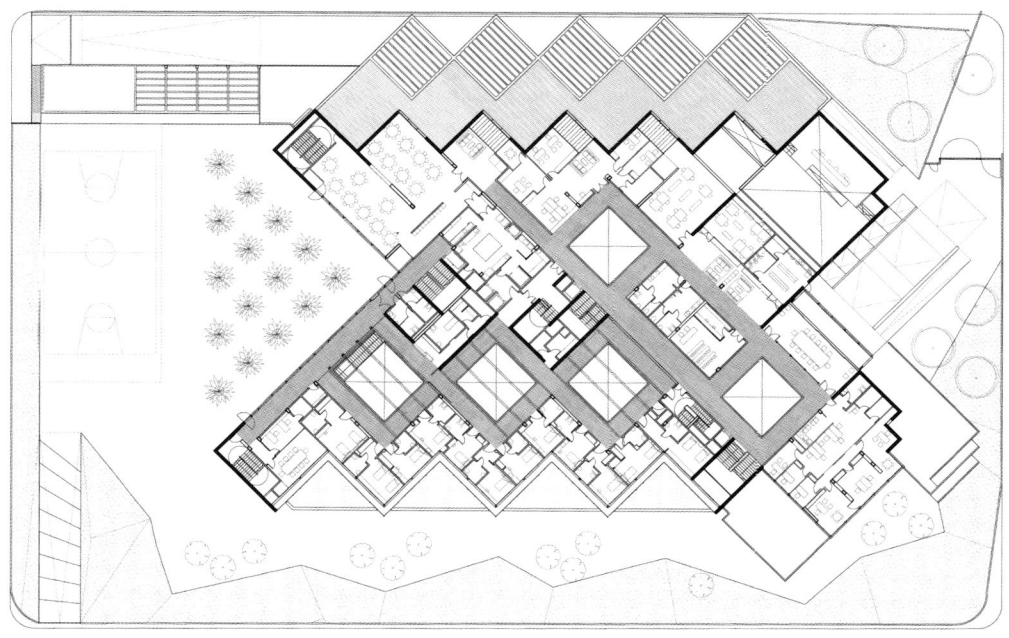

Floor Plans

INDEX

Angela Fritsch
info@af-architekten.de

Bateman Architects
admin@batemanarchitects.biz

Cannon Design
bonnen@cannondesign.com

C. F. Møller Architects
jw@cfmoller.com

CSPE
cristina@cspe.net

Dutch Health Architects
Ronald.SchlundtBodien@egm.nl

dwp
russell.p@dwp-next.com

HKS
slsmith3@hksinc.com

Lifschutz Davidson Sandilands
ben@ing-media.com

Michael W. Folonis Architects
g.sun@folonisarchitects.com

Mitchell Architects
nathan@mitchell-architects.com

Mullen Heller Architecture
antonio@mullenheller.com

Nord Architects
simon@nord-web.dk

Peñín Architects
estudio@amann-canovas-maruri.es

RTKL
info@rtkl.com

VMX Architects
info@vmxarchitects.nl

VOA Associates Incorporated
contactbeijing@voa.com

weinbrenner.single.arabzadeh, architektenwerkgemeinschaft
kieser.ch@wsa-nt.de

ZGF Architects LLP
info@zgf.com